Art and Creativity in Reggio

This book explores the contribution of art and creativity to early education, and examines the role of the atelier (an arts workshop in a school) and atelierista (an educator with an arts background) in the pioneering preschools of Reggio Emilia. It does so through the unique experience of Vea Vecchi, one of the first atelieristas to be appointed in Reggio Emilia in 1970.

Part memoir, part conversation and part reflection, the book provides a unique insider perspective on the pedagogical work of this extraordinary local project, which continues to be a source of inspiration to early childhood practitioners and policy makers worldwide.

Vea's writing, full of beautiful examples, draws the reader in as she explains the history of the atelier and the evolving role of the atelierista. Key themes of the book include:

- processes of learning and knowledge construction
- the theory of the hundred languages of childhood and the role of poetic languages
- the importance of organization, ways of working and tools, in particular pedagogical documentation
- the vital contribution of the physical environment
- the relationship between the atelier, the atelierista, the school and its teachers.

Three illuminating dialogues, the first between the author and a group of pedagogistas, and the others between the author and a group of designers and pedagogistas, examine the relationship between the atelierista and those actively engaged in working with young children.

This enlightening book is essential reading for students, practitioners, policy makers and researchers in early childhood education, and also for all those in other fields of education interested in the relationship between the arts and learning.

Vea Vecchi worked as an atelierista at the Diana municipal preschool in Reggio Emilia for over thirty years, doing pedagogical research and documentation in the area of children's many languages. She now acts as a consultant to 'Reggio Children'.

Contesting Early Childhood
Series editors: Gunilla Dahlberg and Peter Moss

This groundbreaking new series questions the current dominant discourses surrounding early childhood, and offers instead alternative narratives of an area that is now made up of a multitude of perspectives and debates.

The series examines the possibilities and risks arising from the accelerated development of early childhood services and policies, and illustrates how it has become increasingly steeped in regulation and control. Insightfully, this collection of books shows how early childhood services can, in fact, contribute to ethical and democratic practices. The authors explore new ideas taken from alternative working practices in both the western and developing world and from other academic disciplines such as developmental psychology. Current theories and best practice are placed in relation to the major processes of political, social, economic, cultural and technological change occurring in the world today.

Art and Creativity in Reggio Emilia

Exploring the role and potential of ateliers in early childhood education

Vea Vecchi

Routledge
Taylor & Francis Group

LONDON AND NEW YORK

First published 2010
by Routledge
2 Park Square, Milton Park, Abingdon, Oxon, OX14 4RN

Simultaneously published in the USA and Canada
by Routledge
711 Third Avenue, New York, NY 10017 (8th Floor)

Routledge is an imprint of the Taylor & Francis Group, an informa business

© 2010 Vea Vecchi

Typeset in Garamond by
GreenGate Publishing Services, Tonbridge, Kent

British Library Cataloguing in Publication Data
A catalogue record for this book is available from the British Library

Library of Congress Cataloging-in-Publication Data
Vecchi, Vea.
Art and creativity in Reggio Emilia : exploring the role and potential of
ateliers in early childhood education / Vea Vecchi.
p. cm.
Includes bibliographical references.
1. Art--Study and teaching (Early childhood)--Italy--Reggio Emilia.
2. Creative ability in children--Italy--Reggio Emilia. I. Title.
LB1139.5.A78V43 2010
372.5--dc22
2009038564

ISBN10: 0-415-46877-9 (hbk)
ISBN10: 0-415-46878-7 (pbk)
ISBN10: 0-203-85467-5 (ebk)

ISBN13: 978-0-415-46877-0 (hbk)
ISBN13: 978-0-415-46878-7 (pbk)
ISBN13: 978-0-203-85467-9 (ebk)

For Alice and Mattia

Contents

Acknowledgements

Writing a book always means being indebted to the many forms of intelligence and competency deriving from different areas of work. For this reason, I would like to thank my two editors, Gunilla Dahlberg and Peter Moss, who have carefully and knowledgeably given suggestions on the contents, on the language used and on possible misunderstandings arising from translation.

My thanks also to the two translators for their skilled and sensitive work, Jane McCall who translated the book and Leslie Morrow who translated the interviews, and to Michela Bendotti my publishing co-ordinator who acted as a bridge between all the different requirements of publishing and the many, varied forms of social relations.

A sincere thank you to all those people who, despite their many work commitments, have contributed to enriching my thoughts in their interviews. My thanks to Anna Barsotti for supporting the idea of a book on the atelier, and to all the atelieristas, teachers and pedagogistas who lent me fragments of their projects to illustrate my thinking. Thank you to the *Centro Documentazione e Ricerca Educativa dei Nidi e delle Scuole Comunali dell'Infanzia*, to the *Istituzione Scuole e Nidi d'Infanzia del Comune di Reggio Emilia* and to *Cooperativa Coopselios* of Reggio Emilia for authorizing publication of the photographic material.

A special thank you to my husband Tullio for patiently standing by my side, and trying to make my style of writing more comprehensible to those outside the area of Reggio Emilia pedagogy, and also to my son Michele for his precious suggestions on the structure of the book and for keeping me up to date with accounts of his children as they grow up.

Thank you also to my grandchildren Alice and Mattia, who make it possible for me to see things with my own eyes and in a different way from school, and who keep me constantly informed on how children grow up today.

Travelling companions

The atelier work I coordinated was not only made possible by children's intelligence but also by the intelligent and impassioned work of many people: teachers, pedagogistas, cooks and auxiliary staff, succeeding each other over the thirty years I worked in the *scuola comunale dell'infanzia* Diana and other institutions in Reggio Emilia. I remember almost everyone with affection but obviously my work was interwoven and developed above all with teachers, especially those who remained longest at the *scuola comunale dell'infanzia* Diana and came to form a stable reference group. Let others not be offended if this is, above all, the group I feel it my duty and pleasure to mention; listing them (in the order they began working at Diana) means considering them co-authors of atelier work in the school.

Magda Bondavalli, head teacher when the school opened (soon after 1970, head teachers have long since disappeared), was the only one of us with any educational or organizational experience. An extremely reliable person and gifted with great patience both with children and adults, she had a subversive vein she always kept vigilantly under control, but which let her gaily accept new things with curiosity.

Giulia Notari has genuine and natural individual originality, which as a teacher she brought into educational projects. Some of her distractions are memorable, and she was an enchanting story teller, for children and adults alike. She was the author of projects and proposals that have left important traces in Diana's history, some of which were used by Gianni Rodari in the *Grammatica della Fantasia* (1973a).

Laila Marani was a teacher at Diana school for only a few years, but left traces and memories of an extremely lively mind standing outside standard frameworks. In love with culture, she laid the plans, worked for and founded the Documentation and Educational Research Centre of the municipal schools in Reggio Emilia in 1980.

Laura Rubizzi is a person of great intelligence and sensibility, capable of listening to children's specific individualities. In her daily work, I believe she is one of the teachers best representing the educational philosophy of Reggio. She is the only person from the original group still in the school, and often co-ordinates new research projects with the children.

Paola Cagliari, a sensitive and scientific mind, did not work for many years at Diana, but she and Laura Rubizzi formed one of the most successful teaching pairs because they were strongly attuned in character and culture. She took her degree while working at Diana, including a thesis on spatial orientation, a project we co-ordinated with children aged three, four and five years. For many years she has been part of the co-ordinating team of pedagogistas for Reggio schools and particularly active in the area of projects on continuity in primary schools and other schools for older children.

Marina Mori has a memorable capacity for organizing and educating with affectionate impetuosity and gaiety. Socially committed, extremely generous, with a strong aesthetic sense, the children she worked with for three years generally did the best drawing work. She has left the school to become part of a group of teacher trainers, working in various schools in Reggio.

Paola Strozzi has a striking rational intelligence, is enamoured with study and research, generous, with little acceptance of the routine of daily organization. Her readings were synthesized into notes that she then distributed among us. After taking her degree while working at Diana she also became one of the coordinating team of pedagogistas for Reggio's municipal schools.

Marina Castagnetti is a teacher who, as well as caring for environments and beautiful documentation photographs, knows how to conduct a conversation in English and possesses a capacity for relations that made her the person most suited to receiving and welcoming visitors. She became the reference point for the various film directors, photographers, architects, pedagogistas, administrators, and other people with different backgrounds and interests circulating in the school for many years. For some years she has been at the Documentation and Educational Research Centre.

Evelina Reverberi, after many years teaching in *nidi* with children under 3 years moved to working with 3–6 year olds in Diana. She is one of the people most welcoming of diversity I have ever known, both with children and families; I believe she was and still is very much loved for this. She is a very capable planner and manager of events for family participation. She has made a personal decision to work with children with special needs, but without doubt is a precious presence for all children and teachers in the school.

Sonia Cipolla is a teacher whom I did not have the time to get to know very well, or to work with very much, because she was at home on maternity leave twice during my last years at Diana. In the short time we spent together I much appreciated her intelligence and capacity for reflection.

Tiziana Filippini is another long-standing presence at the *scuola comunale dell'infanzia* Diana, in multiple roles. At the age of eighteen she became part of the Community-Early Childhood Council as a citizen; after receiving her degree she taught in the school for a year; then she was present as mother of Elisa; and finally as pedagogista, a role she has had now for many years and in which she continued after I left. She has responsibility for professional development in the city's co-ordinating team of pedagogistas and for the Documentation and Educational Research Centre in Reggio Emilia. It is, however, difficult for me to think of her in the specific role of pedagogista, because in our many years of working together, first with Malaguzzi then at Diana, she was above all a travelling companion, her competencies both similar and different to mine, an informal person, and willing to get involved in new things.

Naturally there are many more people I should thank and mention in brief portraits, among the teachers and cooks, auxiliary staff, pedagogistas and parents at Diana and other schools. So many, a multitude I would like to hold in a large, affectionate, grateful embrace.

Vea Vecchi

Note on Reggio Emilia terminologies

Reggio Emilia is a city of about 1,650,000 people in the Emilia Romagna region of northern Italy, about 60 kilometres west of Bologna. It is an old and prosperous town, which has invested part of its wealth in developing a network of more than thirty early childhood municipal centres, for children from birth to 3 years and from 3–6 years (the network itself is part of one 0–6 service, located in the city's education department). This educational project began over fourty years ago, led initially by Loris Malaguzzi, first head of the municipal early childhood centres, until his death in 1994; a great pedagogical thinker and practitioner, Malaguzzi plays a leading role throughout this book.

Today, Reggio has gained a worldwide reputation for its pedagogical work, evidenced by the tens of thousands of people from all over the world who have visited Reggio in recent years and the number of centres in other countries that acknowledge the influence of Reggio's pedagogy. This pedagogy has featured in several books in the series *Contesting Early Childhood*, and is the subject of one of them, *In Dialogue with Reggio Emilia: Listening, Researching and Learning*, by Vea Vecchi's long-standing colleague, Carla Rinaldi (2006). Vea herself refers to some other publications that provide further perspectives on Reggio.

In this book we have used the Italian terms for the two main types of early childhood service found in Reggio Emilia and the rest of Italy: the *nido* (plural *nidi*) is a centre for children from around 3 months up to 3 years; the *scuola dell'infanzia* (plural *scuole dell'infanzia*) is a centre or nursery school for children from 3 years up to compulsory school age of 6 years. In Reggio they use the term 'municipal schools' to refer to the centres for young children – both *nidi* and *scuole dell'infanzia* – that are either directly managed by the municipality of Reggio Emilia (we use the term 'municipality' for local authority) or managed for the municipality by cooperatives or other non-profit organizations; this term is also used in the book to refer to this network of services.

The staff working directly with the children in *nidi* and *scuole dell'infanzia* are referred to as 'teachers'. But there are also other groups of workers who play an important role in Reggio's municipal schools. Apart from auxiliary staff (for example, cooks and cleaners), whose important role is acknowledged in several places in this book, there are *pedagogistas* and *atelieristas*. *Pedagogistas* have a higher degree in psychology or pedagogy, each working with a small number of municipal schools to help develop understanding of learning processes and pedagogical work through, for example, pedagogical documentation (a method discussed at some length in the book). *Atelieristas*, whose background is often in the visual arts, work alongside teachers in Reggio's municipal schools, often from an *atelier* (workshop) in a *nido* or *scuola dell'infanzia* where they support and develop children's and adults' visual languages as part of the complex process of knowledge building. The *atelieristas*' role and practice is a central theme of this book.

One other issue of terminology should be flagged up at this early stage of the book: the distinction between the Italian words *programmazione* and *progettazione*. In Italian, the verb *progettare* has a number of meanings: to design, to plan, to devise, to project (in a technical-engineering sense). The use of the noun *progettazione* – translated in this book as 'project' – by Reggio educators, however, has its own special meaning. It is used in Reggio in opposition to *programmazione*, which implies predefined curricula, programmes, stages, and so on. The concept of *progettazione* thus implies a more global and flexible approach in which initial hypotheses are made about classroom work (as well as about staff development and relationships with parents), but are subject to modifications and changes of direction as the actual work progresses. As Carla Rinaldi puts it in her book in this series, project work 'grows in many directions without an overall ordering principle, challenging the mainstream idea of knowledge acquisition as a form of linear progression, where the metaphor is the tree'.

It is not easy to find a term in English that could describe this process precisely as experienced in Reggio Emilia. Some writers in English have used terms such as 'emergent curriculum', 'projected curriculum' or 'integrated curriculum' to describe the overall way in which the Reggio teachers plan and work with children, with colleagues, and with parents. But these terms are (as the reader will discover) inappropriate, derived from methods or ways of working developed and used elsewhere; their use renders invisible the otherness of Reggio. We have chosen, therefore, to keep with the Italian word *progettazione*.

Gunilla Dahlberg and Peter Moss
Series editors

Series editors' introduction
Invitation to the dance

Gunilla Dahlberg and Peter Moss

A pioneering life

This is the eighth book in the series *Contesting Early Childhood*, which we jointly edit. One experience that has run like a thread through the series is the pedagogical work of the Italian city of Reggio Emilia. It has been a source of inspiration to authors from outside Italy (Dahlberg and Moss, 2005; Olsson, 2009; Lenz Taguchi, 2009). But we have been fortunate to have two books written from inside Reggio Emilia itself, by leading figures in the development of this extraordinary local project, the first by Carlina Rinaldi (2006), and now this book by Vea Vecchi. Carlina's book – *In Dialogue with Reggio Emilia* – drew together articles, speeches and interviews from over twenty years to give a unique account of the evolution of Reggio's pedagogical work. Vea's book has been specially written for the series (and translated from her original Italian manuscript), and provides another unique insider perspective, both on the general pedagogical ideas and practices of Reggio and, more specifically, on the role and contribution of the atelier and atelierista to this educational project (both terms are introduced in the note on terminology preceding this introduction and explained at greater length in Chapter 1).

The book is also unique, at least in our series, in the way it connects different levels and stories. It is part memoire of an extraordinarily creative and active professional life, mostly spent working in Reggio's municipal schools, specifically Vea's beloved Diana school (for children from 3–6 years); the personal and the professional are interwoven, in a welcoming and informal style that includes many anecdotes, so you end up feeling you have become friends with the author. It is part conversation, both in the sense that Vea seems to be talking with the reader, but also in the literal sense that the book includes a number of conversations between Vea and work colleagues. It is part reflection, in particular about a lifetime's work and more generally about the pedagogical work of Reggio Emilia and its schools and the 'pedagogical contribution that the presence of an atelier and the work of an atelierista can make to schools and educational work in general'. This reflection has the profundity of someone who has spent many years engaged in pedagogical documentation of the highest order, in other words who is accustomed to thinking about, interpreting, negotiating, evaluating and experimenting with complex processes and relationships. And because documentation means making children's learning processes and pedagogical practice visible, presupposing 'being able to discuss real, concrete things' (Hoyeulos, 2004: 7), Vea's book is full of richly documented material drawn from her own and others' everyday practice and includes a strong visual element.

The book tells a personal story of Vea's work in Reggio since she was appointed as one of the first atelieristas in 1970, a pioneering job in a pioneering project. But it also tells a collective story of how a city took responsibility for the education of its young children. This has meant a continuous project of combining political and ethical values, including a strong commitment to democracy, with processes of research and experimentation. This is fertilized by a great collective curiosity and openness to diversity which has resulted in a desire to border cross and a strong leaning towards trans-disciplinarity, 'the way in which human thinking connects different disciplines (languages) in order to gain a deeper understanding of something'. In telling the collective story, Vea introduces many participants in the Reggio project, not only teachers, atelieristas and pedagogistas, but also children, parents, administrators and politicians – and Vea emphasizes that 'a good relationship with the municipal administration and the Mayor are too important for our school culture... for us to leave to chance'.

Among the cast of players in Vea's story, one stands out for his influence, vision and insight: Loris Malaguzzi, the first director of Reggio's early childhood services ('municipal schools') and one of the great pedagogical figures of the twentieth century. It was Malaguzzi's 'courage and determination' that introduced ateliers and atelieristas into the schools, and which afterwards defended them against any possible cuts (the same is true of school kitchens and cooks, which Vea says are not paired with ateliers and atelieristas by chance, for Malaguzzi thought both important to his idea of early childhood education). What emerges from the book is a picture of a man of enormous energy, imagination, curiosity, perseverance, creativity and political awareness; a manager who was always involved with everyday practice; a provocateur of the people he worked with, but also offering intense stimulation, empathy and support. Little wonder then the sense of devastation when he died suddenly in 1994, but also the sense of achievement that Reggio was able to survive this huge loss and find its own life after Malaguzzi. If Malaguzzi showed great courage in pursuing an educational project, so too have his colleagues and the whole city in taking that project forward and making it truly their own.

Contesting early childhood

The aim of our series is to question and contest dominant discourses and actions in early childhood and offer alternative narratives of an area that is now made up of a multitude of perspectives and debates. We have long felt that the pedagogical work in Reggio Emilia is not a case of 'best practice' of a universal early childhood education (the same only better as some would see it). Rather Reggio offers a case of doing early childhood education in a way that is qualitatively different to so much current early childhood education based on a normalizing project of developmental stages, prescribed technologies and predetermined outcomes. A decade ago we suggested that Reggio had a pedagogical practice that might be viewed as 'postmodern' (Dahlberg, Moss and Pence, 2007); while in our first book in this series we suggested that Reggio was an example of making ethics and politics first practice in education and that its 'pedagogy of listening' could be seen as exemplifying the ethics of an encounter (Dahlberg and Moss, 2005). Whether or not Reggio or our readers agree with these particular readings, we think there is no doubt that Reggio represents something very different to the mainstream, an experience that truly contests the dominant early childhood education.

You feel this from the language that Vea uses throughout her book about everyday practice, so different from the predictable and desiccated language of so many English-language books, articles and reports about education: connections and intensities, research and experimentation, curiosity and surprise, gaiety and tenderness, theories and interpretations, and much else besides. Let us take a specific example: Vea uses words such as 'magical' and 'wonder', which for many may sound romantic, but which to us suggest something very interesting. Giordano Bruno, the scientific father of Galileo Galilei, was burnt at the stake for his ideas, proposing a reconciliation with the magical, but not as irrationalism; magic for him stood for the allying of knowledge and the power to act (Massumi, 2002). It is actually this pragmatic understanding of magic that we think may be put to work in the pedagogical practice in Reggio Emilia, a kind of 'miraculation of forces and agents' as Brian Massumi has expressed it.

Vea's language, including her love of metaphors, is used to support and express well developed ideas that provide the pedagogical work of Reggio with its distinct identity. We want to look at three of these ideas that are central to the book: learning and knowledge; the role of poetic or expressive languages, and therefore of the atelierista, in learning and knowledge creation; and the importance of organization and tools.

Learning and knowledge

Reggio's educational philosophy, Vea says, is based on subjectivity, dialogue, connection and autonomy. Learning is a process of knowledge building, recognizing that knowledge so produced is inescapably partial, perspectival and provisional and not to be confused with information. One approach to learning is transmission, or reproduction, and Vea acknowledges that this 'brings certain advantages and can produce appreciable results'. But Reggio, she adds, has chosen another approach: one based on the 'understanding of problems through experiment, trial, error and testing', a 'pedagogy of listening' where the learner develops theories, shares them with others, redevelops them in a pedagogy that emphasizes the importance of relationships, listening ('one of the foundations of our work is the careful, respectful, tender "listening" with solidarity to children's strategies and ways of thinking') and avoiding predetermined results. In this approach to learning, new thinking, new ideas and new perspectives are highly valued, though established knowledge is also respected. Vea expresses this approach in a statement that makes it clear that it can apply not only to younger children but also to children and young people in compulsory schooling:

> It is important to society that schools and we as teachers are clearly aware of how much space we leave children for original thinking, without rushing to restrict it with predetermined schemes that define what is correct according to a school culture. How much do we support children to have ideas different from those of other people and how do we accustom them to arguing and discussing their ideas with their classmates? I am quite convinced that greater attention to processes, rather than only the final product, would help us to feel greater respect for the independent thinking and strategies of children and teenagers.

Schools, she adds, need to consciously take a position on '*which knowledge* they intend to promote': in short, these are alternatives, and choices of a political and ethical nature must be made between them. She contests an idea of teaching that chooses to 'transmit circumscribed "truths" in various "disciplines"'. Her choice and position is clear, 'to stand by children's sides together constructing contexts in which they can explore their own ideas and hypotheses individually or in groups and discuss them with friends or teachers.'

Reggio and Vea place great importance on process, not just product or outcome, which in any case cannot and should not be split and set up in opposition as often happens today. She also attaches great importance to connections in processes of knowledge construction and sees much modern education as structured instead in a compartmentalized way that divides rather than connects disciplines, subjects and languages, fragmenting reality and making the development of thinking and understanding far more difficult. Instead Vea puts forward 'proposals for learning that do not hurry to fence the world in more or less rigid categories of thought; but, on the contrary, seek connections, alliances and solidarities between different categories and languages or subjects'.

The unpredictability of learning in this approach to education, arising from the synaptic dynamic of relationships and new connections, contests the idea of learning as a process of linear progress and development, in favour of learning as an uncertain, unpredictable and intensely creative activity, with new understandings created unexpectedly and shooting off in new directions. The image of knowledge here is not like a staircase, where you have to take one step after another, which is similar to the tree metaphor of knowledge that remains so prominent in education; rather the image is the *rhizome*, something which shoots in all directions with no beginning and no end, but always *in between*, and with openings towards other directions and places. It is a *multiplicity* functioning by means of connections and heterogeneity, a multiplicity that is not given but constructed.

The role of poetic languages and the atelierista in learning

It is here, with mention of connections and languages, that we come to the role and contribution of the atelier and atelierista to learning and education. The name 'atelier', Vea tells us, was chosen because they felt it was the most suitable metaphor for a place of research where imagination, rigour, experiment, creativity and expression would interweave and complete each other. The atelierista works from (but not always in) the atelier, and has an artistic but not an educational background; she is more an artist than a teacher, but works closely with teachers in schools, both engaged with processes of learning. Her contribution is to introduce what Vea variously calls an 'aesthetic dimension' or 'poetic languages' into the learning process. What do these mean? And what do they contribute to learning?

Reggio is associated with what Carlina Rinaldi (2006) calls the 'fantastic theory' of the hundred languages of childhood, though she goes on to add that reference to a 'hundred' is arbitrary and chosen as a very provocative statement giving different languages not only the same dignity but also the possibility to communicate and connect with each other. Vea explains the concept of languages in the following way:

> We (in Reggio) consider *languages* as the different ways used by human beings to express themselves; visual language, mathematical language, scientific language, etc. In a conversation on the relationship between pedagogy and atelier, Claudia Giudici, pedagogista, puts it like this, 'When we speak of languages we refer to the different ways children (human beings) represent, communicate and express their thinking in different media and symbolic systems; languages therefore are the many fonts or geneses of knowledge'. *Poetic languages* are forms of expression strongly characterized by expressive or aesthetic aspects such as music, song, dance or photography.

We, like the educators in Reggio, think that this theory is especially provocative at a time when mainstream education seems increasingly focused on, even obsessed with, just two languages: reading and writing, and indeed the hundred languages came out of political discussion in Italy in the 1970s about the reasons for and consequences of privileging these two languages from the many available to children. The theory relativizes these two, not devaluing them but situating them among a much wider range of languages, all of which have an important role to play in learning and life. It asks, why these two more than others? What happens if we neglect other languages? What can other languages contribute to human flourishing?

So part of the process of learning through relationships and other connections involves working with a range of languages – and one role of the atelierista is to stimulate the role of 'poetic languages', especially the visual ones, 'if aesthetics fosters sensibility and the ability for connecting things far removed from each other, and if learning takes place through new connections between disparate elements, then aesthetics can be considered an important activator for learning'. The atelierista supports connections, or as Vea more poetically terms it 'the dance', 'between cognitive, expressive, rational and imaginative'. An aesthetic sense is fed by empathy, an intense relationship with things; 'it does not put things in rigid categories and might therefore constitute a problem where excessive certainty and cultural simplification is concerned'. The task here is not only to connect but break down the constraints created by mono-lingualism, closed-off disciplines, preconceived categories and predetermined ends.

What is central to Vea's thinking and the book is that the atelier and atelierista are at the heart of learning, key partners with teachers, not technical specialists who transmit specialized skills and help children produce nice products, nor purveyors of a particular subject that children can dip into every now and then (the twice a week 'art lesson'), 'we always did things in such a way', says Vea of her work, 'that the atelier expanded out into the classes and school… We always worked on projects and it was the progress of these that determined children's presence in the atelier'.

In addition to the atelierista as educator (though not teacher), Vea explores some other roles and contributions. There is the ateleriesta as a guide for border crossing between the world of art, architecture and design, equipped as a sensitive antennae for contemporary issues; as a go-between and coordinator, keeping the group of teachers together and acting in solidarity; as a lens for the school community, helping it to see children and adults in a certain, aesthetic way; and the atelierista as provocateur, the 'persevering defenders of *non-obedient* processes'.

Organization and ways of working

The third idea that comes through clearly in the book is the great importance attached by Reggio Emilia to organization and ways of working. For us, Reggio Emilia exemplifies the potential for working with democracy, experimentation and the ethics of an encounter, and has managed to do so, constantly evolving its thinking and practice, over more than forty years. This extraordinary power of sustainability and renewal has not happened by accident. It owes a lot to a gifted educational community and to the deep political and cultural values embedded in the city of Reggio Emilia; it has depended on sustained political, administrative and popular support; and it has benefitted from a wealth of international relationships, dialogue and recognition. But it has also arisen from an attention to creating conditions where democracy, experimentation and encounter can be sustained, and where thinking and doing, working hand in hand (for there is a strong antipathy to splitting theory and practice), has constantly been open to evaluation, reflection, dialogue and new directions.

Vea provides important insights into these conditions. Some have been organizational, for example the introduction and development of new models of working: new roles, in particular atelieristas and pedagogistas, and new patterns of working, in particular moving from the individual teacher working with a class to teachers always working in pairs. Other examples include strong systems for professional development of educators and parent management committees.

Some of the conditions have involved tools and ways of working. Vea writes about a number, but two are of particular importance. Pedagogical documentation is a vital part of the pedagogy in Reggio, what Malaguzzi's biographer describes as 'an extraordinary tool for dialogue, for exchange, for sharing... (that for Malaguzzi meant) the possibility to discuss "everything with everyone"' (Hoyuelos 2004: 7). Vea sees it as the origin of the atelierista, whose evolution she believes 'together with that of Reggio Emilia pedagogy, stems above all from the birth and diffusion of observation and documentation of learning processes'. This book provides an important contribution to a growing literature on the purpose and practice of documentation, a tool of great value for planning, researching, evaluating, professional development and supporting democratic participation (for other, complementary sources see Dahlberg *et al.*, 2007: Rinaldi, 2006).

Project work is also integral to Reggio's pedagogy and its understanding of learning, and the atelierista plays an integral part in project work. Project work, Vea explains, means 'work in which adults (teachers, atelieristas, pedagogistas) make initial hypotheses and seek to have a deeper understanding of an area or topic but where key elements for moving forward come from work with children and careful analysis by adults of what is happening along the way'. The project then provides a supportive context for learning as knowledge building, evoking

> the idea of a dynamic process, a journey that involves uncertainty and chance that always arises in relationships with others. Project work grows in many directions, with no predefined progression, no outcomes decided before the journey begins. It means being sensitive to the unpredictable results of children's investigation and research (Rinaldi, 2006: 19).

A third type of condition, which Vea gives much attention to, is the physical environment of the school, not only the buildings but the furnishings and fittings. She values this for a number of reasons: for its contribution to learning; for its contribution to well-being and the aesthetic experience it offers; for its ability to express values, ideas, images and emotions; and for its capacity to allow, encourage and 'educate ways of seeing, exploration and sensibility'. She is a fierce defender of the importance of an environment that is beautiful and well cared for, 'we are convinced of the right to beauty in a healthy psychological relationship with surroundings'.

The importance Vea attributes to the environment has been a stimulus to important projects of research and dialogue in Reggio between educators (atelieristas, pedagogistas and teachers) and architects, which have led, among other things, to close working relations between Reggio and designers and manufacturers of innovative furnishings and other equipment.

This attention to organization and tools has been qualified by some important considerations. These conditions for sustainability and renewal should always be determined by values: political and ethical practices precede technical practice. Management is closely in touch with practice, not least through pedagogical documentation and regular dialogue with educators; in this respect, as so much else, Malaguzzi set an important precedent. Last but not least, good work takes and needs time: time for preparation, time for listening, time for documenting, time for discussion, time for reflection and time for pleasure. Vea reserves some of her most scathing comments for those tendencies in modern education that lead to hurried and, therefore, superficial work.

This seems to us to get to the heart of the matter. If education is about technicians transmitting information and skills and delivering predetermined outcomes against predefined norms, then it needs little time for children or educators to think or work. But if it is a democratic process of building knowledge through complex and creative relationships and processes, then education requires commensurate time.

Concern, hope and excitement

Vea, it is clear from her book, looks at contemporary developments with some concern. She appreciates the great challenges to be met if an ambitious local project like Reggio's is not to weaken and fade away. She is highly critical of most schooling today and of teacher training, which does not prepare students to be sensitive to aesthetics nor to understand the powerful role that aesthetics can play. Instead, teachers are often 'excessively seduced by techniques and tend to propose them with children using only a simplified knowledge of their expressive potential'.

While in the wider society she sees evidence of 'a hurried, superficial culture that tends to diminish a sense of wonder... Superficiality, lack of concentration, hurriedness – all are things we suffer in more or less obvious ways, immersed as we are in background noise which is constant and all-pervasive'.

But despite these strong notes of caution and expressions of deep unease, what comes through this book above all is a passion for researching strategies in children's thinking and for working by their side to construct richer, more complete knowledge; a deep pleasure in relationships with children and adults alike; an abiding joy in work as an atelierista and educator; and fierce pride in what has been accomplished over the decades in Reggio Emilia and its schools. Now retired from her former job as atelierista at Diana school, Vea today is as busy as ever, working in Reggio's Loris Malaguzzi International Centre. Her international reputation has grown over the years, as many thousands have seen her work first-hand in Reggio or heard her speak in other countries.

Vea's story of her work with the aesthetic dimension and poetic languages in schools and learning processes is, above all, a source of hope for all those who believe in the possibility of an affirmative and inventive pedagogy: a pedagogy that is open for connections, affect, intensity and emergence; a pedagogy that is open to children's potential and has the capacity to listen to expressive events – events of intensity and affect – and to be open to that which has not yet been put into words; a pedagogy that finds joy in the unexpected, dares to follow projects in motion without knowing where they may lead, always prepared for surprise and risk; a pedagogy that adds to the world rather than subtracting as is all too common in education. In a world obsessed with quantification, reductionism, normalization and predetermined outcomes, this pedagogy gives cause to believe in the world again.

We can find other causes for hope, in particular that the work in Reggio Emilia may be in step with some important developments beyond its borders. Like Vea, we think that there is a long history of relegating the poetic languages; that in education the idea of the hundred languages and the value of aesthetical learning processes are still not taken seriously; and that they are at odds with what Vea refers to as the 'traditional culture and education', indeed may be viewed with deep suspicion as subversive of them and much else besides. Yet, as Vea shows, many important scientists have recognized the importance of these languages and the importance of beauty. A change seems to be taking place, as more and more scientists are questioning whether these languages should be split off from a cognitive core. Michael Thaut, professor of music and professor of neuroscience, is one of them. He argues both that 'the brain thinks in multiple languages' and that 'music and the arts in general are now proposed as precursors and cognitive prerequisites for the development of higher cognitive functions and the emergence of verbal language' (Thaut, 2009: 2).

Vea's work is cause not only for hope but also for excitement. Like other books in our series, Vea explores new theoretical perspectives and shows their relevance to the field of early childhood education – in fact, to all education. The excitement is generated by what has been done so far, and by the potential for further work, exploring new theoretical perspectives and putting them to work. Vea, it is clear, is not recounting a linear project with a beginning, middle and end, but a rhizomatic project with no beginning and no end, where one is always in between, and with openings and lines of flight, shooting off in many directions.

Vea is herself hinting at some possible directions to be explored, which might provide us with more understanding of what happens when connections, intensity and affect are augmented. We think there is a need for new theoretical perspectives to more fully take account of what is going on in Reggio's schools. What, for example, might chaos and complexity theories have to offer?

A book, like this one, that offers both hope, from its account of what has been done, and excitement by opening up glimpses of what is still to come, is very special and very precious.

References

Dahlberg, G. and Moss, P. (2005) *Ethics and Politics in Early Childhood Education*. London: Routledge.

Dahlberg, G., Moss, P. and Pence, A. (2007) *Beyond Quality in Early Childhood Education and Care: Languages of Evaluation*, 2nd edition. London: Routledge.

Hoyuelos, A. (2004) 'A pedagogy of transgression', *Children in Europe*, 4, pp. 6–7.

Lenz Taguchi, H. (2009) *Going Beyond the Theory/Practice Divide in Early Childhood Education: Introducing an Intra-Active Pedagogy*. London: Routledge.

Massumi, B. (2002) *Parables for the Virtual: Movement, Affect, Sensation*. Durham: Duke University Press.

Olsson, L. M. (2009) *Movement and Experimentation in Young Children's Learning: Deleuze and Guattari in Early Childhood Education*. London: Routledge.

Rinaldi, C. (2006) *In Dialogue with Reggio Emilia: Listening, Researching and Learning*. London: Routledge.

Thaut, M. H. (2009) 'The musical brain – an artful biological necessity', *Karger Gazette*, nr. 70.

Chapter I

Introduction

> But the atelier was most of all a place of research (...). We have
> always found it a privilege to be able to encounter the fascinating
> multiple games that can be played with images: turning a poppy
> into a spot, a light, a bird in flight, a lighted ghost, a handful of red
> petals within a field of green and yellow wheat...
>
> (Malaguzzi, 1998: 74–75)

Little has been recounted to date of ateliers in Reggio Emilia's municipal
schools for children from 3 months to 6 years, and their contribution to constructing a pedagogical identity in the schools. Ateliers have been discussed by
people external to the group working in Reggio Emilia, but from Reggio itself
only Loris Malaguzzi, in a few sober and lovely pages in *The Hundred Languages
of Children* (Malaguzzi, 1998: 49–97), has spoken about them. He entrusted
ateliers in schools with a mission that held within it a wish: that the atelier act
as guarantor for the freshness and originality of an approach to things.

Now, after thirty years in the atelier of the *scuola comunale dell'infanzia* Diana, I
would like to talk of ateliers (for readers not familiar with ateliers, I end this chapter
with a short note). I do not intend to attempt at rigorously situating ateliers in an
historical context, nor do I propose an autobiographical story. What I do propose,
filtered through memories of personal experience, is reflection on the pedagogical
contribution that the presence of an atelier and the work of an atelierista can make
to schools and educational work in general, the extent to which expressive 'languages' can be advantaged and evolved when they are woven into a pedagogy that
considers them important for the processes of knowledge.

In the absence of precedents, teachers like myself with a background in the arts
called to work in the municipal schools in Reggio Emilia were given the name
'atelierista'. This name was invented for a completely new kind of work, and the
name contains a clear and immediate reference to the nature of that work.

The term 'atelier' harks back romantically to the studios of Bohemian
artists, and in pedagogical thinking in Reggio it has been revisited and
reinterpreted to become synonymous with places where project work

– *progettare* – is associated with things taking shape through action; places where brains, hands, sensibilities, rationality, emotion and imagination all work together in close cooperation. Our everyday language contains and implies an infinite series of virtual meanings made to emerge at intervals by cultural currents and emotional waves, assigning them with new value and meaning. In the international pedagogy connected with Reggio Children, the term 'atelier' – together with the presence of an atelierista in schools – has come to have a clear, shared value. It stands for the presence of something giving a direction to educational thinking, in which the aesthetic dimension has a new importance and appreciable pedagogical and cultural value.

I have divided this book into chapters that deal more specifically with certain topics that, to my mind, represent the Reggio philosophy, *seen from the point of view of the atelier*. I have purposely avoided exploring and reflecting on the broader issues of Reggio philosophy in order not to risk generalizing and repeating ideas now well known. Other people are better placed to do this and in some cases have already done so.

What I would like to do is to outline the culture of the atelier and some of its distinctive traits; a culture which has been capable, together with children, teachers, pedagogistas and families, of producing a form of mutual confrontation and dialogue – in Italian we say 'confronto'[1] – between different approaches and ways of thinking that has shown itself to be so *bubbling* with possibilities and potential ways forward in Reggio Emilia's educational practice and schools.

Many voices other than my own make an appearance in this book: pedagogistas, teachers, atelieristas, architects, graphic artists and administrators. For example, you can hear the voices of two pedagogistas talking together in Chapter 4, the voice of an administrator in Chapter 5, and two architects in a conversation with three pedagogistas in Chapter 7. Their intelligent contributions enrich my opinions and in a small way represent the work of interweaving and exchange of opinion between people with different competencies, which forms the basis of the work in Reggio Emilia's *nidi* and *scuole*. They are just a small part of the multitude of people who have contributed to constructing our reality: the children, the people working in the *nidi* and *scuole*, pedagogistas, administrators and families. These conversations, which were recorded, transcribed and edited to maintain the rhythm of spoken conversation, have had to be cut because they proved too long for the available space. Selecting was not easy and I hope the acuteness and passion of the contributors can be sensed.

I would also have liked the voices of other teachers and atelieristas to appear in the book because many people, many competencies, have contributed to the invention and making of ateliers in the schools of Reggio Emilia. However, limitations of space made this impossible.

The contributions taken from various authors quoted in this book should not be seen as a collection of erudite citations. The thoughts of these people have been my travelling companions while writing. When we contemplate a particular theme, I believe we often find phrases and thoughts in material we chance to read that feel close to our own thinking and clarify it; a sort of virtual round table that can be amusing at times.

I would like to specify just one more thing. In this book, I have freely alternated personal ideas with examples of school practice which more clearly communicate the atelier's role and make it possible to get past the too specific, restricted confines to which schools and culture would have it relegated. For greater clarity and rhythm in reading, a different character has been used for these stories.

Note on the atelier

Ateliers as spaces, as opportunities for techniques and expression, are present both in the *nidi* and *scuole dell'infanzia*, however, the person of the atelierista is only present in *scuole dell'infanzia*. This is not because we consider the atelierista's role to be of little importance with small children but because atelieristas are considered simply too expensive for schools like the *nidi* which have high running costs. However, the 0–6 pedagogical project has made it possible for exchanges of competencies to take place between *nidi* and *scuole dell'infanzia* and this is clearly visible in Reggio *nidi*.

I hope that an idea of what an atelier is will emerge, at least in part, from reading the book. There follows a brief description for those readers who have never visited the municipal schools in Reggio Emilia.

Figure 1.1 The atelier and atelierista (author Vea Vecchi) in the *scuola comunale dell'infanzia* Diana

Working with possibilities offered by the available space, the atelier should be large enough to contain several children and activities and connected, visually and otherwise, with the rest of the school. It will be equipped with tools: tables, containers for materials, computer, printer, digital cameras, easels for painting, surfaces for working with clay, an oven for ceramic work, tape-recorder, a microscope and other equipment depending on the funds available. Together with digital material there will be a large quantity of traditional materials: different types of colours for painting and drawing in different consistencies and shades; black, white and red clay, oxides of different colours, colours for ceramic work; wire in different thicknesses, cutters, recycled and discarded materials... and many more. Tools and materials that make it possible for the children to have experiences in which their thinking takes on different forms (visual, musical, dance, verbal).

The atelierista is a person with an artistic background who comes into schools through a public examination. She does not have an educational background – she is not a qualified teacher. Her professional development and her work with children in schools is strongly supported through relationships with teachers and pedagogistas and specific activities such as documentation.

Chapter 2

Aesthetics/Poetics

It would be truly naïve to imagine that the mere presence of an atelierista might constitute an important change in learning if the atelier culture and the pedagogical culture do not reciprocally 'listen' to each other or are not both of quality. To introduce an atelier into a school means that materials available for children's use will most probably increase in number, that techniques and the formal qualities of final products will improve. Above all, however, it is an approach, the relation *with* things that must be activated through certain processes where the aesthetic dimension is a significant, fundamental presence.

To my mind an indispensable premise for ideas about the atelier is a reflection on the role of *aesthetic dimensions* in learning and education in general – and a topic deserving of deeper evaluation and understanding. The topic is a difficult one but must at least be mentioned, for among Reggio pedagogy's most original features is an acceptance of aesthetics as one of the important dimensions in the life of our species and, therefore, also in education and in learning. While in Reggio schools the role of an aesthetic dimension can be felt immediately, the opposite is usually true and the world of education generally keeps a distance from the subject. I do not think a true understanding of Reggio pedagogy is possible without due consideration of this issue; an issue which can be approached from various points of view and studied in different ways. For my part, I will discuss it mainly with a view to giving far more attention to the role of atelier and atelierista in places of education and in learning.

Undoubtedly it is difficult to say simply and clearly what is meant by an *aesthetic dimension*. Perhaps first and foremost it is a process of empathy relating the Self to things and things to each other. It is like a slim thread or aspiration to quality that makes us choose one word over another, the same for a colour or shade, a certain piece of music, a mathematical formula or the taste of a food. It is an attitude of care and attention for the things we do, a desire for meaning; it is curiosity and wonder; it is the opposite of indifference and carelessness, of conformity, of absence of participation and feeling.

The *aesthetic dimension* is certainly not only these things. On the level of education it deserves deep thought and I am confident its presence, together

with awareness of it, would raise the quality both of relations with the surrounding world and of learning processes in schools and in education. With
the help of some stories to illustrate, I will try to argue how sensory perception, pleasure and the power to seduce – what Malaguzzi called the 'aesthetic
vibration' – can become *activators of learning*; how they are able to support and
nourish kinds of knowledge not based uniquely on information; and how, by
avoiding simply definable categories, they can lead to the sensitive empathy
and relation with things which creates connections.

I believe everyone senses on entering Reggio Emilia's municipal schools
how the presence of an atelier and atelierista gives them particularly well cared
for physical environments, including striking products and documentation by
children and teachers. However, not all visitors fully appreciate their positive
educational value. Reflection is needed in order to understand to what extent
Reggio Emilia's recognition of aesthetics affects not simply such appearances,
but a way of 'doing' school and consequently learning by children and adults
and the pedagogical philosophy. This is the most difficult part of the story to
tell and we can attempt to do it through examples and personal experience.

Aesthetics as meta-structure

It is as well to clarify from the beginning that for us educators in Reggio
each discipline – or rather language – is made up of rationality, imagination,
emotion and aesthetics. Cultures which rigidly separate these qualities and
processes of thinking inevitably tend to subtract part of the processes from
the various disciplines or languages. They recognize the rational part of an
engineer, the imaginative part of an architect, the cognitive part of a mathematician, the expressive part of an artist and so on, in simple categories.

In this act of fragmentation and exclusion of some of the processes which,
I repeat, belong to our species' way of thinking and constitute a biological inheritance that is probably ancestral, cultural resources are effectively
diminished and there is a consequent impoverishment in the overall quality
of concepts and thinking.

Rationality without feeling and empathy, like imagination without cognition and rationality, build up partial, incomplete human knowledge.

Various philosophers and thinkers when considering aesthetics have located
it in the border zone of tension and vicinity that exists between rational and
imaginative, between cognitive and expressive. This tension and vicinity
tends to bring a greater degree of completeness to thinking. Gregory Bateson
defines aesthetic sense as 'responsive to the *pattern which connects*' (Bateson,
1979: 9) and adds, '*The pattern which connects is a meta-pattern*. It is a pattern
of patterns' (Bateson, 1979: 11), to be thought of '*primarily* (whatever that
means) a dance of interacting parts' (Bateson, 1979: 13). Some pages later he
cites a discovery by Goethe, 'a considerable botanist who had great ability in

recognizing the nontrivial (e.g. in recognizing the patterns that connect). He straightened out the vocabulary of the gross comparative anatomy of flowering plants' (Bateson, 1979: 13). Taking leaves as an example, Goethe argued that the terminology used to name their various parts was unsatisfactory, using words which are too abstract, too far removed from the life built up by related structures. Saying 'stem' has little meaning if it is not placed in a relationship of growth and life with other living elements.

> 'A stem is that which bears leaves.'
> 'A leaf is that which has a bud in its angle.'
> 'A stem is what was once a bud in that position.'
>
> (Bateson, 1979: 17)

Bateson comments on these botanical formulas with a more general consideration, 'The shapes of animals and plants are transforms of messages' (Bateson, 1979: 18).

I, too, will attempt to use the plant world to support my thesis. Leaves appear to be a favourite subject for school work for various justified reasons. But too often and too quickly the leaves become leaf corpses far removed from the 'pulse of life' which ought not to be lost during the course of investigation, whether in drawing, natural sciences or other.

Drawing close to a leaf and considering it to be a living organism generates a sense of empathy that keeps the level of interest high in children (and adults) for sustained periods of time. It gives the eyes lenses of 'solidarity', which in the end often give direction to ways of seeing and thinking, modifying processes of understanding of the leaf in question and simultaneously the quality of understanding of the entire plant world (see Figures 2.1, 2.2, 2.3).

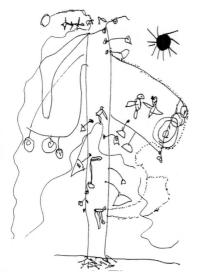

Figure 2.1 Drawing of a tree. 'I think trees are alive because they make apples, they make leaves, they make wind.' Marco, aged 4 years, *scuola comunale dell'infanzia* Diana

Figure 2.2 Clay trees with roots. 'The roots are very, very important because they are the tree's brain.' Giuseppe and Giulia, aged 5–6 years, *scuola comunale dell'infanzia* Diana

Figure 2.3 An open seed in a tree. 'The seed already knows how it has to become.' Vittorio, aged 5 years 6 months, *scuola comunale dell'infanzia* Diana (author's comment: a small tree foetus with the DNA already written inside it)

As I said earlier, it is not simple to demonstrate these claims. In final products those like myself with a background in the arts and possessing a knowledge of visual languages can pick up on – in drawings, sculptures, verbal language – signs of a relationship between artist and leaf which is culturally and emotionally complex. As far as formal qualities of final products are concerned, this complex approach confers on drawings and other forms of representation stemming from different techniques and materials a particular kind of sensibility and originality, which would rarely be found otherwise. An empathetic attitude, the *sympathy* or *antipathy* towards something we do not investigate indifferently, produces a relationship with what brings us to introduce a 'beat of life' into explorations we carry out. This 'beat of life' is what often solicits intuitions and connections between disparate elements to generate new creative processes.

Aesthetics as activator for learning

I would also like to mention briefly the point of view of Kant – with the inevitable impertinent superficiality when dealing with one of the undisputed prodigies of philosophy – who sees aesthetics as a border area where 'reason and imagination do not concur except within a tension' (Deleuze, 2000: 9). Kant and other writers speak of thinking as a sort of mobile threshold, a continuous back and forth between challenge and reinvention, reformulating faculty structures and domains, and how this tension is often a source of renewed paradigms and, therefore, a producer of creativity.

If we believe these claims – which naturally require evaluation by people with other competencies – we can establish a first basic connection; *if aesthetics fosters sensibility and the ability for connecting things far removed from each other, and if learning takes place through new connections between disparate elements, then aesthetics can be considered an important activator for learning.* If all of these things are even only partially true, it is difficult to understand why the aesthetic dimension is usually so distant from the world of school, so extraneous to formative experience for future teachers and pedagogistas.

Earlier I said it would be naïve indeed to think the presence of an atelier and atelierista is sufficient to guarantee the aesthetic dimension becoming an activator of learning. Continuous dialogue is needed between an informed atelier and pedagogy that is both sensible to 'poetic languages' and aware that these are often characterized by a different way of seeing, more profound, anticipating the future, in order to construct innovative spaces together of great interest for education and learning.

Because I refer often to 'languages' and 'poetic languages', I should make it clear at this early stage what I am referring to. In Reggio pedagogy, a choice has been made to extend the term language beyond the verbal and consider *languages* as the different ways used by human beings to express themselves; visual language, mathematical language, scientific language, etc. In a conversation on the relationship between pedagogy and atelier, Claudia Giudici, pedagogista, puts it like this, 'When we speak of languages we refer to the different ways children (human beings) represent, communicate and express their thinking in different media and symbolic systems; languages, therefore, are the many fonts or geneses of knowledge'. *Poetic languages* are forms of expression strongly characterized by expressive or aesthetic aspects such as music, song, dance or photography.

The particular form of educational observation and the documentation of processes used in Reggio schools for some time, testifies to the fertile relationship between poetic languages and pedagogy. During this documentation and analysis of processes, the aesthetic dimension *expresses* its powerful energy, and demonstrates its ability for developing new connections. In the following pages, I will try to provide stories that make this clearer.

I think schools in general do not take account of the aesthetic dimension in learning because, in the vast majority of cases, they consider it to be superfluous; perhaps pleasing but neither necessary nor indispensable. A doubt arises: could it be that the freer approach to problems and irreverence towards consolidated forms of knowledge – typical of those working with aesthetics – represent for traditional culture and education potentially subversive components? A traditional education is often based on rigid paradigms, unchanging over time and with no doubts or uncertainties. An aesthetic sense is fed by empathy, an intense relationship with things; it does not put things in rigid categories and might, therefore, constitute a problem where excessive certainty and cultural simplification is concerned.

Beauty as an aspiration and right of the species

Perhaps an important point to agree is that the pursuit of beauty and loveliness is part of our species in a deep, natural way and constitutes an important element in our humanity; a primary need. A rapid, superficial glance at the history of mankind is sufficient to find, in each age and culture, in objects that have come down to us, a constant presence of care taken with form and attention towards an aesthetic dimension. Gestures of care, research into the quality of form and beauty are testified to in objects which are not only great works of art but ornaments for the body and simple objects for everyday use. This form of inspiration can be found in all peoples and cultures, past and present: to aesthetisize, understood and experienced as a filter for interpreting the world, an ethical attitude, a way of thinking which requires care, grace, attention, subtlety and humour, a mental approach going beyond the simple appearance of things to bring out unexpected aspects and qualities. This aspiration to beauty and loveliness is too often demeaned by the dominant current culture that underestimates the significant psychological and social repercussions of doing so.

It is neither comfortable nor simple to speak of beauty and aesthetics in a world afflicted by injustice, poverty, repression and cruelty. Beauty and aesthetics may seem ideas so ephemeral and far removed from our everyday lives that we feel almost ashamed to speak of them. At the same time we can sense how they counter apparent fragility with an extraordinary strength and resilience that derives from this intrinsic fragility itself.

I would like to quote the ideas of two different authors, which reflect the most dramatic aspects of this contradiction. The first from George Steiner is terrifyingly true and distressing, 'Fascism and the Apocalypse of Auschwitz did not arise in a desert, but at the centre of high culture in Europe. Only 200 metres separate Goethe's garden and the gates of Buchenwald' (Steiner, 2006: 43). The other is by Andrea Branzi who writes, 'The question of aesthetics is *the* serious political issue of the future; in the sense that either this system will prove capable of less ugliness, or it is destined towards social collapse and political refusal' (Branzi, 1997: 25).

Like many others I personally believe that beauty and aesthetics are generative resources for women and men and that to propose them as inalienable and fundamental rights would greatly benefit all humanity.

Poetics

In an informal meeting in a municipal school during one of his most recent visits to Reggio, scholar Jerome Bruner spoke of how in his lessons he prefers to substitute the word 'Poetics' for 'Aesthetics'. The statement struck me greatly, not simply because they are the words of a great *maestro* like Bruner, but because it also made me feel the word 'poetics' as less abstract, less lofty-sounding, almost more humanly tender.

Aristotle's Poetics goes beyond the specific confines of the particular poetic production he is discussing (theatrical representation) and his philosophical reflections assume meanings that can be extended to all human communication in which poetic qualities are expressed. The word 'poetics' becomes extended to include all the languages of the arts, structures of knowledge and underlying processes. 'Aesthetics' and 'Poetics' are different terms for describing concepts and processes that are very close to each other. In simplified terms, we could say that 'Aesthetics' is a system of values and 'Poetics' is a project of values of a more subjective nature in which 'the task of a poet is not to say what has taken place but what might take place (Aristotle, 2007: 3) and where creativity and rigour flow together. Creative thinking develops when it knowingly searches for 'how plots must be composed for the poem to come out well' (Aristotle, 2007: 19).

In what ways have the aesthetic dimension and poetics contributed to identity in the municipal schools in Reggio Emilia? Through which channels have they been demonstrated to be most incisive? How has the presence of a poetic approach extended traditional pedagogy with certain values? Is there a risk of superficial aestheticism, an aesthetic facade, a process that some people, in particular pedagogues, accuse us of from time to time? These are some of the questions to which I will try and bring my point of view in various chapters of the book.

An aesthetic sense

It is as well to recall once again that an *aesthetic sense*, precisely because it is an integral part of the species, easily spills into different fields of knowledge and runs across the various disciplines. It is not uniquely connected with art but becomes a 'way of researching, a key for interpretation, a place of experience'. When mathematicians admit that often, from among various hypotheses, they choose the one which presents the most elegant and beautiful formula they are effectively confirming this attitude. Here are some more examples.

Primo Levi, chemist and writer, defined the structure of a material (*Allosan*) as 'graceful' and commented, 'It calls to mind something solid, something properly connected', adding 'to say lovely (*bello*) is to say desirable' (Levi, 1994: 182). Paul Dirac, a founder of quantum mechanics, said that 'a law of physics must possess mathematical beauty' (in Atiyah, 2007: 47). Hermann Weyl, another mathematician, has written, 'I think certain qualities intrinsic to mathematics make this subject closer to the creative arts than to other experimental disciplines' (in Atiyah, 2007: 47).

I think the best way to explain what mathematicians mean by the concept of beauty is through comparing maths and architecture. Architecture draws many of its qualities from its overall visual impact, from the artistic nature of its design, from the engineering that underpins its structure and the sophisticated care for detail in decoration. Various experts work concurrently on different parts of a construction that ends up by being permeated with a constant tension between aesthetics and functionality. Mathematics can be seen in the same light; an abstract building, whose elegant structure expresses an overall project of extreme beauty where the refinement of detail can be admired in its intricate argumentation and whose solidity is constantly reinforced by rigorous technique and the intrinsic usefulness of its innumerable applications. In both maths and architecture it is possible to list qualities the sum of which create beauty: elegance, precision, profundity. In the end however, the aesthetics of maths begins to exist only when it finally becomes visible to our eyes.

(Atiyah, 2007: 47).

There are similar examples in all professions and disciplines. At the same time, however, it should be recognized that, as for all cultural activities, an aesthetic sense has to be supported and defended with constancy.

When, at the end of the 1960s, Loris Malaguzzi chose to introduce in every municipal school an atelier organized by a person with a background in the arts, his decision was and is more revolutionary than may at first appear, for it has brought a new way of seeing into schools and into the processes of learning compared with customary views and pedagogical tradition. What we are talking about is a different vision of problems.

Without diminishing their value, we need to get beyond the materials and techniques introduced into schools by the atelier, even though they are extremely important for the processes they promote and their acquisition of competencies. We must go beyond materials and techniques to stop and look at processes of empathy and intense relations with things which the atelier promotes, to think how atelieristas are capable of proposing themselves as guarantors of the fact that an expressive, emotional part as well as a rational, cognitive part will always be present in every discipline, or language.

In Reggio's experience of ateliers and work with visual languages – by nature sensitive and close to the other poetic languages – the *aesthetic dimension* has found significant, tangible expression through eyes, ears and hands that are capable of simultaneously constructing and feeling emotion.

Suggestions from art

The atelier takes many suggestions from the arts, both past and contemporary. It does not stop so much to look at products as to catch the suggestions that artists, with their sensitive antennae, give us through their works of art. I will give examples for a better understanding:

- the quality and transformation of light during the day (this is particularly evident in Monet's *The Water Lilies*)
- signs (drawn or painted) as writing, as narrative
- how one subject never presents itself through a single facet but through multiple points of view, not as a total of these but with a complex identity
- how colour sings and expresses itself through various hues to reach the point of expressing chromatic uniqueness, as in the works of Klein
- materials perceived as chromatic substance as in Burri's works
- body art where the physicality becomes gesture, rhythm, total participation
- video art, where time and movement are an integral part of the work
- ambience music where the traditional contrast between sound and noise is lost and through sensitive listening everyday life becomes music
- Luigi Ghirri's photography in which form and concept are abstract and colour becomes chromatic music
- concept art in which metaphor becomes a story
- and other examples could be added.

I could go on at length because there are truly many, many *eyes, ears, gestures*, emotions, perceptions and forms of protest offered generously, sometimes angrily, by art and artists.

It is important to understand that the suggestions are not so much on a purely formal level. Rather, they materialize into equally numerous new concepts and new types of relations with the world; which is why references to the world of art and its values should above all be re-experienced and reinterpreted in teachers' ways of working and in children's imaginations. These processes of exchange, vicinity and kinship with the world of art have given rise to ways of working and structures for educational practice, and generated a culture and approach to things which quickly and visibly diffuse throughout schools: to the environment, classroom proposals, processes and final products.

In an educational project, listening is a difficult but indispensable practice that must be learned. Aesthetic tension, with its empathy, searching for relations and 'connecting structures', together with its grace, humour, provocations and non-determinism, supports the process of listening.

Aesthetics/ethics

No-one denies the risk of a superficial aesthetic attitude, which could cover up fragile or poor contents. For in today's society a powerful process of standardization is being acted out, based on dominant cultural models transmitted through mass media and in which beauty is very often devalued, exchanged and sold off in its most futile, superfluous and luxurious forms. This shameful devaluation certainly cannot be attributed to the nature of the aesthetic dimension; it is the fruit of a misunderstanding, or worse, of a betrayal. In our understanding of the word, aesthetics is a promoter of relationships, connections, sensibility, liberty and expressiveness, and its closeness to ethics appears natural.

In educational terms, I would speak of a need for an inseparable union; the surest of unions for keeping all forms of violence and oppression at a distance, making aesthetic sensibility one of the strongest barriers to physical and cultural violence. Since aesthetic experience is also principally the experience of freedom, it is no coincidence that avant-garde aesthetic research has always been and continues to be greeted by hostility in all dictatorships.

Aesthetics/epistemology

Drawing to the conclusion of these brief reflections, I chanced to pick up a copy of the talk given by Professor Mauro Ceruti in Reggio Emilia. Ceruti, Professor of Philosophy of Science at the University of Bergamo, chaired the commission that prepared the *Indicazioni per il curricolo per la scuola dell'infanzia e per il primo ciclo d'istruzione* (*Guidelines for curriculum in preschools and the primary cycle of education*), circulated in 2007 by the Italian Ministry for Education and approved for use in nursery and primary schools. I must say that reading his words about the guidelines could not have made me happier. Because as well as his intelligent thoughts on schools as places of research, in the last few pages (in felicitously synthetic thinking) Ceruti deals with the topic of art as 'deeply epistemological and pedagogical' and how art must not be 'confined to a museum framework, otherwise its aesthetic – and, therefore, epistemological – potential disappears, because the real danger is that of museumizing art'. Soon after he states again, 'epistemology and aesthetics are synonymous'. Why is this? Perhaps because, 'we have even lost the meaning of the word aesthetic. In our everyday experience and I think in the activity of criticism, when we transformed it into an academic discipline. Aesthetics means caring for our sensibility towards relations' (Ceruti, 2007).

I found the same aesthetics–epistemology word pair in a recently published book on synthetic morphogenesis ('The generation of simulated forms starting from algorithms and biogenetics and the generation of artificial living forms starting from recombinations of genetic information', Berardi Bifo and Sarti, 2008: cover) in which nothing can be rigorously anticipated:

> [...] What we are interested in is the point where aesthetics and epistemology meet. For this reason we will look into the magnifying glass given to us by artists. [...] We must start from sensibility, from physical and conceptual perceptions, and also from the sensation of unease the intimate interweaving of things sometimes provokes in the epidemic tissue of subjectivity.

When we speak of aesthetics we speak of our bodies. From this point of view we can have a better understanding of what is meant by art. The work of art is to create antennae. Antennae which perceive all that is intolerable, discomforting, hateful and repugnant in the universe that we ourselves have created. Antennae capable of harmonizing us with the happy constellations of existence, showing us technical and epistemological paths out of the darkness, for freeing us from oppression, for dissolving violence.

In this sense our book is a book of aesthetics. But at the same time it is a book of epistemology.

(Berardi Bifo and Sarti, 2008: 8)

The authors add, 'Epistemology is the science that studies the phenomena of our mental attitudes, our attitudes towards knowledge... ' (Berardi Bifo and Sarti, 2008: 9)

I cannot but feel enthusiasm for this marriage of epistemology and aesthetics referred to by people from different disciplines, and bringing aesthetic experience back to an experience of life and relations, removing it from perhaps too solemn an area and returning it to the everyday processes which help us to sense how *things dance together with one another*. My plea is to listen carefully to the many appeals which have been made about how not reflecting on the tie between epistemology and aesthetics, how not considering them synonymous, deprives us of a deeper understanding of things, 'I hold to the presupposition that our loss of the sense of aesthetic unity was, quite simply, an epistemological mistake' (Bateson, 1979: 19).

Chapter 3

A general overview

An irreverent hypothesis

Many ateliers have been started up in recent years in Italy, but also elsewhere in Europe and the world, but these are external to school *curricula*. Unquestionably the fact of their presence is positive, but their role in relation to schools is very different to that of ateliers situated within the curriculum, tightly interweaving with all other disciplines.

My invitation is to reflect on and evaluate how important it could be to have a larger presence in schools of languages defined somewhat simplistically and arbitrarily as 'expressive': visual, musical and physical languages; and above all to what extent attention towards the expressive qualities and *aesthetic dimension* of all disciplines could contribute to giving knowledge a dimension of greater completeness and *humanity*.

The question we should be asking is to what extent and in what ways the processes of learning and teaching could change if school culture welcomed the poetic languages and an aesthetic dimension as important elements for building knowledge. The hypothesis makes many people smile, as if it were a surreal request; perhaps because it is that far removed – too far removed – from everyday reality. Certainly schools exist that are working in this direction but these are isolated cases and have a limited impact in terms of numbers on the formation of knowledge in the world. Instead, this irreverent hypothesis has partly been realized in Reggio Emilia's early childhood centres – our municipal schools – where it is actually possible to observe and reflect upon the strange and unusual educational phenomenon that has been constructed there. Rather than speaking in the abstract, the Reggio educational project makes it possible for me to discuss real, verifiable situations.

Why should this have happened in Reggio Emilia? According to Andrea Branzi's recent essay on the city, Reggio Emilia is an innovative place (the most highly innovative in Italy) because we find here many cultures, traditional and new, united with a strong and natural passion for thinking and doing, 'A sort of natural energy which manifests itself in a highly sophisticated form of spontaneous vitality' (Branzi, 2007: 236). I would like to think this is truly the case, and certainly on encountering Reggio pedagogy, first recounted by Loris Malguzzi during a conference and then on entering the schools and working there, I was fascinated, perhaps engulfed by the vital energy alluded to by Branzi, and by the dream of an educational project in which professional and cultural backgrounds like my own (a diploma from Modena Art Institute and a teaching certificate for art education and history of art which I took in Florence) would take on shape and meaning; quite the opposite of my brief prior experience teaching in secondary schools, in which the subject of art was then, and continues to be, considered of secondary importance.

Although the Reggio schools were only starting on their educational journey, when you walked into them you could feel the energy, the optimism of a community working to a high degree of social and ethical awareness; awareness that over the years has taken shape in a strong common vision – to understand the peculiar qualities of which simple analysis of the ways teachers are educated and trained is not sufficient. Perhaps the social and cultural situation at the time, or maybe the words of Malaguzzi, were capable of deeply motivating the work of teaching young children which elsewhere had so little social recognition. Perhaps there was also an awareness (or a hope, or a possibility) that through our work we were contributing to different ideas of learning and knowledge to those then circulating which were so unexciting culturally.

A multiplicity of languages

It has always been my impression that in the area of education, the concept of *knowledge* needs to be defined in deeper ways and with greater awareness so that it can develop and evolve in conditions of greater excitement and cultural vivacity, a sort of instinctive sensibility and swiftness in responding to cultural stimulus. And to better define the word *knowledge* I would combine it with other words such as *trans-disciplinary* (a term proposed by Edgar Morin), *co-participation*, *solidarity*, *humour*, *tenderness*, *grace* and then, not least, *beauty*.

I believe that in work like mine, which deals with education, one of the objectives should be clarifying what kind of knowledge we are working for. Perhaps all this has been said many times before and by authoritative people, but that does not prevent us from taking up the theme again: how the development of thinking is limited by systems of teaching that tend to separate the different disciplines; how by working in this compartmentalized way we come to break reality up into little pieces and make a more general, more complete understanding of things more difficult; how this division poses obstacles to opportunities for grasping elements capable of establishing connections which constitute the support, the strong links, in comprehensive networks of knowledge.

This should not be interpreted as an invitation to give up the necessary and positive depth of knowledge in disciplines. However, it corresponds to an idea that enriching our knowledge of a discipline ought to lead to the desire for connection and dialogue with other areas of knowledge. I say 'ought to' because the initial separation of disciplines causes and supports ever-greater specializations which, in the end, are revealed to be myopic and to truly enrich neither individual nor collective intelligence. This is one of the reasons that has led to Reggio Emilia pedagogy's preferred use of the word language in the place of discipline and when I say 'language', as I have explained before, I do not mean only the customary spoken languages in the traditional use of the word, but all those ways of communicating through which human thinking is brought to reflect, dig deeply, ask questions and make interpretations in different areas such as science, music, architecture, painting, cinema, mathematics, etc. to take in all areas of human communication.

Every language has its own grammar, its own specific nature, but it also has a structure disposed towards communication and relation. Structurally speaking a language is open to communication. When in Reggio pedagogy we declare that a child possesses and 'speaks a hundred languages' – by which we mean the many communicative possibilities with which our species is genetically equipped – we are hypothesizing that learning processes take place in which several languages (or disciplines) interact together. I believe research and discovery in the area of the neurosciences, which are now well known, have confirmed the extent to which our minds and our sensations form a continuum. Therefore, conscious of the fact that our minds and sensations exist in continuous connection, we believe that opportunities and the freedom for analysing each complex problem and situation through the filter of more than one language supports one of the brain's natural, biological capacities; and that encouraging relations between processes and the flow of one into the other activates different areas in the brain's structure, so giving greater richness and completeness to thought. We understand, however, that these biological capacities need adequate contexts, materials and rhythms in order to achieve and express this growth.

These declarations have led us to design and plan our school environments, the materials used, procedures practised, the professional development of educators and the things proposed with children so that there is a real possibility of the hundred languages being able to develop through the synergies created, and of the observations and documentation we produce being capable of carefully viewing this interweaving of languages.

I hope it is clear we are not aiming simply to collect a series of discipline-based points of view for a topic. What we are proposing is a sort of *trans-disciplinary fertilizer, full of vitality* capable of welcoming different ways of thinking, not afraid of 'interference' and 'contamination' but considering them to be a possibility and not 'off the subject'.

Personally I am convinced, and I have declared this on more than one occasion, that the richer and more complete a language, the more it is able to welcome and enter into synergy with other languages. However, this means that each language must be treated by adults and with children for its rich structure and expressive possibilities. This is certainly not a simple aspect, for the languages each one of us knows deeply are few and in many we are practically semi-literate and this limits our ability for listening to the processes of children.

What to do? To begin with we can give children and ourselves the opportunity that comes from not immediately creating hierarchies between languages, understanding the richness that arises from this. We can offer school education where different languages are treated in both specific and interdisciplinary ways and we can continue to try out and use languages in practical ways in everyday teaching by forming groups of teachers with different areas of competency who can plan and share experience together.

From this point on I will start to alternate my reflections with episodes whose authors are children of different ages; brief stories capable of giving a livelier face to the words of a profession like my own.

Crowds

We would need to be deaf (and unfortunately teachers often become deaf through erroneous forms of educational programming) not to capture, in initial conversations among a group of children starting a project to look into impressions of crowds, how they relate to reality through intertwining perceptions so that borders between 'languages' are continuously and repeatedly crossed.[1]

Four boys and four girls discuss and define their images of a crowd in two separate groups.

Girls' group

'When there are a lot of people, they make a huge din. People make a lot of noise with their footsteps.'

'Children can get lost.'

'People are passing by with their shoulders all squeezed.'

'You can hear talking and shouting… some people go right, some go left, some go straight on; downhill, uphill, one way, the other way, anyone who wants to goes wherever they want.'

'It's a carpet of people walking and moving.'

'The girls have a nice smell.'

'And the girls have mini-skirts, tights, jeans, ballet pumps, trainers, or heels, trousers… not the men, they don't have nice clothes.'

Boys' group

'There was a flood of people near my house, all in a line. All you could see were heads, lots of heads.'

'I was in the middle, but when there are lots and lots and lots of people it's a big problem because you can get lost.'

'On the television I saw lots of people, you could see lots of t-shirts, lots of jackets.'

'People breathe and sweat, there's a smell.'

'I look carefully at each person, I can see them everywhere. If a person goes the other way I can see their back.'

'When the crowd is really crowded your mummy picks you up or your daddy takes you on his shoulders, and all the view you can see is heads.'

'At night a crowd is very very dangerous because it is all black.'

'The young people all like wearing black. Black is their favourite colour.'

Everything is already here in the words of the children, in their definitions of a crowd, in the consonance and differences we can pick up between girls and boys. Teachers have here all the indicators for a project that will allow them not to betray the point of view of the children, which already anticipates and contains a synergic use of languages.

It is sufficient to listen to children for us to understand that *trans-disciplinarity*, the way in which human thinking connects different disciplines (languages) in order to gain a deeper understanding of something, is not a totally separate theory from reality or a *teaching commandment*; it is a natural strategy in thinking, which is supported by our initial hypothesis that opportunities for combination and creativity in a plurality of languages enriches children's perceptions and intensifies their relations with reality and imagination.

Literary critic and eclectic writer George Steiner urged us all to find a unitary vision once again and considered the schism between humanities and sciences to be a principle impediment in our culture. 'For Plato and Aristotle, and also for Leibniz and Valery, mathematics was the music of thought. Leibniz said "when God sang, he sang in algebra". A marvellous expression; to sing in algebra' (Steiner, 2006: 46). Marvellous indeed; an expression that communicates a beautiful, impassioned idea of numbers that in no way depreciates the rigour of this discipline or the difficulties of studying maths.

Mathematical explorations

Alice has just turned five and for some time, like many children of her age, has had a real passion for numbers; a myriad of situations prompt her to count, to add and subtract, to break down the same number and put it together again in different ways and she is trying out play with multiplication. She amuses herself by working out which numbers are defined as even, which as odd and why. She adores inventing her own mathematical problems – and solving them and starts these by saying 'What if...?' in a suitably enquiring tone of suspense. She is trying to disentangle and understand the days of the week properly, and evaluate the passage of time. One day Alice asked me, 'If it takes me an hour to go 10 kilometres, in half an hour do I go 5 kilometres? How many kilometres can I go in three quarters of an hour?'

With this last part of her question she lost her way, partly because I was not able to supply her with a completely clear answer. A teacher in a class of 5 year olds that I consulted for a brief exchange of views on this problem confirmed that many children have an interest in numbers and showed me material that she and her colleague had for the most part created themselves in order to support and evolve this interest.

Can it be possible that this passion and curiosity is so easily extinguished when children get to compulsory school? That numbers *cease to sing* for them? Is it really a question of greater difficulty? To what extent are difficulties in teaching exacerbated by confining maths to a narrow category, artificially limited and extraneous from the start?

Malaguzzi often said that in learning *effort and pleasure* come together; this is the path we need to look for and go down with the children; not the simplest perhaps, but neither in the end is it so terribly difficult.

There follows a series of stories on this theme, different in subject matter and with children of different ages.

Mathematical compositions

Small sticks of similar length and pebbles of various shapes and sizes (flat, round) were proposed with some 4-year-old children. They were asked to connect each stick to a pebble; a way of making the well-known mathematical concept of one-to-one explicit.

It is interesting to note how children carried out their task and how their attention was given to a sense of space and shape as well as to numbers. I challenge anyone not to notice how solutions to their problem have also pursued the beauty of formal composition (see Figure 3.1).

Figure 3.1 Mathematical compositions, children aged 3 years to 3 years 6 months

The power of zero

Christian, a little boy of 5 years 8 months, has made a drawing to visualize his mathematical theory, 'A zero has united all its strength to make numbers up to infinity'.

Again it would be difficult to separate qualities of form and aesthetic from cognitive qualities (see Figure 3.2).

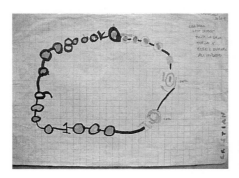

Figure 3.2 The power of zero: visualization of a mathematical theory, Cristian, aged 5 years 8 months

The sunflower

For some time we had observed how children were sensitive and attentive to the play of light and shadow, which means in turn that teachers must also be so. If not, documentation of an episode such as the one recounted here would have been impossible, and impossible, therefore, for it to have had a continuation. Two children aged about two years were walking around their classroom and stopped when they were attracted by a ray of light coming through the window.

'It looks like a surprise.'

'It looks like a piece of sun… It's a sunflower' [in Italian *girasole*; gira=moving, turning, sole=sun].

In two simple sentences the children let us see into the seed of knowledge: the wonder, curiosity, and ability to construct new connections.

After welcoming the ray joyfully and with curiosity the children specify it is a ray of *sunlight* and in an extraordinary leap of thought calmly assert that the ray moves round in connection with the sun. In an intuitive and illuminating likeness they suggest an analogy, voicing it through reappropriating a double noun to confer a precise identity on the phenomenon they have observed – it is a *girasole*, a tournesol. I do not know if the child uttering the word was familiar with the flower of the same name; perhaps yes, perhaps not. Children are sometimes capable of invention and intuition of a remarkably scientific nature, in the same way as they are capable of connecting pieces of information in such unexpected ways. I am always moved by children's approach to the phenomena of reality and as in many other similar episodes this story seems to me to be an extraordinary combination of rationality and poetry because children's ways of seeing interrogate the world, marvel, and create hypotheses.

After noting the children's conversation the teachers *gave more space* to the sunlight and organized the environment so as to let the sun make shapes and plays of shadow and light. The presence of sunlight has become ever more *fluid* and capable of creating wondrous contexts. This sensibility towards light, which had been observed on various occasions, also struck the architects and designers with whom we work on a regular basis and they too became more sensitive to this idea, to the point of including occasions for creation of light-phenomena in their design projects that await the possible exploration of children.

The overhead projector

Sunlight, artificial light, light and shadows; it took the contribution of the atelier to transform an overhead projector, rather a banal object which is usually used for talks or lectures, into an almost magical instrument of unexplored potential for the children.

Overhead projectors have been a constant presence in Reggio centres for some time (and also now in many schools around the world). They are tools for making interesting discoveries in science and the perceptions, for suggestive games and exploration, and are capable of creating fantastical stage scenery.

They are almost magical when they make materials placed on their transparent surface into precious things and they create absolutely extraordinary visions when they project giant images of various objects and materials onto a far surface (see Figures 3.3 and 3.4). 'Look! Look how marvellous', exclaims a 4-year-old girl, inviting classmates and teacher to participate in the joy of an unexpected and enchanting experience. Inside classrooms, projections become wondrous and changing backdrops for narrating stories or physical immersion in images. They can also become surprizing sources of discovery when we compare the mirror image of an object with its position in the original, or when the projected image of an object grows or shrinks depending on its distance from a light-source. The latter is a phenomenon even many adults find difficult to manage, so that very often their predictions (and actions) are exactly the opposite of correct interpretations of the optical phenomenon.

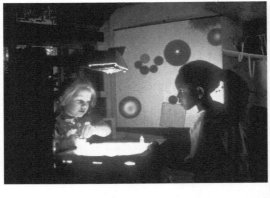

Figures 3.3–3.4 Projecting with the overhead projector

Documentation of a project[2] on light coordinated by an atelierista included this conversation between two children aged about four-and-a-half, recorded while they were exploring a hairslide positioned on top of an overhead projector and projected onto a white wall (see Figures 3.5–3.7).

Figures 3.5–3.7 The hairslide, Lucia and Marco aged 4–5 years, *scuola comunale dell'infanzia* Gulliver

MARCO: The image is different when it gets to the wall – it turns round and in my opinion there's an electronic system going all this way and then it goes high up there and then onto the wall.

LUCIA: And the system transports pictures of objects.

MARCO: Perhaps the minor tube has a picture inside it and takes it to the mirror... into a secret passage, a short cut, and then takes it as quick as it can to the wall.

LUCIA: The picture in the mirror has to run to get to the wall. The mirror (the small mirror in the overhead projector) makes it turn the other way.

MARCO: As if the hairslide were doing a somersault.

LUCIA: A somersault on the wall. In the light bulb you can see a picture of the slide... the slide does a somersault on the wall.

MARCO: No, first it does one on the mirror.

LUCIA: You need a lens like ones in binoculars.

MARCO: A lens to design a somersault.

LUCIA: Mystery solved.

In this brief dialogue each one of us can grasp or interpret various aspects. We cannot help but recognize the intelligence, the inventive and analytic ability that the conversation contains, the ability for listening to others that brings the children, naturally and with lively intelligence, to proceed using the logic that went before. They realise the projected image has been inverted compared to the original and because a tool is involved, there is undoubtedly an 'electronic system' that transports the image on its 'way' and transforms it before arriving at the wall, a 'secret passage'. The journey imagined by Marco and supported by Lucia is adventurous, somewhat mysterious but unquestionably interesting. It is Lucia who specifies that 'the system transports a picture of objects' clearly differentiating the real world and the projected world; parallel worlds with different rules and lives. On the way the object encounters a mirror, an element that is familiar to the children and, although they do not analyse it thoroughly, they perceive the phenomenon by which reflected images turn upside down. In fact it is the mirror that catches Lucia's attention and to which she attributes the phenomenon that makes it turn things 'the other way'. Then we have the playful and irresistible image of an object doing two daring somersaults; first into the mirror and then a running somersault onto the wall, to make its passage from the real world into the projected world. And here 'the mystery is solved'.

Teaching cannot forget beauty

Is it so mistaken to believe in the possibility of learning in which wonder, ethics, beauty, pleasure and rigour are the basis of knowledge?

In his book *Giustizia e Bellezza (Justice and Beauty)* Luigi Zoja discusses how growing complexity has eliminated beauty because 'it is an obstacle to efficiency, speed and the financial measuring which ever more exclusively guides society. It has to be admitted: aesthetic values simply tend to be anti-functional and anti-economical' (Zoja, 2007: 22, 23). Later he concludes his argument with a hopeful thought on beauty's inevitability:

> Beauty triumphs in itself and through itself. Beauty is a completely different thing from eliminating ugliness and in fact does not require this. [...] Since we need positive tasks and not only moralism lamenting the ills of the world, we secretly turn to aesthetics as a free, instinctive complement to ethical issues. Offering beauty is naturally right. It immediately makes the world better, it requires no crusades against wrong, it curries favour with no murderous ideologies. It is generous (and, therefore, ethical) precisely because those close to it benefit from it, not only the creator or commissioner.
>
> (Zoja, 2007: 23)

The task of teaching cannot forget beauty. The issue is a serious one and difficult to deal with in education. Again Zoja warns us that 'those who are not able to see the beauty being lost for ever cannot reach the heart of injustice and, therefore, lack the necessary awareness for confronting it' (Zoja, 2007: 38). Much of the world around us seems ever more inclined not to recognize beauty, or worse, not feel a need for it and the damage caused by its absence is more serious than would at first appear: the absence of relationship with environments ever more carelessly and grievously maltreated; housing that is more often about profits for builders than attention to a culture of habitation; lack of care and solidarity for places; widespread vulgarity; ever more deafening and constant background noise. The daily message we often receive is contrary to beauty and contrary to knowledge, which recognizes in beauty a vital seed of civilization.

Reggio pedagogy has welcomed this seed, attempting to defend and give it sustenance down the years; considers poetic languages and forms of art to be a vital presence in learning curricula; has desired ateliers and atelieristas in the same way that it has defended schools having their own kitchens and taking care with food; has resisted and continues to resist financial pressures that view ateliers, kitchens and beauty as luxuries and, therefore, not vital. But clearly Reggio pedagogy is a microscopic presence in the international world of school education and certainly cannot oppose current society past a certain point.

Perhaps, however, the stubborn defence of these things, which are seemingly less defensible in rational argument, has in part contributed to Reggio pedagogy's long life, almost half a century, in a network of public, municipal schools that have become a point of reference and hope for so many teachers in different countries and cultures.

In a recent book, Andrea Branzi draws attention to the importance of working on 'useless things', a quality which represents an abundance of energy and generosity and which is significant on an anthropological level. He discusses the fact that the development of all civilizations and societies has started from the energy for things often perceived to have no use: art, poetry, music; pleasing things, and that these, not just functional objects, have made it possible for civilizations to develop. On a social and political level, it is important to transform a flower into a precious gift.

There is a lovely poem by Danilo Dolci (Dolci, 1970) in which I find the expression of one of the reasons the Reggio Emilia approach has been successful throughout the world: that fascinating mix of realism and utopianism which makes us openly welcome others with their ideas and cultures without ever ceasing to dream of them as different to the way they are; we embrace a reality which all too often punishes childhood with the optimism to go on believing that each child has the right to someone with a project for their future and development, in the conviction as the poem says, that 'each one of us grows only by dreaming'.

The exhibition from Reggio Emilia entitled *The Hundred Languages of Children* that has travelled the world for almost thirty years, bears Loris Malaguzzi's initial declaration that makes it resonate with the poem quoted above, 'This is an exhibition of the possible'. In these words Malaguzzi consciously announced to the public that the quality of the projects exhibited was not present throughout the entire network of Reggio schools, but that we dreamed of achieving this quality of education and practice for all the schools and that we would work towards that end.

We have managed in part, but I am completely convinced of the fact that *only by dreaming does each person grow*. Just as I believe that thinking each child is born with the possibility of expressing her/himself in many languages makes education and schools capable of speaking many languages. Consciously and persistently.

I am convinced in the same way that Reggio pedagogy owes much of its attraction internationally to the fact that it continues to dream and work on certain aspects, i.e. that it considers beauty and processes promoted by poetic languages to be important for learning.

This does not mean, as some people have insinuated and at times also declared, that we make children in Reggio schools live in school environments too artificially beautiful and good compared with the general conditions of society; but that the teaching profession cannot afford not to consider problems of ethics and aesthetics. During a television broadcast seen throughout Italy I have heard a well-known journalist, the wife of a noted Italian politician, declare she would never send her children to a Reggio school because they were *too lovely*, that children should experience reality, which is not lovely, from the start. In declarations of this kind can always be found a form of *violence towards dreams*, especially towards change for the better, which I find slightly terrifying.

We must work with constancy and commitment, without forgetting our proposals of ambitious and tender objectives on the way. Could it be that tenderness in education is seen as a form of weakness and permissiveness, that it should always be countered with useless and unjustified severity? Is it the age old, ever updated ambiguity existing between authority and authoritativeness? Only the ancients seem disposed to go to the heart of the issue. When asked in an interview, 'How can we get back to schools which are places you go to learn?' Edgar Morin replied simply, 'With love. And it is not my idea, I am simply quoting Plato' (in Lilli, 2007: 49). More than anything else children ask for attention and love.

Difficult children

It once happened that I was documenting and observing 4- and 5-year-old children who belonged to the category defined as 'difficult' because they are often in conflict with other children, and often it is difficult to involve them in proposals for classroom work. These three children were trying to make a construction but spent most of their time arguing and pushing and shoving each other. In a deliberate but natural way the teacher introduced a fourth child, who demonstrated very good relational competencies to the group.

The most interesting aspect resulting from this child's inclusion was a recording of the language that he used. Very often he used the other children's names, and used the plural – we – in the project context, 'Shall we add this object?' and 'Then shall we transform it into a spaceship?' He asked the others' consent for things he proposed, using expressions such as 'Do you like it?' and 'Do you agree?', and suggested ways of continuing their play. The overall image of his verbal and body language gave the idea of both proposing and requesting collaboration. It emerged very clearly that what the other children lacked was not the desire to work together, which was what they perhaps desperately wanted, but a sort of literacy in the language of relations.

Following this we gave greater attention to these children, documenting them for example in positive situations. Results were not always immediately obvious but the climate of mutual trust between children and teachers unquestionably increased.

It was, therefore, very moving when one of these three 'difficult' children left a beautifully coloured autumn leaf on the atelier table. When I thanked him, perhaps excessively, he replied with some embarrassment, making little of it, and said 'there were lots of them anyway and I didn't know what to do with them all'. I continued to find a lovely leaf on my atelier table for some days.

Collective intelligence

Children, together with their families, bring all aspects of external reality into school and this is the reality we face every day; it is never a very easy reality. However, precisely because schools and knowledge do not exist in artificial bubbles cut off from reality (and just as well), I believe schools need to consciously take a position on *which knowledge* they intend to promote. Schools can do this through consciously and essentially making ethical and aesthetic choices expressed not so much in preaching that is more or less moralizing, but more than anything else by their approach to things, the thinking and doing that give concrete value to what is meant by knowledge.

Values are concretely expressed in the quality of proposals and educational 'procedure', in continuous exchange with a contemporary world, in an idea of teaching that chooses not to transmit circumscribed 'truths' in various 'disciplines', but rather to stand by children's sides together constructing contexts in which they can explore their own ideas and hypotheses individually or in groups and discuss them with friends or teachers.

What Pierre Lévy calls collective intelligence emerges forcefully in Reggio schools, 'The common sharing of cognitive capacities, abilities and memories of people participating in a flow of information. A flow requiring communities of imagination not only of news' (Lévy, 1996: 65). I believe Reggio Emilia's municipal schools are places which have practically supported and informed such a flow: through people with their widely differing characteristics that have worked in the schools; and through the different competencies that have come from the outside, from Loris Malaguzzi to pedagogistas, psychologists, neurologists, architects, designers and artists (of which more later), a *transdisciplinary* world with certain shared ideas on humanity and knowledge.

Children's theories

One of the foundations of our work is the careful, respectful, tender 'listening' with solidarity to children's strategies and ways of thinking. Careful however! These are children who feel free to express their opinions and who trust in the fact that they will be listened to carefully and respectfully. It is no coincidence that Jerome Bruner recalls that what struck him most on first entering the Reggio schools was a teacher who was listening to a child's theories on how shadows are formed. He emphasizes how this listener was interested and serious, because the child was putting together a theory the credibility of which was not important. What was important was the process that led to the construction of the theory.

Alice (aged 4 years 11 months) lying on her mattress suddenly says, 'I think brains have books all around them. We say "Brain! read the rainbow book!" and we think of a rainbow. The brain is surrounded by millions of books where lots of things are written and the books are what we think'. Some months later, the same girl, Alice, walking through a meadow says, 'Where do they get the colours we use? Perhaps they collect lots of dead butterflies and make colours from their wings. No perhaps they use grasses?'.

How children make theories is fascinating. The presence of rationality and imagination and such close intertwining between them is found only in the theories of great thinkers; in children's theories there is also that highly empathetic approach to things which is highly developed in children and a sensitive filter for understanding and connecting things.

It is not easy to make a lot of people understand the important consequences of adopting a particular approach towards the various languages or disciplines for both children and teachers – the differences that can be created in knowledge with a certain *angle* or way of proposing a language. I will attempt to make this idea clearer, though I find it difficult to give an account of how things can be proposed with children because we offer them not only words and actions but a certain relationship with the world. In this relationship proposals are generated by a combination of words and behaviours that accompany them: gestures, tone, expressions of the face and body. I will try to recount this complexity anyway, in two examples, while declaring once again that ateliers should be guarantors of processes in which cognitive and expressive aspects are never separated, where the rational must never be divided from intuition and where we seek to keep alive the wonder and excitement learning produces.

Reflections on colour

A colour is not a colour if it does not possess an expressive identity, 'Orange is a laughing colour' says a 3-year-old child as he paints. 'Black is all colours' declares a child of two-and-a-half after exploring the large mat set out by teachers and created by bringing together black materials of different consistency and tactile qualities.

If a teacher knows Yves Klein and has been moved on observing his famous *Blue Klein* paintings, she will more easily recognize the same emotion in a 3-year-old boy painting at an easel when the first thick brushstroke of blue runs down from the top of the sheet and he excitedly shouts; 'Look! look what this blue is inventing!'

A drip of blue paint rolling down a sheet of paper tracing unexpected shapes and pathways. Perhaps the difference that derives from the contribution of an atelierista consists simply in this: being able to understand the poetics of colour and be excited by their evocative, expressive power together with the children. It is no small thing, believe me.

But what more usually happens? Colours are grouped together in elementary ways, without distinguishing quality or shade and no care taken in making a 'house of yellows or blues' or of other colours, putting together in a single, simplified category shades of colours extremely different in terms of luminosity, material, consistency and tactile quality. Or children are given the opportunity to discover that together red and yellow make orange, red and blue create purple, yellow and blue make green, in the belief that this constitutes a vaguely scientific, easily reproducible technique, giving simplified, uninteresting information that lacks the wonder of discovery and immediately sets up elementary, simplified categories – reassuring for some – where the extraordinary and *subversive* vitality of colour is imprisoned.

It is different to let colours express their different identities in complex, subjective relationships with children. For a certain shade of yellow changes if the size of the area it covers changes; if an object is rubber or velvet or satin; if a yellow is juxtaposed with a similar shade of colour or with a complementary one; or placed in a particular quality of light. Shades of colour can be discovered and gathered in nature just as they can be tasted in certain foods. Colours can acquire great power of expression through words or painting; they can be played or danced; palettes with different shades can be made up with powdered colour or materials gathered outdoors as in artisan workshops in past centuries, and many shades can be found on computer screens and used with programmes for graphics like Adobe Photoshop, which children are capable of using perfectly well to change the colours and shades of their drawings.

I have seen a 3-year-old girl determinedly search for a particular shade of pink – a colour to express happiness – and use it on the computer for her name, and then look for a sober shade of green as a colour for her name when she was sad.

I will pause here although there could be many, many more illustrations for aspects of colour. Nor should it be believed that everything I have said is too sophisticated for young children.

All of us are born equipped with an extremely refined sensibility for perceiving colour; but as with other perceptive abilities it is the brain that must practice decoding. To achieve this task it is important for it to encounter adequate contexts, otherwise we lose opportunities for *seeing and tasting* the things around us. We are not helped in this task by a hurried, superficial culture that tends to diminish a sense of wonder, our interests and emotions, and *brands* learning with a stamp from which aesthetics has been eliminated; the aesthetics of actions, of intelligent perceptions and of time and rhythm; aesthetics that develop together with reasoning and emotion.

Empathy

I believe a teacher's task is to stand by children's sides and with thoughtful intervention when needed, promote the quality of relations children readily have with things around them and what they are doing. I would like to repeat: an aspect I find detrimental to children's education is proposals for creating things with hurried actions, in too short a time, and insufficient quality of relationship to the subject of their work, too often in this way allowing standardized and purely formal relationships to develop. This 'hurriedness' often leads to actions with little meaning, to learning a mechanical use of materials and techniques, without emotion, without intense or gratifying relationships.

An intensity of relationship is perhaps the first, instinctive, significant way of approaching things suggested by the world of art, but it also suggests acts of attention and care towards the things we do and distances us from the indifference which is one of the worst ways of learning. Taking care means not considering problems of a very practical nature to be irrelevant, problems which unfortunately are only too common, such as having to inhabit schools with dirty walls, or hastily written signs stuck to windows and walls with pieces of brown sticking tape, 'rude' acts which do not take into consideration the feelings of other people, everyday things, small or large, which require attention and emotional participation. Superficiality, lack of concentration, hurriedness – all are things we suffer in more or less obvious ways, immersed as we are in background noise that is constant and all-pervasive.

Children naturally approach things with a strong sense of empathy, and recent studies on the brain are very interesting in this respect. A group of neuroscientists in Parma (a town next door to Reggio Emilia) has made a discovery, which is also of particular importance for education and learning; we are born with a mechanism in which neurons (called 'mirror neurons') respond to motor stimulation with a visual representation of the gesture and the gesture's final objective, not only when we produce it ourselves but when it is made by others (Rizzolatti and Sinigaglia, 2006). This means that we are born with a sub-strata of neurons which require the presence of others; we could define the process activated by these neurons as mutual relations embodied. If, therefore, we consider empathy to be an important vehicle for learning, this suggests proposals for learning that do not hurry to fence the world in more or less rigid categories of thought; but, on the contrary, seek connections, alliances and solidarities between different categories and languages or subjects.

Here is another example to clarify what I mean by care in our approach to things and how I believe proposals for learning can make the process concrete. There is a well-known phenomenon of psychology and the perceptions that establishes the way certain shapes, colours, sounds or other sensorial experience can simulate other forms of reality through a process of substitution; a broom handle that becomes a horse for riding by children is a famous example narrated by Gombrich in *Meditations on a Hobby Horse and Other Essays on the Theory of Art* (1963). This process of substitution is often used in art and it is not a coincidence that young children also use it because they are particularly open to allusive connections that can be made between things.

Materials can allude to realities – re-evoking, narrating or representing them – in personal multisensorial memory processes, connections of a sensory character.

Landscapes with snow, sunlight, fog or autumnal atmospheres, etc. can be visually narrated even by very small children using different techniques and methods, including those that are material-based and non-figurative. It is important to understand that these processes require sufficient time and phases for quality exploration.

Undoubtedly a useful first approach is to establish an intense relationship with the reality being investigated. Especially with very small children this phase is fundamental for the quality of development of subsequent phases: spaces and an environment that can be explored by the child herself using all her senses in a context of interpersonal relations – what we might call 'the right acquaintances'. A second phase might be to look for different materials together with children, letting them make the choices. Materials can be of different size, colour, substance, with different qualities of touch and sound; but they should be capable of triggering memories of personal experience. Our minds are capable of connecting very different planes and levels; a sense can call to mind a memory and narrate a reality by recollecting it.

Encounters between children and materials are generally extremely rich in suggestive qualities, memories and meanings, without much intervention on the part of the teacher.

By delving into materials children remember, choose, interpret and easily attach certain materials to a real sensory experience. Looking for materials to represent a certain reality can take on a theatrical nature and as children recollect their experience they often tend to use the tone of voice and mime the body language they consider most suggestive and suited to narrating the experience they are intent on remembering.

Representations of experience can be encapsulated in a sort of physical performance with child and material in dialogue together and to which children happily abandon themselves. This theatrical situation is sometimes accompanied by projecting images of the explored reality onto walls, floor or ceiling in the space where children are exploring materials.

More often the dialogue woven between child, experience and representative material is made more evident and becomes visible through the creation of a product; tactile, visual, sonorous or all of these. The close presence of an adult is intended to be such that, as children create their products, they are reminded of past experiences and feelings, so that as they give shape to materials (visual, acoustical or other), these traces of past perception and emotion are incorporated.

The mental image each child constructs is an assembly of parts, which gives each 'author' a special way of seeing their own work and that of their companions. Children can easily see analogous elements in the products of their classmates, which reinforces the memory of something experienced individually and collectively.

Some years ago journeys of this kind were experienced and recounted in teacher workshops in different parts of Italy, but what happened in these? On more than one occasion I found this entire sophisticated and delicate process speeded up and rushed, important phases entirely skipped in order to immediately get to the point of obtaining a final product. The pedagogista of a school in northern Italy showed me drawings by 5-year-old children done with coloured pencils. By their nature pencils leave faint, opaque traces. Near the drawings were packets of white tissue and the pedagogista told me, '… then we'll have the children rip up the paper and lay pieces of it on top of their drawings, so they look foggy'.

I tried to explain to the pedagogista and other teachers that there may be differences between a technique mechanically applied to obtain a result that is an appropriate representation of a situation being examined, which is what they were trying to do in this case; and, by contrast, results obtained with a more complete process that is careful not to lose the value and meaning of work being done, which is what we should always try to do. The teachers listened, apparently not very convinced, and I struggled to explain the difference between the two ways of working. I had the impression they evaluated my way of working as over-refined and thought that it would not actually change the final quality of the work to a great extent. I continued, explaining that the end result of the products they had shown me would be a simplified, conformist picture of fog, and that in all probability it would be far removed from the children's perceptions.

Then I asked if the children had at least explored fog and how. They replied, 'No not yet. But it will be getting foggy soon' and that this particular activity was part of a teaching programme (written in perfect pedagogical language) in which they were expected to explore different kinds of weather conditions using suitable drawing techniques. Fog was one of the conditions.

It could be the teachers were partly right and that, in the end, especially with very young children, the final product obtained using the two different approaches is not very different. What changes completely to my mind are the traces left by the work done and the meanings that children take away with them. This difference is in the construction of a different approach to things and reality, a different attitude that increases and informs the quality of our relations with our surroundings. The difference lies in seeking to avoid losing the children's wonder and curiosity when they look at things; avoiding standardized relations.

Playing with metaphor

One of the most important areas of attention for an atelierista or teacher should be learning to develop journeys for work that do not 'betray' children or their different interests and senses; and which learn to use the children's very sensitive antennae, which are capable of lending new and rich ways of seeing the world to adults. In my opinion, among the various educational philosophies available to us, attention towards the entire process is the one that makes a difference and constitutes a platform for the forms of knowledge I would wish to see. I believe the entire process of alluding to reality which substitutes certain elements with other apparently unrelated ones, as the previous example shows, can generate a metaphorical process of great interest if it is conducted well by children and teachers.

We know that art, like children, makes wide use of metaphor. I do not wish to go into a comparative analysis of the metaphorical processes used by artists and children, but I believe we can all agree with the evaluation that constructing metaphors is a mental operation giving unusual, unexpected and very often, totally original results. I believe metaphor corresponds to an investigative attitude towards reality, to participation that allows our thoughts to open out and break down the rigid boundaries that are usually constructed. I see metaphor as a genuine system for organization of intellectual development; for this reason and because I think of it as 'celebration thinking', I believe it is useful and amusing to use – frequently, naturally and with a light touch.

Much has been said and written on verbal metaphor. But there is very little on non-verbal metaphor, which uses other languages and which children in my opinion also use very often. Reinterpretations in visual metaphor are not limited to the element of form as many maintain. Substituting one form with another similar form and the consequent substitution of meaning is certainly the most obvious aspect and the one we encounter most frequently. However, we should not underestimate other elements like colour and material. If, for example, we take the image created by a 4-year-old boy in which an old brass dip pen has been transformed into a war spear, obviously the shape of the pen has led to analogy with a spear. But we cannot know to what extent the colour, and especially the metal material of the pen, have also contributed. Just as we cannot know how much the green of a peapod, and not simply its shape, has contributed to its transformation into a grasshopper (see Figures 3.8 and 3.9).

I say this because the journeys using materials described above make it possible to do small pieces of field research into non-verbal metaphor.

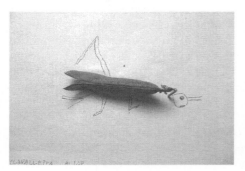

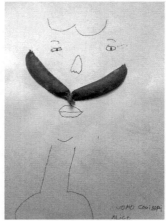

Figure 3.8 Metaphors with pea pods, Alice aged 5 years 10 months. A mermaid

Figure 3.9 A man with a moustache

How do metaphors manifest themselves, and at what age? What sensory form do they take? Are the metaphors of girls different from those of boys? Several years ago in the *scuola comunale dell'infanzia* Diana, I remember we did some research which attempted to give credible answers to these questions and we built up a visual documentary with material gathered. I feel these areas of research need to be taken up again and reworked in new ways, updated and more deeply explored, because children change very rapidly, both as individuals and as part of the evolution of society over time.

Field research is the most effective way for all teachers to develop their own interests and improve professional work. Field research, or at least an attitude of research, is often closely related to the quality children and teachers experience in a process: observation and documentation are its tool and filter. But I will discuss this in later pages.

Choosing atelieristas

As far as 'languages of expression' and techniques are concerned, different tendencies exist in the field of education; one is to specialize certain teachers in this area, another is to request that artists contribute or come in and teach. In both instances, the initiatives are worthy because, although in different ways, both approaches seek to highlight and support in practical ways the importance of the 'expressive languages'. However, some doubt remains as to whether people making these choices are clear about the different learning processes that follow for both children and teachers, and what evaluation is made of them.

I would like briefly to reflect on this idea. I am quite certain that when Malaguzzi chose to introduce people with artistic backgrounds into Reggio's schools without giving them a specialized role (in the sense that their work was not limited only to the languages of art), this was a radical and courageous choice producing renewal and significant new interpretations both in the ateliers and in pedagogy; and to which this book would like to bear witness. When instead artists are asked to work with schools, their background does not, generally speaking, include specific knowledge of children. If artists do not manage to enter into a close dialogue with a pedagogy that embraces the languages of art and is also aware of and respectful of children's strategies, then their contributions are almost fatally destined to be limited and unidirectional, visits in which the artist will tend to transmit a personal view of things and leading to operations of a kind revealed to be the opposite of ideas on personal freedom close to artists' hearts. So, unfortunately, very often their way of educating does not give the hoped for results, at least not for that area of pedagogy that believes creativity in early childhood exists and has its own points of view and strategies.

At the same time there is nothing in the educational training of most teachers to prepare them to be sensitive to aesthetics or consider aesthetics a powerful element for understanding and connecting with reality, i.e. formative of culture in the broadest sense of the word. That is why teachers are often excessively seduced by techniques and tend to propose them with children using only a simplified knowledge of their expressive potential rather than informing sensitive dialogues with reality. Often they demonstrate much greater concern for the final products than for the processes that generate them and they find it difficult to accept new or different schema from those they have learned in art courses. Here again that *busy thinking* which accompanies the work of children tends to be lost or, at the very least, not emerge.

We cannot over-generalize, and I do not exclude the possibility that artists and teachers exist with the gifts of listening and relations and poetic sensibility towards children and reality. Nor can I deny that there are situations where the above choices (artist or teacher) encounter suitable environments for educational renewal. However, I believe this is neither simple nor very common, and a great deal of awareness is required for these conditions to be created.

Having said that, the choices exercised in Reggio Emilia have not been without risk nor have they automatically ensured either the quality of atelieristas or, effectively, the quality of processes in pedagogical renewal. The thinking and possibility promoted by the choice Malaguzzi made in the mid-1960s requires reflection and renewal, 'each one of us grows only by dreaming' (Dolci, 1970).

Art schools and art colleges need new thinking and new teaching, because people educated in these institutions often find it difficult to go beyond the usual cultural scheme of things and to *establish sensitive listening* with children and with their surroundings. There is, however, in Reggio pedagogy a distinctive trait that is essential for supporting the pedagogical value that can come with the presence of ateliers and is also capable to some extent of resolving the problem of individual professional quality; this is the strong presence of pedagogical philosophy intent on embracing poetic languages for their fundamental role in learning and knowledge.

At the same time we also need to be aware that the necessary journey for growing and evolving children's different creativities is long and complex, at least this is how it has been for the atelieristas in Reggio schools.

I remember a question Francesco Tonucci, pedagogista, researcher and renowned illustrator, with whom I worked on various occasions, used to ask insistently over and over again, and I fear we have never really given it a totally satisfying answer. The question was this, 'How is it that by looking at children's drawings I can recognize which schools the drawings come from?' and he would continue posing this question about the role and influence of teachers and atelieristas. Tonucci kindly left the last part of his question unsaid, i.e. how much did this contradict our claim to be listening to individual children?

To my mind recognizable provenance of work owes more to situations in the 'environment', the *cultural humus* which is characteristic of each individual school; conditions caused by intertwining, the result of mixing many different characters, personalities and cultures and the more or less felicitous coming together of these components. All this was, and is, more important than the presence of the atelierista and her personality.

If I might make a comparison, which is perhaps a little prosaic, I would like to remember that foods assume a very different taste and character depending on the environment they grow in; sun, air, water, soil and grass determine different tastes, smells and shapes, sometimes significantly so, in genetically similar products. Then, as now, another important factor has to do with which interests people were very involved in and trends circulating in schools at different times. For example, perhaps there was a greater use of or greater care over real-life drawings or investigating classmates, or portraits were being dealt with in a particular way; people's different perspectives could create a particular climate. It could happen sometimes that for a period of time, much attention would be focused on children's abstract representations or that, on the basis of a chance conversation, for a time certain animals became a preferred subject for work.

However, it is also true that it has been much less easy to distinguish the school of provenance for children's work for some years now, partly because we have learned to be more careful in our intervention and avoid interfering with the original quality of individual children's work. We have managed to replace our initial aesthetic parameters, which stemmed from a knowledge of adult art, with more appropriate evaluations for the languages of children. It takes great care and long periods of time to learn to listen to what is different – and children are different. In order to achieve good results though, we must have a good knowledge of the languages of Poetics and the languages suggested by materials (above all, an *approach sensitive to surroundings*, a *poetic way of seeing*) and of the strategies of children's thinking.

Naturally the cultural level in an environment continues to be important in the end, affecting both children's products and those of teachers, so that above all the issue is the quality of process that the children and teachers and atelieristas are able to develop together.

Ateliers and workshops

Today in Reggio Emilia the term 'atelier' is seen to be slightly inappropriate. But it is defended with a suitable lightness as distinct from traditional 'laboratories', which often involved insufficiently thought-out proposals and action; hurried work was often superficial and approximate and final products, generally culturally and aesthetically rather poor, were the focus of attention rather than quality in the entire process. In a school education, although repeating things is an important part of learning and its pleasure, motivation is often lost along the way and the proposed action, the choice of a certain technique or another, risks becoming reduced and simplified, leaving little trace in the person using it – a sort of fast food in technique and ability. I am speaking on a general level, though perhaps I should not, because there is a great deal of variety in 'laboratories' and the people who work in them, and these differences need to be respected. However, the superficial attitude I mention is much more widespread than many believe and should be watched out for carefully, perhaps even in Reggio schools.

Today, more than ever, attention to the project is important because haste seems to have become urgently important for younger generations; when projects exist they are often short-lived and rapidly replaced by ones of even shorter duration. Interests on the other hand are multitudinous, almost greedily so, and have the brief lifetime of an emotion, of a gesture; to the extent that 'acts are very often consumed in the gesture' (Galimberti, 2008a: 278).

I have often recounted, to the point of almost reducing my opinion to a slogan, how ateliers can and must make techniques *become languages*, how the ability to execute a technique must be developed in the context of broader and more complex meaning.

The words might seem over-emphatic, but I continue to believe that using technique and material in this theoretical frame implies an approach for ateliers and on a more general level can make an effective difference to the construction of learning because it requires vitality, and a capacity for relational growth which can go on to light up new interests.

The importance and care given to the entire procedure, the whole process, leading to a final product is one of the elements which, to my mind, distinguishes the atelier and Reggio pedagogy from other places. This importance and care, informed by field research and discovery made possible by observation and documentation, is in response to the intelligence and creative processes children are capable of in an entirely natural way. It is not easy to demonstrate differences produced in this kind of approach or explain how they happen, but I continue to believe the way problems are approached constitutes a condition that, in the end, creates a difference.

I will try to make my thinking clearer by using two illustrations, two testimonials to how precisely in everyday life important differences can be found regarding our ways of being teachers and especially to the importance of 'contexts' in which learning processes take place.

Mattia and going through a hole

The first example is Mattia, 10 months old, who crawls towards a cupboard and by sitting upright manages to reach a ring-shaped handle on a drawer. At the same time he notices a metal teaspoon on the floor. We do not know what association of images or previous experience makes Mattia relate the two things, but he immediately begins passing the spoon through the open ring of the handle. We must consider that it cannot be easy for Mattia to precisely aim the teaspoon at the hole in the drawer handle, but the sound the spoon makes each time it falls on the floor has for him the taste of victory. Mattia continues his game, repeating it over and over again for a long time. Repetition is an effective process for learning, and it is also clear that Mattia is curious, interested and gratified by this game made of a precise sequence of actions requiring motor and perceptive ability and, in all this, the small sound made by the spoon falling to the floor is included.

Mattia will probably try to transfer such an interesting experience into other contexts and re-experience the feelings of curiosity and satisfaction the game has given him.

At this point there might already be an initial difference in what people mean by a teacher's work. One person might observe the scene appreciatively, but let their interest end there because they do not see it as relevant to the work of an educator. Another teacher might carefully observe this small event, annotating all Mattia's explorations, because they are considered useful material to reuse with other children after suitable reflection. The teacher who has documented Mattia's game can thus begin a project offering a small context to children of the same age, situating it in an environment where other children can reproduce the significant phases in Mattia's explorations, highlighting and varying certain aspects of the perceptions such as size (both the hole through which the object is passed and the object itself), the degree of difficulty in passing the object through the hole, the height from which it falls, the materials it is made from and the surface it falls onto in order to introduce different, varying sound effects.

An important aspect of the different behaviours demonstrated by these two educators might be that one has a programme that is defined from the outset and repeated without paying too much attention to what happens in the meantime. The other might have an educational project open to the changes derived from carefully 'listening' to the reality around her, with suggestions coming from observing the children strongly predominating. When practical proposals start from interests shared by children and teachers, they have a much greater chance of success for both because the entire journey is followed and supervized by teachers with a proper understanding of the basic qualities and, therefore, much more curious towards and capable of proposing interesting adjustments and interventions on the way.

The latter of the two teachers is also aware her proposal will not necessarily be successful with all children and does not negatively evaluate children showing no interest in it. Individual variations always exist and should be included in our hypotheses: a child might not be attracted to that particular game at that particular moment, or may try twice and then grow tired and abandon it; or instead a child might find the situation fascinating and continue playing alone for a prolonged time.

It is true that an adult could also invite a child to put an object through a shape, and the child might also learn the technique and become very interested in the game. But we must be aware of an apparently small but very significant fact: not all learning comes about through things offered by adults. Especially if the adult intervenes with an excessive insistence on practice and repetition, what the child is partly robbed of is the invention of the game, independently discovering the game and deciding how long it should last. Many games designed with the best of intentions and defined as 'intelligent' present us with closed and completely defined mini-contexts, which allow for very little variation; one of the limitations and unknown factors connected with these games is the degree of interest they create and their ability to extend direct learning done through them.

I fully understand that not all learning can be done independently; but it should not be forgotten that spontaneous motivation constitutes a first important spark and a good foundation subsequently for learning processes that take place in the best possible way.

I believe teachers need to always bear this in mind, making efforts to seek out proposals and ways of building interesting contexts that let individual children and groups of children set out on adventurous thought and action in the most subjective, autonomous way possible; teachers must be aware that education can rarely be planned simply, with direct responses to their offers. Doors must instead be left open for all the possibilities arising when we *listen* to children and their extraordinary capacity for inventing creative, new situations.

The black rubber column[3]

The situation is not very different in this second example where some older children are encountering new materials and tools. The problem is one of how to stimulate motivation and let children be authors of their own projects to the greatest extent possible.

A group of 5 and 6 year olds is exploring spaces inside the building that will become the Loris Malaguzzi International Centre for Childhood in Reggio Emilia (discussed further in Chapter 10). The children are particularly interested in two large empty rooms with two rows of parallel columns running down their centre destined for exhibitions. 'These columns are beautiful but too similar. Each column is a column' the children comment. What emerges strongly from the children's words is an important element, a central element; their strong desire for 'individuality' in collective groups to be recognized and given importance. This topic is of great ethical and social importance and should always be taken into consideration when working with children. It is a topic I do not intend to deal with here because I would like to concentrate on an aspect that might appear to be of secondary importance and has to do with procedures in educational practice. I say of *apparently* secondary importance because, in fact, our everyday actions are concrete manifestations of the educational and social values we wish to promote and develop.

The children debate this issue of individuality among the columns and resolve it with a proposal for making them different – personalised wrappings – column by column – which they call 'clothes'. This will allow the columns to change appearance and become distinct from each other, but it will also transform perceptions and relations within the entire space. The idea for these clothes was probably generated by the children's discovery of small differences and tiny details found on column surfaces, such as different textures and imperfections produced by the hand-made wooden casings for pouring concrete.

The children perceive these irregular surfaces as 'the column skin', so generating the children's desire to give each column back its individuality.

After making sketches of the columns the children make prototypes of *garments* using different materials and techniques. The following account is just a small part of a much longer project and has to do with making a *black rubber wrapping* for one of the columns. To my mind it is a clear example of how techniques can be learned in interesting, adventurous contexts, which make trial and error possible without demotivating children, in a different situation (but on a deeper level much closer than it seems) to Mattia pushing his spoon through the drawer handle.

The children go out on a visit from school and into a shop to choose and buy the material they will use for a prototype and then, back at the atelier, work begins on making the clothes using some of the techniques they have already tried out.

Paolo begins drawing shapes directly onto the rubber with a white crayon. The shapes are geometric and the teacher asks, 'Now what shall we do with the shapes you have drawn?'

Paolo says, 'We'll cut them out'. The other children in the group agree. Cutting out requires the delicate work of anticipating the organization of spaces and volumes, which lines to draw and how thick to make them. The same shape can be cut or its outline cut several different ways. Cutting out effectively involves redrawing shapes and requires children to work on predicting how to alternate gaps and intact pieces, which they are unlikely to have seen before. It is difficult and completely new work.

To give the children practice before cutting definitively into their rubber, the atelierista decides to make several copies of Paolo's shapes on black card – black like the rubber – and distributes them among Paolo and his friends so they can explore different strategies for cutting before the actual work itself.

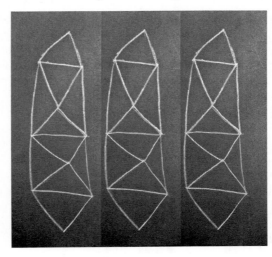

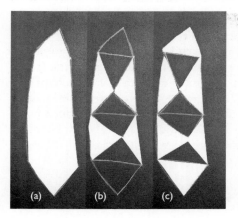

We can see the two children's variations, Paolo and Alessandro, in this
first drawing. Paolo begins to cut
under Alessandro's vigilant gaze.

The first cut is around the perim-
eter of the shape (a) and it comes away
entirely; in the second shape (b) Paolo
symmetrically cuts two pairs of triangles. The central triangles come away.
On the third shape (c), Paolo also cuts
the two top triangles. Some pieces
come away. Alessandro who is still
watching says, 'We need to cut less'.

Paolo asks for a fourth shape, the same
as the others, and on it he draws two
lines, one inside the first triangle and
one outside. He comments, 'This way
first we cut a piece inside and then
outside'. His cutting corresponds
exactly to his plan for leaving an
opportune border. Paolo adds another
line and cuts again. The children concentrate hard and work in silence.

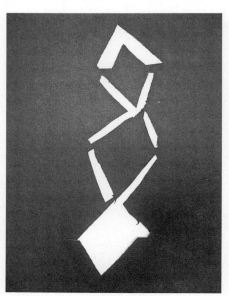

The finished shape. The final cut
has caused a piece to come away,
but Paolo decides that it is fine
anyway and observing the shape he
comments, 'I didn't cut right down
to the end, otherwise this piece in
the middle would have come away
and wouldn't be there and it [the
shape] wouldn't be as nice'.

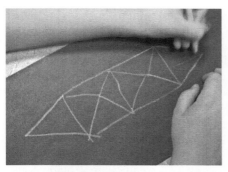

Pietro's shape. Starting with the same drawing and having observed Paolo's work, Pietro announces, 'I would like to put different things on it' and with a red pencil he changes the original shape by making a cross in the top triangle.

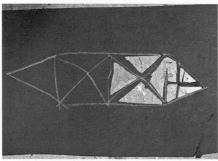

Drawing and cutting, he proceeds. Then at a certain point he changes method, 'Now I'm going to cut the lines, not the black part'.

The finished shape. Andrea and Pietro are working side by side. Andrea also likes the idea of varying the initial drawing by tracing new lines in red pencil and so he adopts his friend's method.

This method will subsequently be adopted by several other children with some differences in the construction process. One method generates different construction processes.

For example, Andrea holds his work up to the light and uses this *light drawing* several times to check his work during the course of cutting this and other shapes. He has added seductive traces of light to the traces of red pencil. This is another suggestion that other children will take up.

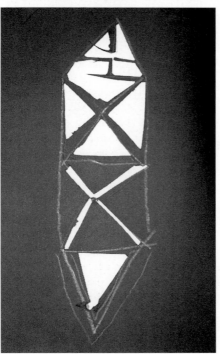

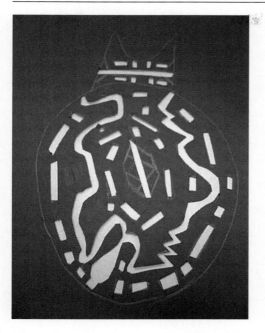

The 'contagion' that takes place between children is an interesting and often creative process. As the children continue their work they become more skilled and throw themselves into extremely risky drawing and cutting.

One last comment about children's ways of thinking. Rather than throw away the small shapes they have cut away, Paolo arranges them in a composition and emphasizes his sense of their shape by outlining them in colour. 'We can attach these onto the column as well', he says. Children rarely discard a piece of hard work by throwing it away. Each piece of a final product is perceived to be part of the whole, part of a process. Material we might consider disposable has a different value for children. But they never lose sight of their final objective.

Before the children arrive at a finished column they will need to deal with many more problems; however, they will never lose sight of the final objective, in this case creating a prototype column.

The finished prototype column

Good documentation, of which I have had to give an extremely summarized example, which I hope is clear, does not need many comments but I would like to make just one on the subject of 'contagion' among children. If we bear in mind the discovery of mirror neurons referred to above, we can locate 'contagion' in the area of initial simulation of intentional gestures by another; a strategy for learning which in the story we have recounted is immediately developed into a variation that becomes the agent of exploration for other trials and discoveries.

There are many, many pages to the study notebook written by the atelierista who followed the entire project. Reading it is as interesting and fascinating as reading a mystery story; we are never sure what might happen next but before the end we discover the many surprises that children's ways of thinking can create.

One of many reflections generated by stories like this is the difference between transmission of technical abilities by teachers in situations where development of a manual ability becomes the primary objective and the attitude of the teacher in the project presented above with an approach based on giving children time to realise what problems exist in order to deal with and resolve them independently or through observation of work by friends. The techniques and children's actions are placed in broader contexts with more general understanding of problems through experiment, trial, error and testing.

Not that the first approach to the problem – directly transmitting techniques – is mistaken. It brings certain advantages and can produce appreciable results. However, it is clear that in Reggio our choice is for the second way of working. We believe teachers of this kind can better support and develop creativity and personality in individuals and groups. The way of working and process lead more effectively to a greater understanding of problems and are, therefore, also more suited to reconceptualizing and resolving them in other occasions and contexts.

Malaguzzi used to say that the work of a teacher is for 'professional marvellers'. The definition is truly beautiful; a message of hope for such a delicate profession. If we are not capable of waiting for the awareness that what children's research generates will probably surprise us and also surprise them, then our job will almost certainly be less interesting and less fun, the climate of learning different and probably less productive for both children and teacher.

The worst doubt or risk is being content with the obvious, to stop looking for what is new and unexpected, and in the end no longer seeing things through the eyes of the children before us. It is my impression that Reggio today also needs to consciously and lucidly renew the significance of a pedagogy in which Poetics has such an important place and in which aesthetics continues to play the role of important connecting structure for learning processes. For when their values and meanings are not constantly explored, even the best habits can 'evaporate' into nothing more than an opaque series of gestures and customs that have lost their vitality and sense. Truly this would be a pity for, I believe, the presence of ateliers, the way they have developed over time and been situated in knowledge processes, is one of the most original features in Reggio pedagogy. It would be no small loss.

Chapter 4

The bicycle metaphor

There can be no discussion of Reggio Emilia ateliers without relating them to the pedagogy Loris Malaguzzi pursued; a pedagogy sensitive to the poetic languages and not rigidly contained in preconceived formulas; insufficient to hurriedly classify it as being part of a pedagogy it refers to, such as socio-constructivism – however interesting and clarifying it may be. Malaguzzi the pedagogista was extremely attentive to contemporary life, curious and interested in reflection and developments taking place around concepts in other disciplines, and he brought this knowledge to the pedagogical discussions he made and maintained with teachers. Those who worked with him well remember the wonderful meetings that were held where Malaguzzi, always an avid reader, brought us his latest findings, always extremely up to date and, particularly in the 1990s, related to the areas of neuroscience and scientific philosophy. These readings were reinterpreted and related to pedagogy, something he did without ever losing sight of that vital part of pedagogy connected to small children, and through his attitude even neuroscience was conferred with a particular form of tenderness and *humanity*.

In his reviewing and discussion of contemporary events, politics also became part of a social and pedagogical context, to be understood and debated. When the school year finished in the *scuola comunale dell'infanzia* Diana, at the end of June or beginning of July, it became our habit, which we never gave up, of asking him to visit the school for a chat. During the course of these free conversations, with great liberty and frankness, he brought us his opinions on Reggio Emilia, on the cultural, political, social and pedagogical panoramas in Italy and other countries. This intelligent comprehensive vision was extremely useful for bringing us up to date generally, enriching our knowledge and making it possible as a group – when we returned to school after the summer – to choose priorities in the projects we would develop with the children. It is deeply regrettable that we foolishly neglected to tape these meetings.

However, in those conversations we learned a way of working and thinking which, as far as possible, we have continued to apply through reading and reflecting, either alone or better still in reciprocal exchange with others. Like any human activity, pedagogy requires us to have ears alert to the things around us; especially pedagogy because it deals with education and the precious part of humanity which is children. Otherwise it risks losing contact with the centre of its reflection and practice – children – and becoming transformed into a discipline based simply on a series of rules that can be applied, often too sure of itself and 'crystalized' in time.

In a discussion of psychology, Umberto Galimberti says there is a need for awareness that disciplines connected to psychology are perhaps just one of many episodes in history in which human beings have attempted an interpretation of themselves. I believe the awareness that psychology is not an exact science applies even more to pedagogy.

Sometimes – to tell the truth very often – it is my impression that reading important past educators and psychologists orients educators' ways of seeing children too rigidly; their eyes and ears do not sufficiently see and listen to what children actually do and say. The subject of children is not static over time, or the same in every era, because both the culture and society in which they form change very rapidly. Pedagogical and psychological knowledge, therefore, should always be open to channels for listening and interpreting and avoid becoming filters that are too short-sighted or opaque for reality to pass through.

One aspect I have often encountered in the world of pedagogy is a lack of correspondence between the premises of the reference culture – declarations of intent – and translations of these into practice in real relationships with children. It seems to me that a pedagogical background tends to separate the theoretical part from practice in quite a clear-cut way and treats practice as the poor sister. In reality, this separation impoverishes both, and people who are responsible for schools and for professional development should give this aspect their careful attention. About this subject Malaguzzi used the metaphor of riding a bicycle: to go forward we have to push both pedals and maintain a good balance; one pedal represents theory, the other practice; pushing only one pedal does not get us far.

Current (2007) proposals by the Italian Ministry for Education include *Indicazioni per il curricolo per la scuola dell'infanzia e per il primo ciclo d'istruzione (Guidelines for curriculum in preschools and the primary cycle of education)* and here again the same lack of correspondence is to be found. The introduction to the guidelines opens up new ethical, social and cultural perspectives and though perhaps appreciating some aspects more than others, a reader like myself on the whole might agree with this first part and begin formulating hypotheses for feasible and interesting journeys in practice. However, reading the second part, which refers to fields of knowledge, we are confronted with language of a more restrictive nature, a reduction in cultural openness and the consequent limits on the imagination and practical possibilities that stem from this.

Perhaps I have a diffident attitude towards a certain type of language and terminology, and perhaps this irritation makes me unsympathetic to terms such as 'painting–drawing experience' and 'creative–sound possibilities'. To me, it seems they represent an obsolete way of working and I immediately have visions that are not in the least bit comforting and too often seen in schools, memories of proposals for work with children in which a stereotyped conception triumphs absolutely and where the results are work which is rather careless and ugly. It takes the ability of certain teachers to make children's work ugly!

I only hope that the fields of knowledge will be filled with reflection and imagery during professional development, work-groups and workshops, which distance themselves from the kind of language that fosters the courage to embrace children's points of view – seemingly so distant sometimes from what schools actually work on.

The sea ball

A little boy about two-and-a-half years old has made a ball from damp sand, compacting it down, and runs to throw it into the sea. Coming back up the beach he shouts happily, 'a ball of sea, a ball of sea!' The compacted sand has dissolved on contact with the sea water and become one with the sea. The ball of sand has become 'a ball of sea'.

I always fall under the spell of these thought processes and the words used to communicate them. How is it possible with a child like this to use terms such as 'diagram of the human body' or 'manual activities', etc.? Worse still, how is it possible to give them simplified models for drawing, banal and elementary, of 'body schemes', as happens in some schools?

To learn *a language* we need to *speak* it often, and the language of drawing needs to be 'frequented' in the same way. Real-life investigation is one of the many proposals we can make and in certain situations the subject can be a friend acting as model.

Respect

In this short story, the teacher Marina Mori was alone with a large number of children, space in the classroom was restricted and documentation was necessarily hurried; however, the processes are interesting. The teacher often finds herself organizing educational proposals in difficult conditions, but she is optimistic the journey will be positive anyway. In this situation on a particular day, a child from the class is chosen to act as model for drawing or clay work.

In this particular case the model is a girl, Sewaa, whose physical and character traits are first observed and commented on by her friends:

'Her eyes are black and big and wide, her lips are big. The bottom lip and the top lip... when she smiles her mouth goes shorter.'

'Her hair is rolled up tight and she has little plaits all over her head.

Sewaa, 'Mummy does my plaits... She always has different hairstyles, her hair is always carefully combed... she's thin, but she has muscles' (see Figure 4.1).

Figure 4.1

The model often intervenes to confirm or refute comments made by her friends:

FILIPPO: Someone told me Theo likes Sewaa too.

THEO: Yes I like her.

FILIPPO: Perhaps he likes her because they have the same skin.

CAMILLA: That's not true because I like Evans and he has brown skin.

SEWAA: I like Theo because he's my friend and I like Ismail who was nearly my friend... So skin colour has nothing to do with it!

CAMILLA: Sewaa is good, and intelligent, because if you say something to her she works out an agreement.

SEWAA: I get angry with the children when they hurt me and then they all say "I won't do it again!" So then I forgive them because... I love all the children, they're my friends...

The proposal for drawing begins and it is customary for us in Reggio to divide children into groups around the model, each group with a different viewpoint: front, back and side. The teacher is aware that, even if they are not very good, she will be able to use the photographs she takes as she circles the children during their work at a later point with the children to discuss the relationship between the model and views of her from the different angles. The teacher chooses to dedicate greater attention to documenting a group drawing the model from the side, because she knows this viewpoint, like the back view, poses the children with interesting problems.

As they draw, the children intelligently check each other's work as they often do, partly to verify, partly to gather suggestions from work by companions.

A little girl, Laura, is wandering around curious and stops in front of Martina's work saying, 'Look it's not right like that, do you think you can see her from the front? You've drawn Sewaa as if she was like this, in front of you... Instead you were supposed to draw her like this... from the side... in profile... with only one eye, only one leg, only one ear' (see Figure 4.2).

Figure 4.2

Then, showing her own drawing, 'Look, like this... the way I've done it', and she puts the two drawings together to compare them (see Figures 4.3 and 4.4). 'You have done her with two arms, two eyes... it isn't like from the side, it's a front [view].' Laura's tone is kind but firm. Martina, who at the start of her classmate's reprimand wore a surprised expression, seems little by little to understand.

Figure 4.3 Laura's drawing

Figure 4.4 Martina's drawing

The teacher approaches and asks in a friendly way, 'The drawing you have done is lovely but, to see it like this, where would you have to be sitting?' and Martina answers, 'There, at that table there' and points to the groups who can see Sewaa from the side.

The teacher does not say the drawing is mistaken, rather she underlines that the drawing is a nice one, neither does she ask the child to redo it, but by her question she sanctions the difference between two points of view: front and side. Highly respectful of the child's sensibility, she does not immediately confront her with a further test in drawing because, by her reply, Martina shows that she has taken a first step towards understanding the problem, which is not simply a drawing problem but conceptual. There will be other times for advancing this awareness she has just acquired.

I like this short and apparently simple sequence of photographs because it high-lights a series of significant aspects that are generally underestimated:

- that learning 'body schema' comes about through very different journeys but that these are always perceptive, affective, cognitive and social journeys.
- that an awareness of children's possible processes, and in this case ones to do with drawing, supports the teacher in making proposals and observing processes developed by the children.
- that respecting and esteeming children makes teachers better teachers, because the importance of the problem that has been posed and cognitive conflict stemming from it should not become more important than self-esteem being built up by children or their sensibilities.

A female pedagogy

I do not know by what reason or virtue Malaguzzi managed not to separate theory and practice, nor from where he got his sensibility for practical teaching which sometimes – Malaguzzi will forgive me – drifted slightly towards the theatrical, although this drama is often part of children's natural aspiration. However, I believe the union between theory and practice for which we con-stantly checked our work has continued in Reggio schools and this has been one of Reggio pedagogy's strong values. It is a difficult value to maintain over time, and needs constantly to be recalled and examined because it is always at risk.

The pedagogy under discussion, Reggio's pedagogy, has been built up in the daily work of many women and cared for by female minds and hands. With few male teachers – and undoubtedly this is a deficiency – women have been capable of building an education in which certain important values are practiced; the value of relations, of empathy, of solidarity, of caring for things, of tenderness and grace; all traits that psychology has traditionally attributed to the female gender, but that constitute richness for everyone.

Atelierista Mirella Ruozzi has taught in Reggio schools for many years and, to my mind, she clearly demonstrates the extent to which a tender and playful way of seeing can guide very sophisticated observation and documentation, capable of gathering information and situations in a very subtle way to tell the story of children, under 3 years of age, in *nidi* with complexity and acuteness. In the *Centro Video* (Video Centre)[1] this atelierista, together with a young assistant, has recently created a large number of documentary videos – documentation which tells the story of children in these centres and where they themselves testify to their own irresistible intelligence and curious marvelling. In a few frames, a recent video recounts scenes from a day in the life of a *nido* and we see situations causing us to reflect on small children's attentiveness to relationships, how they experience these, and we sense even more strongly the injustice of what is too often stolen from too many children on a daily basis.

In the video small scenes such as the following example can be glimpsed.

Four hands playing, tiny everyday stories

One morning a teacher starts playing a guitar, a wonderful object that naturally attracts the children's curiosity. Among other scenes is a sequence where we see two children of different ages (10 and 23 months) touching the strings of the guitar and trying to produce sounds from them. There is no doubt the older girl is more successful. The smaller boy tries to catch the girl's attention; he touches her, pushes her and appears more interested in his relationship with her than in the guitar. The little girl is irritated, she wants to be left in peace to explore the sounds produced by the strings.

Suddenly the little boy performs an action, which combines his desire for initiating relations with the little girl and his simultaneous desire to play the guitar – neither of which has been satisfied until now. After a few failed attempts he manages to take the girl's hand in his and guide it towards the guitar chords; where their hands, now tightly joined, together touch and make the chords sound – thus resolving two problems and his aspirations.

These documentations give us small portraits of children's lives and their points of view; perhaps documents of this kind should be circulated more often as study material in university faculties whose task it is to prepare teachers. I am certain that for many lecturers and future teachers, these examples would constitute precious documentation for getting closer to children and discussing them in ways that avoid the usual barriers between moments of theory and the real work in the midst of children.

Concerning pedagogistas

Malaguzzi *hypothesized* pedagogistas as people who would be capable of not separating theory and practice, with the task of comprehensively supporting pedagogical work in schools entrusted to them. As with atelieristas, this was a further example of another occupation, with a distinct profile, introducing its expertise and 'cultural' background into the multidisciplinary educational context – the school community – which embraced and used their contribution and their deeper theoretical insights as a precious resource. At the same time through a series of requests in different areas, from organization to class work and social events, staff in schools worked in such a way that the profession of pedagogista was carried out in a complete way, without separating theory from practice and practicalities.

The organization of our work in Reggio took all these different elements into account and supported a constant interweaving of different competencies and many points of view.

From what I hear and generally see in schools in Italy and other countries, the fact of having such a large pedagogical team in Reggio Emilia (on average each pedagogista is responsible for four schools (two *nidi* and two *scuole dell'infanzia*)) constitutes a positive distinguishing feature, as too does the existence of ateliers, school kitchens and family participation. We need to be aware of this and ensure we make full use of these important resources. To be honest, sometimes we manage and sometimes we do not.

It is not easy for pedagogistas to intelligently balance different components of society: children, teachers, families, political power in the city and national politics. Above all, it is not easy to coherently interweave the reference theories with what is actually done inside the schools. Perhaps for the pedagogistas the greatest risk to be avoided is repeating beautiful theories without lucidly and constantly exposing them to critical exchange with the reality of the schools they coordinate. The other risk is to declare *reciprocal exchange* as one of Reggio's fundamental values, but then fail to pay it sufficient attention in concrete ways – in theoretical aspects of educational work or during professional development for school staff; or again in exchanging information with other pedagogistas about projects to be undertaken in schools. Although there is so much work to be done, this cannot be taken as a sufficient excuse for not practising this value.

If we were to forgo dialectic exchange between different experiences for too long a time, if insufficient attention were given to developments in pedagogical theory and research in various disciplines, then the pedagogistas in Reggio preschools would lose one of their most important traits, one that distinguishes them from national and international pedagogy: giving shape to theory through educational projects and everyday practice without those theories being betrayed. At the same time, it is important not to be too fond of our theories and leave space for doubt, let our 'listening' to cultural and social reality and listening to children modify the theories we refer to. Critical awareness is something to be looked after very, very carefully.

Vea Vecchi in conversation about learning and atelieristas with...

Simona Bonilauri, a pedagogista since 1982, and Claudia Giudici, a pedagogista, currently on the management staff of Reggio Children and President of the Istituzione Scuole e Nidi d'Infanzia del Comune di Reggio Emilia *since November 2009.*

VEA: Two initial questions. Do pedagogistas recognize the poetic languages as being important for learning? To what extent has the presence of the atelier and the atelierista as a conscious choice contributed to the identity of the pedagogy of Reggio?

SIMONA: Aesthetics is commonly seen as something 'added' to knowledge-building processes; it can be there or not, and whether it is there or not does not affect the validity of the learning processes and the construction of knowledge. I don't share this opinion, because for me aesthetics is innate to the knowledge-building processes.

CLAUDIA: The aesthetics of learning is not a simple topic to deal with. When I began as a pedagogista, I asked myself the same question that we are often asked: What is the relationship between the atelier, art, the expressive languages, pedagogy and didactics? Why do we have a figure like the atelierista in our schools? Wasn't it sufficient to have some specialists go into the schools to conduct workshops on painting, clay, and so on?

The educational experience of the Reggio municipal schools was strongly characterized right from the start by research and innovation. It was a pedagogy that tried to break down the boundaries of traditional pedagogy, that searched for international and interdisciplinary cultural references, not only pedagogical references, so becoming a 'transgressive' pedagogy that right from the start fought against habit and boredom by pursuing change and possibility. I think that the choice made by Professor Malaguzzi back in the 1960s to have the atelier and the atelierista in the municipal schools comes out of this ongoing search for innovation, followed and pursued by crossing boundaries that may be unknown or daring, always trying to interpret the contemporary world.

SIMONA: In the pedagogy of Reggio, art has been used as a force for breaking away from dominant thought. When you try to understand how children learn from a constructivist and socio-constructivist point of view, you realize that it takes place in a multidisciplinary and multisensory way, a way that is already inherent in children, and that the atelier has contributed to highlighting this. When children learn, they do it by interweaving and making connections between the different languages, and this is exactly what school in the traditional sense does *not* do, because it tends to separate the languages, which are defined as different subjects, disciplines, fields of knowledge, etc.

VEA: The term 'language' that we often use casually could easily create misunderstandings...

CLAUDIA: ...we use the words 'language' and 'languages' to indicate the many sources and forms of knowledge of children, of human beings. When we talk about languages, we are referring to the different ways that children – human beings – represent, communicate and express their thoughts by means of different media and symbolic systems. The languages, therefore, are the many sources of knowledge.

Going back to Simona's comment, giving attention to children's ways of learning brings out strongly an aspect that today may seem obvious and banal: children learn through their bodies, sounds, the languages of drawing, painting, modelling, and so on. So what emerged was that the expressive or poetic languages are languages that are in tune – in an emotional, affective, and cognitive relationship – with children's ways of knowing and with each other.

So it was necessary to make a choice that would not betray these processes and the ways of knowing of children, of human beings. It was necessary to introduce in the school an element of *subversion*, with respect to the traditional school and way of teaching, that would render the didactic process more complex, and thus more consistent with children's ways of knowing. 'Didactics' means all the methodologies that support and give shape to the teaching–learning relationship and, therefore, to interpreting and acting on our listening to, and observing, the children.

The day-to-day work of observation and documentation of the children's learning processes has been the instrument of interweaving between pedagogy and the thinking of the atelier, modifying each other reciprocally. Observation and documentation show how children seek beauty through many languages that are empathic with each other, not separate and sequential; how they seek an aesthetics of expression of their ideas and thoughts.

Another essential aspect of the educational experience of Reggio that has always been present is the close connection between theory and practice, not one preceding the other but going along together, indispensable for advancing. Given the importance of this and given the considerations and the reflections on children's way of knowing, it was necessary to make a cultural and organizational choice – the introduction of the atelierista and the atelier – and organization always is or should be cultural. These choices immediately changed the way of teaching, and thus more generally the pedagogical and educational project.

SIMONA: Yes, I think that the encounter between art, cognitive psychology, and developmental psychology required a form of divergent thinking that evolved first as a fertile intuition then as necessary in offering new criteria and strategies for teachers' professional development. Placing the children's knowledge-building processes at the centre led to a transformation of adults' expectations. We try to work on a process of deconstructing our knowledge and our mental schemas.

VEA: Learning to *unlearn*...

CLAUDIA: ...having considered the visual language and the expressive languages not as a separate discipline but as a means for questioning and investigating the world and building bridges and relationships between different experiences and languages, to keep the different cognitive processes in a close relationship. This meant developing a pedagogy that would work on the connections and not on the separation of the fields of knowledge. Hence, knowledge and languages resonate with each other, are in reciprocal relationship and empathy, and it is from this relationship that the children's experiences and knowledge are expanded, increased, modified and enriched. And we, as educators, have to work on this interweaving and these connections.

SIMONA: The atelier is undoubtedly the symbolic place of this work we have done.

VEA: If the explosive force of a choice of this type, of a pedagogy that accepts and utilizes the culture of an 'impertinent' atelier, as Malaguzzi defined it, does not continue to be clearly reflected by the people who live it, there is clearly the risk of losing its *subversive* force and the atelier just becoming an organizational presence.

SIMONA: In fact, I think that in addition to the problem of considering aesthetics or the atelier as an accessory, as we said before, there could also be another drift: the atelier could simply become a *technique*, but for now this has not happened.

VEA: It is a potential risk. The atelier creates various types of products with the help of materials and techniques that imprison or liberate many expressive and cognitive processes.

SIMONA: But technique is the indispensable condition for expressiveness. The force of our atelieristas, and teachers together, has always been to stay in touch with the knowledge-building processes of the children and of the adults and constantly redefining them. So the atelieristas did not become merely workshop instructors, though it remains a possibility and a risk. Fortunately, the children always keep us on track…

VEA: Another risk is working with the materials and the techniques without seeing them as a relationship between many elements where important knowledge-building processes are developed.

SIMONA: But what can we do to ensure that a technique is not an end in itself? I agree with Claudia when she said that we use the technique to understand the processes and not for instructing the children to be 'skilled'. But this assertion, too, should be made with caution, because if a child is skilled at cutting paper with scissors, not only is she satisfied but she also has some specific competencies.

The atelier has given the term 'experience' the possibility to take shape within a large pedagogical project: when Malaguzzi said 'we are engaged with humankind', he meant something global, systemic, not sectorial, that doesn't separate the children's competencies from those of adults and contexts. We have contextualized the techniques, that is, we try to produce 'experiences'. The technique was placed at the service of a project, a larger project than just pedagogy, and it is this that led to the search for other languages. It was precisely this project for and on human beings that led Malaguzzi to the significant intuition of inserting the atelier.

VEA: One of the aspects that is clearly perceived in our schools is the presence of a collective intelligence that goes beyond the single individual or the single school. One of the elements, perhaps the crucial one, I think, for the challenge we're talking about is the intense relationship of people with things: with the environment, but also with all the elements that surround us, with the projects that we do. This diffused empathy requires time to become a lucid and aware 'collective intelligence'.

SIMONA: The presence of the atelier, with this breaking away from conformist thinking, anticipated the theories of complexity, and brought to Italy the idea of learning that is not linear but is multifaceted, that was also confirmed subsequently in the sphere of psychology. This complexity is difficult to live and inhabit on a day-to-day basis and what we are doing, at times, is still somewhat linear, even though each school embodies a complexity of thought and of life that we cannot disregard.

There is also the risk of an 'aestheticizing' interpretation...

VEA: ...the intense relationship with things, whether angry or loving, is one of the bases of art, and where there is this relationship the 'aestheticizing' risk is removed.

SIMONA: Undoubtedly if we keep in mind the individuality, the subjectivity and the relationships, we will have an increase in uncertainty but also an increase in freedom. You can breathe this atmosphere in the air of a school... At the *scuola comunale dell'infanzia* Diana you have a strong sense of this subjectivity, this freedom that also involves time, because there the children have to be able to take time.

On the intense relationship of things, I would go back to the slogan of the 1970s: if you don't have time, compensate for it by the quality of the time. This is also true for adults, because the professional development exchange requires and means taking time, that is, a kind of circuit is formed between experience and subjectivity; I can have an experience only if it is a subjective experience and in the encounter between these two dimensions – experience and subjectivity – there is the aesthetic appeal.

CLAUDIA: Also because, otherwise, all you would need is an atelierista in a school to make a school of quality. But that's not how it is.

Another thing, in relation to what we have already said, is how the atelier has significantly changed the language of the pedagogy, due to both the use of images and the forms of communication. Take, for example, the invention of documentation as a strategy of assessment and of professional development, which is now recognized by others but is certainly original to the experience of Reggio. Ours is a language that has always described pedagogy in a hybrid and multidisciplinary way, so we don't use only one didactic or psychological or sociological language but many others that traditionally belong to other fields of knowledge. This hybridization of the languages must be maintained, despite the hard work it requires.

When I listened to the first presentations of documentation, I was struck by the words and images that were outside the conventions, and how they created new realities and new possibilities for the children. It's a way of communicating that is widely used by the children as well, for example a child who says 'an evening as soft as a blanket'.

VEA: A curiosity: why are so few individual processes documented? If the child is given space, if there is curiosity to understand the strategies used in confronting problems, the relationships, then the documentation of an individual process is always there and is always interesting. Certainly it depends on how much space, how much freedom is allowed to the subjectivity of the children.

CLAUDIA: This is why it's difficult. In any case, on the topic of individuality we risk being misunderstood if we do not qualify it in a group context, because we have always worked on individuality *and* group and this also gives a political meaning to the idea of education.

Another political message that I find to be particularly strong is the desire that our schools should be beautiful – caring for the public environment as having an ethical meaning. But, generally speaking, this is not considered important, especially in a public school.

VEA: Beauty can become a provocative factor. Going into the latest schools created here, there are those who say with a disapproving tone, 'But this is more beautiful than my home!' There is still, many years since the first schools, enormous confusion between luxury, care and competence.

CLAUDIA: Alberto Munari and Donata Fabbri, who have for many years studied the aesthetic processes in learning, assert – I'm going here from memory – that there always exists in us an aesthetic project that leads us to construct and put into context what we are doing according to ways that have their own appeal… and it is this basic aesthetic that stimulates us to improve our interpretative constructs, to give order to our cognitive map, to seduce and be seduced.

SIMONA: I was once asked, 'Is there too much stimulation for the children in your schools?' It was 1980 and it makes me smile because I had a hard time finding a suitable response.

VEA: Especially in small environments like the *scuola comunale dell'infanzia* Diana, the amount of objects, contexts and materials that are visible can give the impression of saturation. The important thing is not to transform the school environment into a sort of museum exhibit.

SIMONA: I look for a clue to understand whether in the schools I go to we are becoming a museum or whether we are still alive. When I'm at Diana and I watch the children moving around, the question is: Are the children choosing? Usually in a museum, at least in traditional ones, you're a spectator. Here, instead, there are children who are researching and *acting* autonomously in different contexts. Their ways of moving around, their autonomy does not come from something 'given' to them, but from an environment that allows you to make choices. With teachers and atelieristas attentive to supporting variation and the possibility of choice, we are far from the static nature of a museum. The atelier has nurtured all this vitality, which we must not lose.

Chapter 5

The long view of organization

Much important work has been written and conferences held on the importance of organization as a creative process and not simply as the application or support of efficiency. So I will limit myself to just some personal reflections that purposely avoid complete or deeper discussion of the topic. What I am interested in doing, however, is making some mention of the effects that organization criteria framed by Malaguzzi had on people like myself who were working and continue to work in the municipal schools of Reggio Emilia.

In a discussion of 'managerial illusion', Pier Luigi Celli (1997) writes of how production strategies and programmes in the business world remain distant from real social problems, thus encouraging hyper-simplification of conceptual tools so that these are now no longer capable of interpreting new complexities – making managerial competency poor in the very conflicts which are now critically important. I believe the same reasoning could be applied to schools. Unless the Italian national school system begins to address important issues of teacher training, including attitudes and competencies in communication and the relations that teachers ought to have, and the different social and cultural realities children and their families are part of, if it does not reflect on today's culture, or invest culturally and financially but continues to be governed by purely financial concerns, then the educational system will be incapable of anticipating and governing change in society and carrying out its important task. What business calls 'human resources', in the context of schools are children and teachers – the future of humanity. They have rhythms and times for accumulating knowledge, relations, values, problems and change which make our schools irrelevant and distant from children and their families, having chosen to transmit a static culture, unchanged over time, with too many certainties, few doubts and very little research behind it.

Instead, the organization and management of public schooling needs cultural, anthropological, ethical and aesthetic choices, guided by philosophy and long-sighted vision. It needs to draw on the strength and awareness that come from the layering and enrichment acquired through real experience, experience that has itself been the product of experiment and research containing reflection, discussion and interpretation of contemporary life in the light of *trans-disciplinary* thinking. It appears to me that the many proposals formulated for schools by different parties following each other into government in Italy have not so far been capable of this approach – or of real change.

I believe Malaguzzi took a long view of organization and this has given Reggio schools a very solid organizational base and great resilience. They have a capacity for self-nourishment in theoretical and practical areas that has constituted a wall of defence for resisting and for maintaining high levels of quality even in very difficult times.

Perhaps I should mention that owing to personal character and family 'culture', I do not very willingly accept rules I do not agree with. This said, I must immediately add that in thirty years of work I never felt this way, for I felt I was working with rules that I clearly perceived to be the ethics of a working group and which supported a large community; I never felt these rules, sometimes stated and sometimes left unsaid, to be a rigid, bureaucratic mesh. Everything was always seeking to maintain a balance between the rights and responsibilities of three components and protagonists in schools – children, staff and families – with a particular concern for children's rights considering, as Malaguzzi used to say, 'they have no unions to defend them'.

Normal school life

When I retired from working at the *scuola comunale dell'infanzia* Diana in 2000 we had never used clocking-in machines (there still are none to my knowledge). Staff in this and other municipal schools practised a strong form of self-regulation; this was not openly declared or explicit but had the effect of being extremely attentive to the rights of each person; above all it was vital for the smooth flow of normal school life. Any incorrect behaviour by one person had too many consequences on the work of others not to be noted and civilly remarked on by the group itself, without recourse to sanctions. Accepting incorrect behaviour in the workplace – an unjustified absence, late arrival or other unsuitable behaviour – without challenge or intervention was seen as a form of complicity. Silence was not acceptable and problems were generally discussed by the staff group at times set aside for self-organized professional growth by the collective group of school workers.

This does not mean there were no disputes. These took place and were extremely lively, but they were always in the context of *conflicts* of a *social* nature and character without excessive reference to personal situations, and problems were always resolved in friendship and dialogue. To my knowledge the border between necessary flexibility and tolerance and complicity and indifference was never crossed in the Diana school.

Important choices

In the early 1970s in the space of a few years, apart from introducing atel-ieristas, other revolutionary choices were made that contributed to building a new public image for early childhood services, such as transforming their name (for example, from *scuola materna* to *scuola dell'infanzia*), introducing male staff into these services (tradition was particularly unfavourable to this), having teachers work together in pairs, giving priority to the entrance of children with disabilities into the school community, and the organization of parent management committees. All these choices were, in their time, coura-geous and anti-conformist. But were they easy choices? Certainly not: on the contrary they were strongly contested even by workers in schools, who did not easily accept professional discussion and exchange with colleagues or being subjected to the judgement of families. The construction of a very different image for teachers and young children's schools (in Italian we say the schools are *of* the children and not *for* children) was truly underway.

There were fundamental organizational changes such as teachers working in pairs together for several hours a day, which made it possible on a practical level to carry out work with smaller groups of children and to have continu-ous exchange between two colleagues. It is ironic to hear people discussing children's 'social abilities' as a fundamental aspect of education and then see how this socialization is scarcely contemplated or supported in the traditional organization of teachers' work. Indeed, the latest school reform approved by the current Italian government proposes, among other things, a return to one teacher per class in primary schools. This has been supported by a majority in the government (thereby saving money) and also by many others justifying their position with nostalgic references to schooldays in the past when only one teacher was present in each class.

Another important organizational feature of Reggio schools was including time during the working week for self-organized professional growth, and this is still the case today.

There were two-and-a-half hours of weekly meetings between the entire school staff – teachers, atelierista, cooks and auxiliary staff – and this activity was run in a completely autonomous way, a cultural and social space which can be very important, on the condition that there is a real understanding of its effective potential. For example, spaces dedicated to self-organized pro-fessional development should not become times simply for establishing a calendar of future commitments, but occasions in which – after reflection and discussion – pedagogical, social and cultural priorities are given to vari-ous programmes. Naturally when I speak of these work groups I also mean to include the pedagogistas, although they cannot always be present at every meeting owing to their responsibilities in various schools and their important role in coordinating strategy and evaluating the work being done.

There were, and continue to be, other ways of organizing development, for example when all schools come together or groups of schools coordinated by pedagogistas. These professional development programmes are often very interesting, but to my mind the weekly self-development sessions between members of a school collective are extremely effective as an element for formative professional growth. They can be fine-tuned to topics raised by the staff of a school and a significant contribution to cohesion in the work group's everyday life. Precisely because this self-organized development is left to individual schools, it clearly does not work in exactly the same way or with the same quality in each school, but it is the task of the pedagogista to intervene in suitable ways, treating each situation individually and encouraging thoughtful discussion. All this in order that discussion of daily activity and the approach to educational work can always be in a climate of cultural vitality and pedagogical research; when this happens then it is rarely necessary to intervene.

Over the last decade, some of the general meetings for professional development have been open to teachers from non-municipal schools in Reggio – services run by cooperatives, private providers and the state – and this constitutes further opportunity for reciprocal exchange.

Another important element in school organization that I have always thought of as resulting from a highly refined psychological sensibility is teachers and other staff lunching together as part of the organization of the working day. Food prepared by cooks in school kitchens is good and nutritious, prepared and presented with care, very inexpensive for staff, and the atmosphere established in a shared lunch is extremely pleasant; three quarters of an hour to step outside the working day. In actual fact time available for lunch is often reduced to half an hour, for children's rhythms do not include 'bells' to measure time out precisely; however, though people can take lunch elsewhere, to my knowledge no one has ever availed themselves of the opportunity to do so, and the atmosphere of socializing and friendship which is created becomes an important part of everyday life in the school.

Changes

Reggio's schools have had the courage to change their organization over time while also maintaining components considered important as fixed points. Changes it has been necessary to deal with since Loris Malaguzzi's death in 1994 have been charted and guided by two pedagogistas, Carla Rinaldi and Sergio Spaggiari, who have travelled a long way with Reggio schools, first at Malaguzzi's side in the role of coordinators then as directors; the two have very different personalities but are often complementary in their professional background and working style. Together with them, an important role has been played by Sandra Piccinini, a young woman who served as *Assessore* for Schools and Culture[1] in Reggio Emilia *Comune*.

Over the past fifteen years, important changes have taken place under their directorship: the conception, preparation and creation of the Friends of Reggio Children International Association and Reggio Children (both in 1994), the latter being a public–private company that the municipality, along with other interested parties, established to manage pedagogical and cultural exchange between the municipal early childhood services and a large number of teachers and researchers from all over the world. Transfer of the municipal schools to the *Istituzione Scuole e Nidi d'infanzia del Comune di Reggio Emilia* (2003), an agency of the Municipality with teaching, pedagogical and administrative autonomy, its own financial budget and its own board of directors nominated by the mayor; and the creation of the Loris Malaguzzi International Centre (2006), discussed in more detail in Chapter 10. How have ateliers changed over the years?

At the start of the 1970s, the situation was very different to the one we are presented with today. Teaching staff in *scuole dell'infanzia* with three classes were organized as follows: each teacher was alone with thirty-two children and one of the three teachers also acted in the role of head of group. Supporting them was a teaching assistant with a slightly lower wage and an atelierista with the same salary as the assistant. Staff worked forty hours a week; atelieristas assisted with children during afternoon naps and took turn to provide adult supervision for children staying at school until 6.20 pm (municipal schools are open after the end of formal school hours, especially for children of working parents).

Today, there are two teachers for each class of twenty-six children in pre-schools. The assistant's role no longer exists and atelieristas' salaries have been the same as teachers' for many years now. If the class includes a child with disabilities (with 'special needs'), another teacher is added to the class and, in recent years, there are 'cultural mediators' for children who do not speak Italian. The working week is now thirty-six hours, of which thirty are spent with children, 2.5 are for group professional development, and the remaining 3.5 hours are put aside for professional updating and development, documentation and family meetings.

For families requesting the extended school day another teacher takes over in the afternoon.

I am quickly describing staff organization to show more clearly how in the very beginning the presence of a role like the atelierista's was not foreseen, and that when first introduced the atelierista had lower wages and professional status. Then, quite quickly, we went from a minor professional role, a supporting role sometimes, to recognition of a much more important role in the school work group. In the beginning, this new role was a subject for debate among groups of teachers because it was absolutely new and relations between different competencies needed to be redefined – between different people when all was said and done – because unconsciously and imperceptibly small forms of hierarchy tended to form. I remember, for example, a lively discussion with an excellent teacher who defended her role, maintaining that she was the only person who should communicate directly with families; she found it difficult to accept that I should discuss children directly with parents without her presence or consent. All these are things that might make us smile today, but naturally each change – and there were so many in those years – needed time to settle down and Malaguzzi was very understanding about this, but also clear cut in his decisions and convincing in his motivations for everyone.

I really believe that introducing the profile of atelierista into schools for preschool age children has opened the way to changes in practice. However, this introduction could have produced much less innovation if Malaguzzi had limited himself to using the atelierista's various competencies in traditional ways; only using them, for example, in a role of support and assistance when teachers were missing; or confined to the role of specialist in techniques necessary to produce work to be admired with children; or again using them as graphic artists for communication with the public. In a later chapter, I will discuss the atelier and its organization with children from all school classes in a more complete way.

The voice of an *assessore*

I would like to finish this chapter on organization by including the narrative voice of a city administrator, Sandra Piccinini who, in her role as *Assessore* for Schools and Culture (responsible for educational and cultural policy in Reggio Emilia's municipal administration) from 1990–2003, experienced many changes, including changes in organization in the role of protagonist (until November 2009 she was the President of the *Istituzione Scuole e Nidi d'infanzia del Comune di Reggio Emilia*).

Her voice is important because it increases awareness that the existence of Reggio's municipal schools, together with the pedagogy and organization we have discussed, has required and still requires open-minded choices, which stand outside traditional approaches; and that Reggio pedagogy must each time win not only the trust of families attending schools but of the various administrators and politicians who follow on from each other to govern the city. And let no one believe this is a simple or automatic task, because even in Reggio Emilia, as in the rest of Italy and the rest of the world, the culture of childhood – and, therefore, of schools – struggles to affirm itself in a way that is adequate to the intelligence and creativity of children.

To my great regret I have had to make cuts to the lovely letter Sandra Piccinini wrote to me recounting the years when she was *Assessore* in the city. The letter was too long for the space available in this book. It was not easy to edit, however, I hope the reader can sense this young city officer's passion and acuteness, even though she defines her character as 'slightly awkward'.

Dear Vea,

You asked me to respond to the question, 'Why a young woman like yourself should have been placed at the head of educational and cultural policy for the *Comune* of Reggio Emilia?', and you asked me not to answer with just 'official statements' but intertwined strongly with personal experience. To answer I went to look at notes I began keeping precisely in those years, such intense years; a sort of diary to conserve the memory of what might have been lost – the details.

I have chosen to alternate two characters: a normal character I used for reconstructing the context of that time (especially for myself), the 'official' reasons you call them, and the *italics* for more personal experience, although it is not always easy to distinguish the two. I hope you enjoy reading it.

We are speaking of the 1990s, difficult to recount because they are still so close, not yet 'history'. Years of change and acceleration in all processes: economic, communication, social. Governing the city meant first and foremost anticipating fluctuations in order not to be governed by events.

Reggio Emilia began to grow again after substantial stability since the end of the war and one of the lowest birth rates in Europe in the 1980s. It was a medium-sized city with a homogeneous character; this is how it was perceived by its inhabitants and academics who have occasionally described it. In the 1990s, the city began manifesting the complexity of contemporary cities: high levels of migration from the south of Italy and the rest of the world, increasing birth rates, increasingly older citizens requiring care and assistance (+15,000 inhabitants in ten years).

Politics

I came from a previous position in administration, through the sort of selection politics carries out in the field. A slightly awkward character, impatient of routine, I was not particularly well loved in more orthodox circles; anyway it happened that young women were called up as part of a slow turnover in generations in local government. This might be one of the reasons for my felicitous encounter with the preschool experience; an experience which was not aligned with {political} parties or unions, but capable of maintaining frank dialogue with politics without accepting its choices in uncritical ways. Perhaps our ambition – together with Loris Malaguzzi – was to influence administration's decisions on issues of education, or make a strong contribution to them. In the history of Reggio, relations with the various currents of politics has seen high and low moments, has not always been easy...

The years in which I was *Assessore* were turbulent from a political point of view, to the extent that in the end they marked the end of an era, and the most difficult decisions were ones which later would *bring* the most profound changes, such as founding Reggio Children, without Malaguzzi, and the decision to give municipal schools a new form of management in the *Istituzione* while starting up a centre dedicated to Loris Malaguzzi.

The beginnings, the most difficult of times...

I was nominated Assessore to the city at the end of July (1990); Loris Malaguzzi was there, in mid-August, in a small office next to mine, and he arrived at the most unthinkable times often on Saturday or Sunday. I was always trying to catch up with things and he would interrupt this with astute questions and original stories, the day would begin to take on a new course... I was learning... he was studying me, and so our conversation began.

That summer, the government approved measures that reduced funding to *Comunes*, so that I was summoned to terribly difficult meetings where there was talk of making cuts, not replacing staff...

I couldn't sleep at night. My friendship with Loris Malaguzzi had not been consolidated, he was diffident but curious, he constantly asked himself, tormented, what needed to be done, the future. He worked in the shadows seeking support and weaving networks that were largely unknown to me. I couldn't take the pace, I fell ill and had to stay off work for a month. Malaguzzi took advantage to have me study and learn a little of the things I didn't know. He gave me proofs of an interview Lella Gandini had made with him, about to be published in The Hundred Languages of Children. *I read it in one sitting, took notes for future conversations... but we never had them.*

It was often like that, conversations were not planned with him, it would happen that you were sitting at the same table for some public occasion and the discussion continued between a pizza, a school visit (often to scuole comunali dell'infanzia *Diana or La Villetta) and the Education offices. This is the way he told me his story of the schools, the conflicts and tensions. Malaguzzi was 'inconvenient', strong enough to do without politicians, but he was passionate about politics, he loved the discussion, was always right up to the minute and exceedingly well-informed, disappointed by the mediocrity becoming widespread.*

Our young mayor Antonella Spaggiari had called him, with a group of experts, to support important decisions in the city and from the seats of city council meetings some were shouting 'enough of the grand and old'; echoes of the 1980s, young go-getters with brilliant careers. The climate around us was not the best. Only the front cover of *Newsweek* (1991), declaring Reggio Emilia's preschools to be the most advanced in the world started a new phase [the American magazine described *scuola comunale dell'infanzia* Diana as the best nursery school in the world], we could catch our breath, and from that moment we worked uninterruptedly on the large and complex project which would take the name of Reggio Children.

We spent several summer evenings in the company of friends – always different – talking of the future in his house in Albinea in the Reggio hills. In the beginning – as often with new ideas – these presented themselves in vague and sometimes contradictory ways, and often one returned home with the feeling the evening had been mostly inconclusive. I used to go there when I was in 'crisis', or after a difficult session in the City Council, or before a difficult meeting.

In the summer of 1992, Malaguzzi had a heart attack, but afterwards he took up work again with a passion (and perhaps smoking). The illness did not make us any closer, I didn't realize it might be something serious. At that point the idea of Reggio Children was beginning to emerge – but we did not have a place... 'it mustn't be a museum', and 'it must contain presences and cultures from all over the world', 'it has to look forward thirty years'... together we would go looking for this place to give the city, once to a cloister, once to a disused warehouse.

His death was sudden, unexpected, on a cold winter morning; we were working at our best on a project that still contained the impossible, and he was afraid he wouldn't be in time.

The pain was one of the worst in my life. From then on everything seemed too big, too difficult for us to be able to do it. Like... an orchestra continuing to play without the Maestro. We could feel people's gaze on us, not only in the city.

Of course he had taught/given us much for us to carry on without him, but it was only then – little by little – that I became aware of the many strong, lovely personalities that surrounded him, making up the pieces of the marvellous (and fatiguing) world of Reggio schools. I became better aware that we all needed to play together, and I didn't yet know the soloists.

But Malaguzzi had taught me one thing: not to be afraid! To work hard, and seek to govern things rather than be governed by them. And so... we worked inexorably, and Reggio Children was born in March 1994, just a few months after his death. It was the best way of demonstrating that the {educational} experience was strong in itself, a way of not betraying Loris Malaguzzi, the best proof of his way of 'making school'.

The Istituzione, a safeguard for local autonomy

We decided to create a new form of management for centres and schools, after months of research and consulting; Reggio Children was ten years old and had travelled many roads around the world; cooperative *nidi*[2] were well established and the very first communal schools were celebrating their fortieth birthdays. The time was ripe, the size and complexity of educational services in the city deserved a specific tool for management.

This was an opportunity for schools to think about their own identities, which like all identities must not be prisoners of the past but 'searched out in the constant flow of things'; in reality schools are constantly modified through their daily habits together with today's children, teachers and parents. But the choice of *Istituzione* was first and foremost to safeguard cultural autonomy in early childhood services at a time when politics was degenerating and invading the areas of culture and communications. To overcome fears the staff might feel in this case, suspecting undeclared privatizations, the key was to clearly express our intentions, talk to workers, with great respect for their work. *Congruent choices, personal ones too, follow the birth of the* Istituzione *from close up. And so came my last day in the City Council as* Assessore, *I was very tense about it, many people said I was passionate in my way of working... I haven't felt nostalgic yet.*

For deeper exploration on the theme of identity, each school retraced memories and a large conference called 'Crossing Boundaries' marked the *Istituzione*'s cultural beginning; there were 'dialogue sessions' showing the point schools had arrived at in their research on emerging areas of learning and knowledge for living in the new millenium.

It was a sort of orchestra rehearsal for the new International Centre dedicated to Loris Malaguzzi. There was no lack of difficulty but perhaps this was something that fascinated me from the beginning, there was very little routine, and when I thought I could sense it I would fight against it. The rest was done by fortunate encounter, many in a place like this.

Chapter 6

An ethical community

On more than one occasion I heard Malaguzzi maintain that even the loveliest school is diminished in educational value if it does not hold participation and relations with families as one of the main values in its philosophy and practice. A different way of thinking considers schools to be the only reference point for education and teachers as the specialists. In this way of thinking, families have a role in the affections and children's upbringing but, because they lack specialist skills, it is cut off from schools. Instead considering schools as important places of learning but not the only ones leads to considering families as bearers of cultural values that enrich the overall culture of school.

Reggio pedagogy has always dedicated a great deal of attention to this aspect, just as it has also taken a great deal of care with its relationship to the city. The strong feeling of suitability of the schools for being public and involving families and citizens has been made clear and evident in various actions intended to bring the importance of education to the attention of many people, in the hope of being able to construct effective participation. It is a very ambitious objective, not easy to bring about and it involved (and continues to involve) all the people working in a school.

In the process of building real family participation, the role of school workers is extremely important. Children, parents and grandparents are in contact with them on a daily basis, and there are often strong relationships with affective implications. However, this does not mean that communication between teachers and families is simple; and over recent years the relationship has become more difficult. What are the reasons?

Perhaps people have become distant from feelings of social participation; perhaps tensions and tiredness exist; perhaps the massive diffusion of very superficial cultural models is responsible; or increasing numbers of families from other, very different cultures; or maybe communication in school is affected by a lack of relational ability. This is not to say that families are absent from meetings, or that management committee meetings are badly attended. However, in order to get to the point of relationships that go beyond a simple educational nature, in order to have real dialogue, we must satisfy a prerequisite: we must be capable of 'understanding the system of symbols of the person we are speaking with, their background values, the culture that supports the position they take'. (Galimberti, 2007). Perhaps our expectations are too ambitious for our real context.

Class meetings and the atelierista's relationship with families

Class meetings have always constituted the main rite in this complex relationship, and much time is spent preparing them by teachers and atelieristas. It is no coincidence that the theme of how to conduct a class meeting was a topic of one of the first books written from the experience in Reggio Emilia (Malaguzzi, 1971). It included a series of articles written by teachers and atelieristas under Malaguzzi's careful supervision. The articles deal with different areas and one, a discussion of class meetings, depicts the work needed to prepare them and strategies necessary for relating effectively with families – how to talk to them about their children and the work being done in school. Reading this book again, there are various elements which are still of interest today and would, perhaps, still be useful for teachers because I do not think family participation is discussed a great deal in teacher training courses.

The issue of daily relations with families and problems emerging from this relationship are today still the subject of much reflection in Reggio schools because, from a social point of view, disseminating a culture of education is an extremely important factor. It is not easy for teaches to learn to listen carefully, to say intelligent things that are not obvious using clear language, to be – in a word – communicators. We do well to recall that such qualities are rightly required of all the school staff, teachers and others, because in the various meetings with parents, and in the everyday life of the school, evaluations and interventions coming from the cook and her supporting staff are also important.

At the start of the school year when responsibilities are usually shared out between staff – assigned by the collective staff group itself – one of the various roles that exists is that of 'reference for family participation'. The atelierista is generally the person responsible for this area of communication with families and the community. Naturally atelieristas are also on the *Consiglio di Gestione* (Advisory Council)[1] and, like other staff, as well as participating in various class and council meetings they also learn to coordinate them and talk with families – to organize events.

What role do atelieristas have in relations with families? I would say they broke new ground, because though in the beginning ateliers acted in simpler, more direct ways than now, their work gave strong visibility to some of children's competencies, for example in paint, clay, ceramic and drawing work, with products which were easily distinguishable from those usually found in early childhood services. The work was decidedly lovely and used references from traditional and contemporary visual culture opportunely interpreted considering the age and imagination of the children. Although we avoided interpretations of a psychoanalytical nature in family meetings, the products of children's work were presented using illustrations and comments that gave parents a new image of their own children and children in general.

Communicating with the public

In 1970 when I began to work in Reggio schools, there were already three other atelieristas, and a more advanced aesthetic than was to be found in most nursery schools which were then called *scuola materna* (literally 'maternal schools'). To me, however, it seemed a very questionable aesthetic, inadequate for representing the quality of educational culture that schools in Reggio were already promoting. I had been teaching in secondary schools and had no educational experience with young children, but my son Michele had just turned five, and from the moment I started working at the *scuola comunale dell'infanzia* Diana, he was my source of observation and experiment for trying to understand what proposals were suitable and interesting for children of that age. Michele's experiments and competencies, reading books suggested by Malaguzzi, my teaching experience, especially with older children, and, naturally, a knowledge of the art world were the first things I referred to in deciding what proposals I would make to the children.

Just two years after *scuola comunale dell'infanzia* Diana opened, we organized an exhibition occupying the entire central area of the school. It was open to the *quartiere* or neighbourhood and to the city, and produced a great noise because in it there emerged an image of children that was truly new for the time, a dangerous child in some ways, capable of interpreting reality in original and unanticipated ways. Since then, municipal schools have always closed the academic year with exhibitions of a more or less complex nature and at the same time we began to circulate small publications containing children's work.

One of the first obvious revolutions the atelier achieved was that of visually communicating with the public. Perhaps it is difficult to understand the significance of this today, because time and habit make it difficult to evaluate differences with the past, but the impact then was surprising. The presence of schools and their documentation reached the whole city in posters, fliers and leaflets announcing conferences, exhibitions and management committee elections. In this sudden growth of initiatives, atelieristas were teachers, graphic artists and designers and it needs to be said their competency was not always equal to what was required; however, it was better than what went before.

At that time, in nearby Modena where I live, my husband's architecture studio freed a room for me, and this became a place where the whole group of teachers from Diana would transfer en masse outside working hours and work on exhibitions and publications because the studio had more effective tools and equipment than the school.

I remember a photocopier of excellent quality arriving in the studio that was capable of printing in A3 format and the sudden consequent progress in our communication. Being able to enlarge images and create the large print needed for communication allowed us to go from text we made using rubber stamps or tracing round metal stencils, to enlarging text written on a typewriter. Not only that but the photocopier, which for those times was truly marvellous, allowed good quality enlargement of images: photographs, objects, flowers and textures of all kinds.

We became skilled in manual cutting and pasting and using 'whitener' to erase, and in this way we made publications which were delivered directly to the *Comune*'s printing press and printed in large numbers. Such a huge leap forward in the quality of visual communication would only come again with the introduction of computers and colour printers.

In open bottles

A kind of photocopy-induced *technological drunkeness* was the basis for a proposal, which perhaps was a little adventurous for the time. Five- and six-year-old children built up self portraits as fictitious travellers – in phases and with the help of illustrations. In a first, verbal phase they recounted an imaginary journey where they perhaps met and fought side by side with a favourite character, or slid down their own nose (as one child laughingly imagined) or made friends with a panther, or opened a fridge full of forbidden foods, or started flying, etc. In a second phase, children were photographed in the positions they considered most suited to the story of their imaginary journey. In a third phase, using the photocopier made available by a shopkeeper friend (photocopiers were still rare objects at that time), the authors cut out, enlarged and reduced, in groups until their imaginary journey had been rendered credible. A publication reporting the twenty-six journeys by twenty-six children in class had a lovely introduction by Malaguzzi who helped us to find a title. *In Open Bottles* suggested a relation between journeys thought up by the children and messages entrusted to the sea in bottles, partly for fun and partly in the hope that a person would find them and reply.

After this we re-examined the play of relations between self and imaginary subjects in different ways; for example, photographs of children and characters the children loved or dreamed of were cut out and placed upright to become a cast of actors interacting with each other and protagonists of many adventures. Using the computer has made operations of this kind much simpler, and we can now introduce voices, backgrounds and music.

I think it is clear how exhibitions and publications for families and the public, together with very lively educational documentation inside schools (covering school walls like a kind of second skin) came to be elements that effectively contributed to forming a new, diffused awareness, a new image for childhood and preschool-aged children, and how this in turn led to greater sensibility for the new role played by ateliers. This new awareness and a new relationship with the city contributed to at least reducing, if not eliminating, widespread, excessive and irritating *childishness*: a certain way of understanding childhood, an attitude tending to position children inside the adult's stereotyped models. Perhaps the reduction of childhood to sweet childishness happens because adults want to salve their bad conscience for how little thinking and economic investment is dedicated to the world of school and education.

Defending choices

Over time, integration with other languages and fields of learning grew stronger and the atelierista's knowledge was more closely interwoven with the teacher's. The atelierista's profile was being built up in a new role, different from the familiar role of educational tradition and families were aware of this. She was not an art teacher, not a class teacher, she was a different person again, perhaps not yet properly defined, maybe requiring more understanding, but positive and important.

Schools for early childhood are expensive to run for municipal budgets and in moments of economic crisis, everyone knew which two positions were at greatest risk of elimination in staff cuts: the atelierista and the cook. These were not considered strictly necessary by many Italian *Comunes* but a luxury that could be done without. This was because ateliers and kitchens in schools by their very nature were not paired together by chance, they constituted (and constitute) an implicit criticism of certain utilitarian and slightly obtuse ways of viewing schools for early childhood. So at the first sign of financial difficulty, various *Comunes* that had initially chosen to follow Reggio's example and introduce the role of atelierista, removed it, together with school kitchens which were replaced by deliveries of pre-prepared meals. Fortunately, Malaguzzi objected strongly to this kind of choice and this was one of the reasons he handed in his notice as director of Modena schools (for a period he was responsible for schools in Reggio and Modena). Obviously it is not easy to persuade everyone how much good education can contribute to society in economic terms, nor is the particular contribution made by poetic languages to knowledge and learning (including the presence of the kitchen) commonly held to be important.

In Reggio Emilia, because of the atelieristas' growing importance for work groups and family opinion, we were quite convinced that if proposals were made by the *Comune* to cut their posts, families would fight by our side to keep them going. I believe attempts to do this have been made over the years, however, the initiatives have always been blocked because of the importance families attach to ateliers and the work of the atelierista. In times of global economic crisis like today's, I am not certain that cuts will not be proposed

parents defended atelieristas from being made redundant

again, nor am I so certain families would have such a protective response. When a choice is courageously anti-conformist, like the presence of ateliers and atelieristas, they must constantly demonstrate and confirm their cultural significance and that their existence is important. And sometimes I feel that cultural tension has been replaced by calm habit whose capacity for persuasion and defence I am not sure of.

Although in the beginning atelieristas were the main means and coordinators of visual communication in the city and with families, over time many teachers have also become attentive communicators. In this regard, evolution is particularly interesting in *nidi* which, as I explained in the introduction, had ateliers but no atelierista. However, teachers in *nidi* and *scuole dell'infanzia* very often come together for professional development generating a level of visual and aesthetic communication that is decidedly unusual for schools at this age.

Events in the city

Annual events exist which are important from the point of view of participation and organization, involving all the schools and the city. These are extraordinary collective inventions in which the role and competency of atelieristas is important for successful results. For example, the event in which work by children in municipal schools was exhibited in several places in the historic city centre and for a day changed the face of the city: shop windows with lady's handbags transformed into animals; ceramic shoes walking out of shops to stroll down streets; trees inhabited by clay animals; sculptures of horses resting in flowerbeds; odour meters collecting good and bad smells from certain places; a large circle of blue stones and emphasizing a circle of trees in a ring-of-roses, and so on – the eyes through which children view and experience places in the city transformed into work which was a visible testament to their way of seeing.

Reggionarra

Other truly special events, and deserving of their own publications, could be added to this. For example, an initiative which began with an idea by Sergio Spaggiari, currently director of the *Istituzione Scuole e Nidi d'Infanzia del Comune di Reggio Emilia*. This consists in storytelling sessions simultaneously held in many city places, where interior courtyards, colonnades, street corners, libraries and schools all welcome, for a day and night, hundreds upon hundreds of children of different ages with their families, to listen to stories with different themes; sometimes told by professional story tellers but above all by parents and students who have participated in courses organized by the *Istituzione* to prepare them, sometimes accompanied by music or dance.

REMIDA

REMIDA is a joint project of the Reggio Emilia *Comune* and Enìa[2], managed by the Friends of Reggio Children Association and sensitive to issues of art and ecology. It has approached city industries, and now organizes the creative recycling of discarded materials from roughly 200 manufacturers. Collected materials are cleaned, selected and organized in large, enchanting rooms frequented every day by teachers from Reggio schools and from the province and by young artists. I have seen trolleys usually seen in supermarkets filled up by teachers (as always many women), enthusiastic at the idea of different materials from the usual ones in their schools and attempting unusual and fun approaches with children. At the same time the REMIDA project aims to diffuse and support wider understanding of problems connected to the entire production process, from design and planning to waste disposal and reuse; education for a sustainable future.

School parties

Apart from these grand ideas and mass participation projects, I like to remember family participation in smaller events, more closely tied to the family's own school, because perhaps here we can capture more clearly the heritage of cultural growth in a community; a growth that has developed partly because of the attention paid towards the languages of the atelier and a pedagogy that is sensitive to them. End of year parties are always times for gaiety but they can turn into something different and more than that for children and families if they are sympathetic to a school's educational journey and culture. The *scuola comunale dell'infanzia* Diana is situated in a public park in the historic centre of Reggio and important public spaces like old cloisters and museums were being renovated at the same time as the innovative project, *Invitation to...*, by artist Claudio Parmiggiani was taking shape. In this project the *Comune* of Reggio Emilia invited five internationally renowned artists to create public artworks in five personally chosen places around the city.

In the context of this city culture, teachers and parents went out to visit and observe the old city centre and choose three renovated places as end points in three journeys to map with children of different ages (4, 5 and 6 years). On the day of the school party, in late afternoon, three processions of children and families formed and along the routes they had decided on unexpected situations arose, with parents as animators. A large zebra suddenly appeared from a street corner; in front of a cafeteria a chicken calmly sat and enjoyed a drink; other characters such as a lady dog with pushchair and a leaping frog joined the procession. Naturally these were all parents dressed as animals using costumes created and sewn by other parents from past parties many years before. When the processions arrived at their chosen destinations, other parents were already waiting to act out short scenes highlighting the characters of the various places. I was only able to see two of these scenes. One of them was in a space containing columns and arcades where mothers had worked together with a mother choreographer and were dancing round columns with appropriate music and long lengths of fabric wrapped around their bodies. They appeared and disappeared, using and amplifying the play of perceptions suggested by the site. And I must say all of this took place with unexpected gracefulness for dancers who were beginners. Instead, sound was a central protagonist in the second site, and the various materials used to build the place – wood, bricks, iron and concrete – were all played by parents, naturally with the support of a previously prepared sound track.

In all three spaces, the final moment was an invitation to participate for everyone, particularly children. In the first place, where the relationship between body and space was central, children became part of this *play* by running and dancing between columns.

In the second site everyone was invited to 'play' materials, and children of 3 and 4 years old used instruments given to them and also used their bodies for dancing. I did not see what took place in the third space but I was told the attitude was similar. Repetition of the party in all three places was planned for parents with children in different classes and to make more complete participation possible for a greater number of children and adults.

Perhaps there is no better way than this of letting parents understand the kind of work being done with children when we speak of the relationship with places, empathy and different languages.

The importance of democracy in public opinion

I cannot forget, however, that everything I have recounted up to now and the best of participation is difficult to conserve; this has always been so, but never before has the risk been so great. I fear an attitude of abdication is afoot, a way of making do, educationally and culturally, that is emerging in Italy in a very strong way. In the summer of 2008, film director Nanni Moretti launched an extremely alarming attack from the Locarno Film Festival, which I fear was not just for the sake of provocation. He claimed that in Italy public opinion no longer exists and blamed this on a large part of the television and newspaper industries that have, he accused, 'devastated' the way of thinking of Italians.

This idea was taken up some days later by journalist Eugenio Scalfari who returned to this idea and commented on it in his usual lucid way, emphasizing the importance of public opinion especially in democratic countries, 'In reality, in these [countries] public opinion constitutes that vital substance on which democracy imprints its own shape'. In the same article he wrote, 'the mirror reflecting the image which citizens have of their country has been broken into many fragments, which only reflects the image and fragmented interests of the person mirroring themselves. So many private opinions and no longer any vision of the common good' (Scalfari, 2008: 1).

Naturally, this short-sighted attitude towards the common good can also be found sometimes in people connected with the *nidi* and *scuole dell'infanzia*. However, the philosophy of Reggio Emilia is convinced that education cannot be fenced off in private places, not even the most beautiful or correct individual school or network of schools, and the project for family participation is a strong, important strand in its pedagogy. Constant reminders and support for this exist in the way staff work is organized and the myriad of proposals for participation. If we do not promote an 'ethical mentality' which includes the good of the community, social disaster is easily predictable.

For many years, Howard Gardner has been interested in this issue and has studied the social importance of a moral attitude. He has arrived at the conclusion that without a private and social ethic, there can be no future survival of the species. In a recent interview he declared, 'My favourite example of an ethical community is a small city called Reggio Emilia', citing as an example the quality of facilities for early childhood, and how a certain ethical and caring behaviour towards children and work functions, 'The tone has already been at such a high level that one rarely encounters compromised – that is, qualitatively or ethically sullied – work' (Gardner, 2007: 3). I share Gardner's evaluation of work in Reggio's schools, but I know how fragile this is, how much hard work and determination were necessary and are still needed in order to cultivate ethics, cultural quality and beauty.

Do families and does the city know about this constant effort? Do they realize? Only partially I fear and two hypotheses can be advanced: either the effort to maintain quality in municipal schools is not noticed because families take it for granted, to the point that some sections of the community seem almost irritated by repeated praise coming from the outside world; or this happens because Reggio Emilia is not an isolated city, and criticisms by Nanni Moretti and comments by Eugenio Scalfari involve and include Reggio families.

Family participation is undoubtedly an important means for strengthening borders between collective ethical responsibility and indifference or fragmentary individual visions of reality. A medium-sized city like Reggio sees thousands of families going through early childhood services run by the *Comune*. It can and must become a terrain capable of building public opinion on the importance of education. Without this support all our work may truly risk extinction. My impression is it has never been more important to discuss with all school staff – teachers and other – ways of being careful, of attempting deeper discussion with families on a daily basis. Never has it been so important to position the ways in which children are educated in broader cultural and social contexts. In management committees and public meetings, we cannot afford to avoid discussion of educational themes: organization, fees, numbers of places available, costs. These are all hot topics interesting everyone but they can lose focus and direction when they become isolated items of information and are not courageously positioned in broader landscapes of cultural reflection. In the same way, we must be very positive in seeking out and using opportunities for exchange and discussion with other types of school in the area – cooperatives, state schools, private schools, schools for children over 6 years – because our future social life is at risk if education is not perceived as a fundamental value.

Chapter 7

Environments

One area in the schools of Reggio Emilia where attention to aesthetics is clearly visible is in the physical environment, not generally found in other schools. What a lot of criticism and what a lot of positive comments Reggio has received over the years on this subject from our various visitors. Reflecting on reasons for this ambivalent attitude suggests the existence of certain widespread and deeply rooted stereotypes concerning education, schooling, learning and aesthetics, and I could recount some startling examples on the theme.

One I remember very well, because it was the first of many other examples, concerns a university teacher who came to Reggio Emilia to lecture on science for our professional development. Visiting the *scuola comunale dell'infanzia* Diana, she walked through the door, gave a quick look round the piazza inside the school (see Figure 7.1), empty because the children were in their classes and commented, 'Do children live here then, or is it a showcase?' I was left speechless and doubt I gave her an adequate answer because I was not prepared for that kind of objection or perception of the environment.

Figure. 7.1 The *piazza* in the *scuola comunale dell'infanzia* Diana

Thinking back, her reaction seems extremely clear and interesting, because it registered a certain mental scheme, and demonstrated her own personal culture concerning school environments and, in the end, unfortunately her culture of childhood. The *scuola comunale dell'infanzia* Diana obviously, despite all its problems of insufficient space and the financial problems we had managing it, stood outside this mindset. It looked too well cared for, too tidy, too clean, too lovely – too everything.

I will try now, many years later, to give an answer to this lady who compared the piazza in Diana to a showcase. Partly she was right: the environment is an element we perceive strongly and it expresses ideas, not only about space but about its inhabitants, their possible relations with the environment and with each other. Built environments are always windows for ideas.

Among other ideas in Reggio pedagogy, we are convinced of the right to beauty in a healthy psychological relationship with surroundings. Inhabiting a place which is lovely and cared for is perceived to be a condition of physical and psychological well-being and, therefore, the right of people in general and even more so of children, all children. The extent to which physical environments influence our construction of identity is not something only we in Reggio believe. However, it seems our cities do not pay much attention to this idea and a certain contempt for beauty can be sensed; more important is the economic return for builders.

I remember a very brief discussion with a city official in Reggio Emilia who maintained that environments are not particularly important because it is the people living in them that make them more or less pleasant. If we take this – I fear widespread – position to its extreme, then city administrations become exonerated from responsibility for the quality of places, placing it instead on individuals. According to some ways of thinking, schools for children, for reasons beyond me, should be rather untidy, should have badly handwritten signs stuck on the walls and doors with pieces of sticky tape, should not be too well looked after, with an occasional coat of paint sufficient to make them acceptable.

Another comment from people visiting our schools, typical especially of people coming from the pedagogical field, is, 'You are very good, but there is an excess of aesthetic care in your work'. An excess of aesthetic care! It would be interesting to hold a debate on the subject, and I hope this book in part manages at least to illustrate some aspects behind our choices.

Certain attitudes, related to care for environments, seem to me to be extremely natural; indeed, I suffer when I visit schools where I note a lack of care, which often approaches or crosses the border into slovenliness. There is often a certain amount of confusion between care, the culture of inhabiting and luxury. So as far as school environments are concerned, I cannot but ask myself how much respect there is for children inhabiting them, to what extent care for the environments they learn in affects their general education.

Fortunately, the importance of environment as an educating agent has been perceived by very many people visiting our municipal schools in Reggio, where the importance of constant care and research into interesting furnishings, materials and contexts by personnel and management has been recognized. We have seen evidence of this in school renovations carried out in many countries around the world. It is my impression that attention towards physical environments has been a kind of starting point from which to begin a journey of evolution for many groups of educators.

How ideas about environments were born

Apart from an artistic background, my interest probably derives from relationships with family and friends that made me highly sensitive to environments and the quality of living. In Malaguzzi, I immediately found an attentive and curious listener on the subject and my architect husband, Tullio Zini, who had worked with Malaguzzi in Modena on the design of early childhood centres was asked, free of charge for very little money was available, to design furnishings for the *scuola comunale dell'infanzia* Diana: tables, chairs, cupboards and containers for children, and a glass wall to separate and sound-proof the area planned as atelier. This latter space, which had not been properly defined or made distinct, faced on to and sometimes became one with a central space in the school then referred to as the *salone* or hall. The project we worked on created a very beautiful, partly transparent wall, highly contemporary and attuned to aesthetic research in the 'radical movements' in architecture during those years (1972).

Once the furnishings had been made, the environment immediately appeared different, as did the image of the child and the school housing the child. So began a highly fruitful collaboration; I communicated to Tullio the impressions and needs I and my colleagues perceived from our observations with children and he would generously supply suggestions and designs, always highly economical and simple to make, seeing as their manufacture was often entrusted to school parents or pensioners in the neighbourhood – former carpenters or smithies. Many of these furnishings, with certain adjustments and reworkings, were taken up throughout all the schools and are still present and functioning, for example the arena steps for morning meetings, atelier workbenches, the double curve of the *dressing-up stand* and the *inhabitable kaleidoscope* (which spread throughout the world) and various others.

Important research

In the 1970s, again with consultancy by Tullio Zini and an artist friend Nino Squarzi, who had already contributed some innovative ideas for the initial project by the architect Millo on indoor and outdoor spaces at Diana, an entire school year was spent investigating how spaces in schools were used by children and adults, the quality in the use of these spaces. This enabled a reconsideration of school spaces, and led to the design of new environments, furnishings, equipment and objects. The inquiry used a means of collecting data that was typical of urban studies. All schools were supplied with several copies of suitably scaled plans of their rooms and the research consisted in recording the position of children, teachers and parents at different hours of the day, marking them on the floorplans with different colours. At the same time, evaluations of quality were made for the use of various spaces with indicators of appreciation by children, acoustics, quantity of space and furnishings available.

This work strongly modified our ideas about spaces inside the school, not only from a functional point of view but also considering conceptual aspects. It was immediately obvious the quality of use of space was worst at two times in the day: the lunch for all children and the time when all the children poured into the school's central hall with excessive overcrowding and unacceptable noise levels. From this moment on, starting from this research, the central hall was conceptually transformed and the metaphor of the *piazza* came to be used; entrances came to be considered as a kind of visiting card, introducing the school and its inhabitants and spaces for communicating with the outside world. From this experience, using pedagogical and spatial imagination, we also conceived the mini-atelier with Tullio Zini's collaboration and this was built immediately afterwards, when we took the opportunity afforded by an act of arson at Diana.

A negative event like a fire became an opportunity for creating prototypes for new environments; the mini-atelier drew on all the observations and reflections we had made before that time and attempted to put them into practice in a concrete way. I will take the time to tell the story of what happened because I feel that much can be learnt from it, some of which, with appropriate reinterpretation, could still be enormously helpful today. I remember that when the fire broke out a colleague phoned me and I immediately rushed to Reggio from my home in Modena. Before my eyes I found the new atelier completely destroyed because the fire seemed to have been started precisely in that place. Together with the new dividing wall and furnishings, the entire archive of work from those first years was burned; the rest of the school was partly damaged and above all the walls were completely black.

I had been looking disconsolately for some minutes when Malaguzzi arrived and said to me in an impatient voice, 'Come on, don't stand here regretting, we have to build it again a better way'. The *scuola comunale dell'infanzia* Diana and the *Consiglio Infanzia Città* (see Chapter 6) were marvellous and immediately organized shifts for cleaning and repainting the entire school with the help of all available parents. More than a thousand hours of work were done, naturally all entirely free of charge, but more importantly we decided to use the event to propose building work at the school, especially extensions to classrooms which were really tiny.

We formed a work group made up of some parents from the management council, architect friends including Mariangela Calzolari, who was a municipal technician and subsequently became responsible for renovation, school staff and pedagogistas. Different hypotheses were discussed, some too fantastic or expensive, however, all useful for building up different imagery and getting beyond usual frameworks. In the end, the idea on which to base work which seemed best and was unanimously accepted was the one proposed by Tullio Zini and it included plans for moving the east face of the school and adding a new row of pillars five metres from the back of the school along its entire length (see Figure 7.2). This solution made it possible to use very simple building techniques and reuse all surviving door and window frames from the old facade.

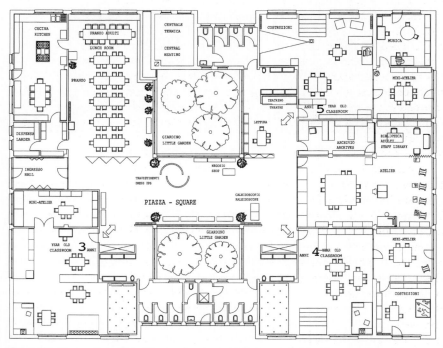

Figure 7.2 Floor plan of the Diana school used for research into the use of spaces

The new dividing wall for the atelier was conceived as a visual screen, a hoarding for presenting work by children. The upper section of the wall was transparent and the lower section, considering the very little money available as is usually the case in schools, was made using the simple expedient of covering a panel of plywood with work by children and protecting it with a piece of flexiglass – making it easy to remove and change work – thus simultaneously keeping the wall and the atelier visually up to date (see Figure 7.3).

Figure 7.3 The atelier window in the *scuola comunale dell'infanzia* Diana

In the *scuola comunale dell'infanzia* La Villetta, created by renovating an early nine-teenth century villa, one observation from the previous analysis of school spaces had been that classrooms organized with L-shaped floor plans best enabled teach-ers and children to organize themselves. Having part of a living space visible and partly screened off allowed less visual interference and greater tranquillity for work in groups. This is why when renovating the Diana school, rather than simply extending classes, the design project created three spaces: the first was a traditional classroom capable of containing all the children; a second small space, which we called the 'mini-atelier', contained large quantities of materials for working with different techniques, was acoustically but not visually separate from the rest of the class for working quietly in groups; and a third small space for group activities could be separate acoustically and visually. This was one of the most important spatial inventions, the one causing the greatest change in ways of working, making it possible and practical to do various kinds of work in small groups and to be able to observe and document children's work.

Furnishings in the new atelier and small spaces were designed by Tullio Zini together with school staff – a large central table, storage for paper using simple bricks as supports for planks of wood, and the same ideas were also used in the mini-ateliers present in each classroom. All this work was done by the municipal-ity's own team of carpenters with help from pensioners in the neighbourhood.

The importance of observation *in situ* became increasingly clear for me after this experience, also the contribution gained from making and imagining new possibilities for inhabiting spaces and the contribution made by exchange and dialogue with people who have specialist competencies; at the same time I understood how important it was for these competencies working by our sides to be of high quality. If renewal is to be more than a word it can come only from this collaboration.

In these first examples of closely woven dialogue between pedagogy and architecture, which would continue over the years and make generations of teachers, atelieristas and pedagogistas more sensitive to their physical environments, the role of the atelierista and her approach to observing children, the importance she gave to certain facets rather than others, and an attention to detail which might generally be considered unnecessary were all significant. There began to be some understanding of the importance of games of balance played by children on lines of shadow, of a feeling of hospitality created for example by large platters of fruit placed in the entrance for visitors, of contributing to a beautiful environment with branches and flowers painted by the children on transparent paper and placed in classroom windows, of capturing the green in the gardens and bringing it into school, of how a graceful arbour of plants climbing over wires put up in the mini-atelier ceiling made it more precious...

Our ability and sensibility in observing how children moved through spaces had also increased. We were better able to perceive aspects of their natural predisposition for establishing a relation with space, how they *taste* space with their powerful but sensitive sense of physicality. Running, jumping, variations in footsteps, hands touching and stroking surfaces; children explore spaces to make their formal, tactile, sonorous and luminous qualities emerge. They feel chromatic qualities and details.

In recent years with the advent of the digital camera, we have been able to observe and confirm this sensibility towards environments through photographs taken by children themselves. It is truly surprising to see the photographs they take, photographs that let us see their ways of seeing, their totally unanticipated viewpoints, such as the importance they attribute to one colour, filling up an entire photographic image with it, the very strong interest in a ray of light entering a window, the *flowering* of a crusty wall, or the play of reflections on a window pane. Ninety per cent of photographs taken by children with digital cameras are details, with girls and boys showing a similar percentage in this preference.

We have begun some small areas of research that have already given us different, interesting elements of information connected to the ages of children, their gender, individual strategies and preferences. This research will be continued for at least two years and aims to collect data internationally.

Pedagogy and technicians

We worked for many years with the technical office in the *Comune* of Reggio Emilia, which is responsible for design, renovation and (in the past) maintenance of municipal schools. Collaboration was not always easy for either of the two parties. Images of childhood and aesthetic frameworks were probably sometimes rather different.

Carla Rinaldi, who became director of municipal early childhood services together with Sergio Spaggiari after the death of Loris Malaguzzi, is highly sensitive to issues of environment and architecture and, together with some of her pedagogista colleagues, she organized a series of meetings and lectures by pedagogistas and architects of quality. These meetings were open to staff in schools and municipal technical offices; city architects were also invited. The reaction from these municipal professionals was surprising to say the least; rather than being pleased at an opportunity for exchange and updating, they took the event as an offence to their professional competency.

When building work is undertaken for school renovation or to bring a building up to new standards, atelieristas, more confident with visual material, tend to become a main reference point for municipal technicians, although everyone working in the school as well as the pedagogista actively participate in the process of critical reflection. However, not all architects and building professionals enjoy this type of participation, which I personally also consider to be precious from a psychological point of view, considering the results it has often produced. Such active participation by school staff often gives rise to particular attention being paid to the quality of living in a space and taking care of an environment, and for children this is a source of education.

The aesthetic quality of an environment requires attention and gestures of care, the maintenance of things and of culture, an attitude of respect for the things around us to which we should dedicate careful thought, organization and financial resources. If children live in well-tended places and see how a community looks after them, they will more probably become citizens who are attentive towards the environment housing them. So for at least twenty years at Diana, groups of parents and school staff regularly repainted the lower parts of school walls – the most exposed areas – and part of the furniture, for though children know how to take care of their environment, there are many of them and they are extremely lively.

A meta-project on environments

In the 1990s, our interest in environments gave rise to a research project carried out together with Milan's Domus Academy[1]. Despite obvious interest in the physical environment of *nidi* on our part and the part of many visitors, nothing can be taken for granted. Michele Zini, one of the architects who worked with the Domus Academy and coedited the book *Children, Spaces, Relations* (Ceppi and Zini, 1998) resulting from the research, took nearly two years to persuade us that it would be useful to disseminate ideas and concepts about young children's environments and to demonstrate the extent to which dialogue between the advanced pedagogy of Reggio Emilia and the advanced design of Domus Academy could be highly productive for advancing ideas and the concrete creation of environments. I do not remember very well the reasons for our caution but perhaps organizing thinking in new ways (and collaborating in the way proposed meant doing this) sometimes needs time to mature and we needed to be convinced that this research pathway really would move us forward.

Once we had clarified the *angle* of the book, we began a series of meetings, which all the participants from the world of pedagogy and the world of architecture and art recall with great pleasure. Our effort consisted in finding words and concepts to represent a kind of environment for children that was far removed from those more generally to be found or imagined in services for children. *Children, Spaces, Relations* helped us clarify, not least of all to ourselves, our values and choices we had made over the course of years and this made it possible for us to communicate these values more effectively with others, at the same time increasing our sensibility towards environments and our capacity for relating to them with practical solutions. This *environmental meta-project for childhood* produced a sort of reference manual for people interested in designing private and public spaces which house children, facilitating conditions of reciprocal listening between the world of childhood and the world of advanced design.

The care we take when we design environments and the care we take when we inhabit them derive from and correspond to an image of the child (and humanity) that is the foundation of the educational philosophy we refer to. We must evaluate in everyday life how much environments allow or forbid, how much they encourage or censor, how much they educate ways of seeing, exploration and sensibility. The extent to which personal sensibilities and culture can grow on journeys of this kind is often underestimated, as are the effects it can have on our relationships with children, the surrounding environment and educational work.

One of the most significant aspects which came from the environmental meta-project was the importance of sensory qualities in environments: light, colour, sound, micro-climate, etc. and how much these influence people's perceptions and overall quality of living. The information and culture we gained from research in these areas amplified and caused greater sensibility in our work with children and considerably improved interventions on the environment by contributing to a more careful, emotive way of seeing the surrounding reality. We know children are born with a very sophisticated sensorial apparatus, equipped to receive a myriad of stimulations, a capacity for learning and growth, which tends to get dispersed by time, because generally inadequate attention is paid to maintaining these capacities or to ensuring children receive adequate stimuli for achieving their potential. If we consider, and this is universally recognized, that our senses are large and precious receptors for collecting and processing information about reality, then we need to find contexts to accommodate this extraordinary natural patrimony and keep it *alive and practicing*. I will recount just a few illustrations, among the many I recall.

Exploring with the senses

Children had been invited to explore the school and investigate the different qualities of light, smell, and sounds present, being careful also to note any variation during the day, during changes in weather and with different seasons. At the end of this work, various spaces were evaluated by children on the quality of these different elements and their variations, using symbols and indicators they created themselves. In a different workshop, atelieristas and teachers were asked to redesign spaces in their schools through an analysis and application of sensory qualities. Another proposal to make with children, simple and also interesting, is to analyze herbs with noticeably different characters such as rosemary, catmint and thyme and try to represent their smells in drawings, then attempt to create sounds and rhythms suited to describing them – and perhaps even try to dance their different essences.

Antonella Spaggiari, who was Mayor of Reggio Emilia for ten years, loves to recount the story of a visit to Diana during which she was struck by the way a small group of 5 year olds was working on the exploration of an onion. Some children were representing the onion's shape in drawings, others were drawing its smell, some were trying to produce sounds to represent it and others still, together with cooks in the kitchen, were breaking onions into little pieces to make them into a salad. This reminds me that many years before, together with the children, we had enacted a sort of 'striptease' on an onion by stripping away its layers one by one and applying these thin layers to a window pane, the veils of the skin transformed into a host of butterfly wings by light passing through them.

Explorations on light led us to bring different tools into school environments for children to explore and manipulate light, in different ways and from different points of view. It is no coincidence, therefore, that the theme of light was subsequently chosen as the main subject in the first atelier organized at the new Loris Malaguzzi International Centre; work based on a scientific approach but also enriched by past experience which was more connected to aspects of expression and environment.

An ecology of place

In my last example, I recalled the experience of having some exemplary aspects and others that it would be better to avoid. Some years after the publication of *Children, Spaces, Relations* (1998), which stimulated much interest and was translated into three languages, we felt the need to take up reflection on environments once again. To do this, we formed an interdisciplinary group to make research on two spaces in schools: entrances and bathrooms, the latter a place to which little reflection had been dedicated apart from thoughts on hygiene and sanitation. We worked together with two young architects (Michele Zini and Francesco Zurlo) and with them we charted a highly interesting journey that made it possible for us to see spaces we used on a daily basis in different ways.

Teachers and atelieristas analyzed these two chosen environments as subjects for research, collecting and documenting their constituent materials and colours and using graphs to visualize the numbers of people using them. Comparing the collected data with recommendations in the 'meta-project for children's environments', the distance separating them became visible. These two environments are both often designed without sufficient attention paid to spaces that children find important. In the case of bathrooms, designs often separate the body and its needs from the pleasure of being in them, and ignore the opportunities they offer, such as the presence of wash basins and water; in fact, the way these spaces were perceived and inhabited by children and adults was documented, clearly revealing the extent to which bathrooms are spaces children frequent joyously and that are almost always underestimated in school design.

At the end of the research, we were able to build up metaphors capable of giving us new thoughts on these two spaces, often considered to be only functional and of secondary importance. It is always interesting when we make concrete choices to have imagery constructed from new metaphors to refer to and use, capable of guiding new models for inhabiting space, and this is true both for furnishings and the living potential of a space.

Once the research was finished and visual documentation had been created that was capable of communicating results to colleagues in other schools, it was time to start the actual process of changing the environments that were the object of the research. Up to this point in the tale, I think the research can be considered effective, formative and culturally precious and it could be a reference for further research into modifying and updating other school spaces. But the second part of the tale must instead make us reflect on how it is possible, so easily and with such superficiality, to dissipate riches that are capable of producing innovation.

At the same time as this research was being carried out, work had begun on rebuilding bathrooms in many schools with the aim of bringing them into line with new safety standards. I believe anyone would find it natural to think that such recently concluded research on an environment would constitute material of great interest and a source of new design ideas. It is not my intention to mete out criticism, but I find it difficult to understand and accept the waste of experience and intelligence that takes place all too often even in little things. I fear, to tell the truth I believe, the recently concluded research and the work undertaken on rebuilding bathrooms never met, were never put together for exchange or related to each other, with the result that once again the part considered 'theoretical' was separated from the practical with all the damage this short-sighted and basically banal dichotomy inevitably causes. This was confirmed by the work carried out producing environments that are rather ugly, anonymous and extremely distant from the image hypothesized in the research done with the schools. (Let no one use the excuse of funding because this issue was not even considered.)

Creating two ranges of furniture

Even in Reggio Emilia, despite the quality of environmental culture existing in our schools, not everything happens automatically, and we need to continue defending our cultural achievements with perseverance and attention. Experience built up over years and which has given great impulse to the sensibility of school staff towards environments, must always be reproposed, reinterpreted and readapted, and each new project or school renovation must be the occasion for research and development of environments. A culture must continuously be informed and develop – because if the opposite happens it regresses and can no longer transmit competencies it has acquired to new generations of children, teachers, atelieristas, pedagogistas and technicians. As the queen says in *Alice in Wonderland*, 'it takes all the running you can do, to keep in the same place' (Carroll, 1998: 145).

By their background and role, atelieristas ought to be *vigilant sentinels* of this attention to environments, and press pedagogical directors so that the culture of environment continues to live on, aware that all this can only be obtained through constant evolution. In professional development courses held by Reggio Children, the theme of environments is always given space and importance. But unfortunately there is always limited time and the subject needs to be taken up on different levels in the workplace and in schools.

There is a very widespread idea that furnishings are a secondary element in environments; instead they are an integral part and their choice reflects in precise ways the image we have of childhood and school environments. For all these reasons, when a young businessman in our city asked us to collaborate on creating a new range of furnishings, we accepted enthusiastically. The work group developing the furnishings included different areas of competencies: the businessman, architects, a pedagogista and atelierista and a contract between Reggio Children and the company stipulating that royalties on the products created would be reinvested in research in schools. This is how the

Atelier3 range of furnishings was born and we feel it truly gives an innovative image of children and schools, to the extent that various companies in the field have also been stimulated to create new ranges of furniture.

Atelier3 totally covered the different types of furniture needed for a school but it did not include a series of elements that could contribute to creating soft, imaginary spaces. To fill this gap, Atelier3 was integrated with a new range made of 'soft' pieces. On the initiative of the same intelligently sensitive young businessman and with the same designers, and with Reggio Children once again by their side for consulting on the new range, PLAY+ Soft was born. Whereas the first range showed a certain design uniformity, the large group of young designers and architects made the furnishings of the new range into a varied landscape.

For the most part this new range of furnishings is composed of soft elements, renamed 'big softies' and this project, more than the previous one, is capable of going beyond preschool environments, and adapting to people of various ages. The project has been capable of entering home environments, shopping centres, bookshops (such as the chain run by Italian publishers Feltrinelli), New York's MoMA Museum, dedicated spaces for childhood like Heathrow airport's new T5 terminal in London and Stockholm's House of Culture and many other projects, confirming once again the extent to which a dialogue between pedagogy, atelier and architecture, which began many decades ago, has given rise to interesting and original journeys now increasingly extending beyond school environments. Rightly so because childhood does not only inhabit a world of schools.

Between art and pedagogy

Dialogues with Places is one of the most recent exhibitions created together with children to inaugurate the Loris Malaguzzi International Centre in Reggio Emilia. The suggestion giving shape to this exhibition came from a project entitled *Invitation to...* conceived by artist Claudio Parmiggiani, who I have already mentioned in Chapter 6 and who is a long-time member of the 'conceptual' art movement in Italy, which goes back to the 1970s. In this project, the municipal administration of Reggio Emilia, with collaboration from private sponsors, commissioned and organized the creation of five contemporary works of art to be permanently situated in various places round the city; spaces freely chosen by five artists of renowned quality: Luciano Fabro, Sol LeWitt, Eliseo Mattiacci, Robert Morris and Richard Serra. In his *Invitation to...* project, Parmiggiani writes, 'For an artist it means electing a place as the emblem of an idea and thinking of it as a voice in his or her work... and through their work communicate the energy, presence and profoundness of this place informing it and giving it meaning... The works are, therefore, expressions of a real solidarity with an environment and its reality' (Parmiggiani, 2003).

We felt the pathways pursued by the five artists to create their works could also activate important and interesting processes with children, such as choosing a place, creating a relationship and dialogue with it, and arriving at the point of designing a piece of work that is attuned to the place and its identity, simultaneously modifying it and enriching it. In this type of journey, important artistic, cultural and social processes are activated which are important also from an educational perspective. The *Dialogues with Places* exhibition (see Figure 7.4) opens with a strong statement, 'Every place has a soul, an identity. Trying to understand that soul and relate to it means learning to also recognize one's own soul' (the word 'soul' is taken from James Hillman's *L'Anima dei Luoghi*, 2004).

Together with James Hillman, many voices have made themselves heard, mournful voices warning us and creating alarm bells, placing care for the environment and its quality in a new and lucid relationship to health, and to physical and mental well-being.

Figure 7.4 The *Dialogues with Places* exhibition

Too often we can observe an apathetic, resigned acceptance of vulgarity and ugliness, a lack of care for environments we inhabit. This degenerative process is culpably underrated; caring for our environment is considered to be an unimportant element of life and culture, not fundamental but a useless refinement, superfluous, or an activity to be carried out at one's discretion. Instead, we believe that today more than in the past, in a situation of social and cultural transformation taking place around the entire planet, in situations of massive *migratory flows* originating in the need to survive, to work, or in tourism, our relationship with environments is an element of enormous importance, because it leads us to a reconsideration of profound aspects connected to cultural, individual and social identity. This general responsibility also involves education.

It is our hope that a sensitive approach to surroundings, in constant daily ways, made up of many actions, of attention and choice, can be a positive element for participation and conscious solidarity with all that surrounds us and with other human beings of all cultures and backgrounds; an indispensable attitude for the future of democracy and the human species.

The Wonder of Learning is a new exhibition created in 2008, a travelling exhibition aiming to update and replace the 1975 exhibition *The Hundred Languages of Children* and organized by the *Istituzione Scuole e Nidi d'infanzia del Comune di Reggio Emilia* and Reggio Children. It contains a section dedicated to this theme of 'dialogues with places' in order to underscore how important the subject is for us and as a practical illustration of possible ways of working with children.

The new Loris Malaguzzi International Centre, where the second phase of building work is nearly completed, has once again drawn to our attention the issue of a culture of environment, the importance and, simultaneously, the fear of beauty. Just as in the 1970s, we continue to hear voices that accuse us of excessive attention towards aesthetics and as always the impression is that there exists a large amount of confusion between professional competency, a culture of inhabiting spaces and luxury. It is saddening after all these years to find ourselves discussing aspects we believed to be more consolidated at this point.

The International Centre has been generated by the pedagogical culture of the municipal schools, and by the attention, hopes and dreams this has awakened in parts of the world. The centre represents a culture sensitive to aesthetics (in terms of connections between structures), which we have built up over many years. To return to where I began the chapter, it is still hurtful to see that certain aspects of this culture, that some of us consider important, are instead perceived by others as a form of *megalomania* and superfluity.

Today in an economic recession involving many countries, there is a need for courageous, lucid and anti-conformist choices. In times of difficulty like this, where both reality and dreams have doubts about the right course to follow, more than any other time we need to be aware that only a culture of professional and ethical rigour and beauty can help us to continue with our hopes. As the poet Friedrich Hölderlin tells us, 'where there is danger, a rescuing element grows as well' (Hölderlin, 2004: 39).

Vea Vecchi in conversation about architecture and pedagogy with...

Carla Rinaldi, pedagogista, Director of Reggio Emilia's municipal schools from 1970 to 1999, Professor of Education at the University of Modena and Reggio Emilia and President of Reggio Children since 2007; and Michele Zini, architect and designer with ZPZ Partners, working with Reggio Children and Domus Academy Research Centre (June 2009).

VEA: I'd like to start from the book *Children, Spaces, Relations: Meta-project for an Environment for Young Children* (Ceppi and Zini, 1998), which is based on a research project that began the ongoing dialogue between Reggio Emilia and the world of design. Michele, your work as an architect designing *scuole dell'infanzia, nidi* and other spaces for children and as a designer of furnishings for children has an important point of reference in the *Meta-project* carried out in the late 1990s. How did the idea for that project come about?

MICHELE: The idea of working on a project about designing environments for children came from the need to find some tools to activate a dialogue between pedagogy, architecture and design. We wanted to make explicit all the ideas and knowledge on the environment that had developed in Reggio's schools, and at the same time to fertilize them with the cultural and technical knowledge and know-how of the world of contemporary design.

There were also some empathies that suggested this encounter: we were reading some of the same authors – Edgar Morin, Gregory Bateson, Ilia Prigogine, Bart Kosko, Marc Augé – studying complexity theories,and visiting the same exhibits of contemporary art. This led me to propose to Domus Academy and Reggio Children a sort of roundtable of research on the environment of young children, applying the work method of the meta-project, which we were experimenting with extensively at that time and which was a current of research in Italian design.

VEA: Carla, you readily accepted the proposal and transformed it into one of the strategic projects of Reggio Children. Why?

CARLA: The meta-project was the discovery, very banal but profoundly true, that we were not constructing a project but *a way of thinking about designing,* the conceptualization of *project design.* For those, like me, who were educated with a concept of project and project design that was dynamic but also specialized, the meta-project became an opportunity to understand in depth this concept of 'meta', going from the project to the meta-project. I think that this was a bold step, which I think is demonstrated by the fact that the book, even though it has been translated into many languages, has not yet been entirely understood in its deepest essence, this 'thinking about thinking' of architecture.

VEA: How did you work on the meta-project?

MICHELE: We applied the holistic approach that characterized all of us from a cultural point of view. We organized a group of people who worked in different fields (art, design, architecture, pedagogy, bio-engineering, interface design, primary design). The job of the two coordinators, Giulio Ceppi and myself, was to elicit contributions, even very different ones, on the subject and have them 'dialogue' without excessively mixing the languages and the approaches; that is, without 'levelling down' the different languages into a single style and language, but rather maintaining a 'semi-finished' level, which would preserve the strength of the differences. Also, the final drafting of the book on the meta-project and its layout, which entrusted comprehension of the meaning to the relationship between text and images and enabled a non-sequential reading, was an attempt to offer something that each reader could personalize, rather than follow one set of rules and a single recipe.

CARLA: The meta-project was an interdisciplinary encounter for *trans-disciplinary* construction. In fact, this experience compelled us, as you often say, Vea, to construct this sort of 'distillation of knowledges', the result of which was the meta-project. We consider inter-disciplinarity to be essential for seeking new answers and new questions, which our times call for. Ours is a true 'season of design', when it is indispensable to dare the new and design the future.

VEA: The meta-project became an approach and a heritage of the world of pedagogy?

CARLA: There was a positive fusion between pedagogy and architecture/design. The book was presented, metaphorically, as a sort of scribbling pad that invited and suggested change. It is not coincidental that almost immediately afterwards we began the research project with Harvard Project Zero on individual and group learning, described in the book *Making Learning Visible* (Rinaldi, Giudici and Krechevsky, 2001). These were enthusiastic and fertile years, where the 'meta' level began to become, if not everyday practice, at least an everyday effort.

VEA: What are the most novel aspects that this research brought to the design of environments for young children?

MICHELE: This work was important because it made visible the boundaries of a field of research that before were hidden. Since then, designing environments for children has become a field that includes different projects that nourish a body of knowledge and are enriched by belonging to an ongoing laboratory of research, which continuously redefines its objectives and for this reason is kept alive and interesting.

   It also shifted the problem from building structures to creating artificial ecosystems made up of furniture, symbols, colours, materials, lights, smells and sounds. It became more evident that it is not only compliance with the regulations that determines the quality of a project. Nor is it simply the architectural quality; there are examples of beautiful buildings that fail to provide a good environment for children. What determines the quality of a project is its capacity to transmit and support a certain image of the child, a child who has a hundred languages and the right to an environment that is rich, multifaceted, complex, well tended, beautiful.

   And finally, this work made it clear how senseless it is to conceive the architecture and the interior design of a school separately, as often happens; rather, they are elements of the same environmental system.

CARLA: For me, this experience represented that famous 'paradigm shift', precisely because it meant overcoming the separation between spaces and furnishings. The encounter between pedagogy and architecture within the Municipality of Reggio Emilia was courageously introduced by Malaguzzi, inspired, I believe, by the great masters of pedagogy like Maria Montessori. It was really somewhat of a cultural 'scandal', the idea that the clients, in this case the pedagogical team and the teachers, and in certain cases also the parents, would sit at the same table as the architect. Usually it was the architect who would 'deliver' a house or, in this case, generously deliver a school to the teachers. This was the first sign of this concept of 'doing school', in both the metaphorical and literal sense, involving the team in building a 'school of thought' to make a three-dimensional school.

VEA: Carla, can you talk about the context in which the culture of the environment of young children originated in the schools of Reggio Emilia.

CARLA: When I first started working in Reggio in 1970, it was an extraordinary moment, in which the design of the *scuola dell'infanzia* Diana had just been completed by the architect Millo, who worked for the municipality. The real turning point was with that design. I started when the project was initiated for the *nido* Arcobaleno with the architect Carta, who had taken to heart the lessons of Diana, challenging our knowledge of such young children – which meant challenging our own ignorance, because in that period (1972–1974) there weren't other *nidi* conceived as educational environments from which to take inspiration, apart from the corporate day care centres at Olivetti. In fact, the architectures of the ONMI (Opera Nazionale Maternità and Infanzia), created during the Fascist era to provide welfare services, offered a design based primarily on welfare and healthcare. The first *nido* designed and opened in the 1960s in Reggio Emilia, Cervi, embodied that health-oriented stereotype.

The *nido* Arcobaleno broke down this approach. Architecture has always had a powerful role in our experience, since architecture shapes the pedagogy, it is one of the strongest influences. So when you make architecture you actually renew the pedagogy; the architecture is not only the architecture of the building, but it determines and modifies the pedagogical architecture. So in reality, architecture and design are in relation with pedagogy, and this gives rise to an extremely generative moment, a moment of crisis, and the crisis is accentuated with the involvement of the teachers and the pedagogistas as protagonists. When this involvement happens, the teachers began to feel legitimated, encouraged to think about the spaces of the school, to imagine them, to want them different. They felt this as a duty and a right and they considered the space to be a fundamental part of the relationships, of the learning and of the communications that developed in the school.

VEA: A space that is subject and protagonist?

CARLA: The space is no longer simply background, but a key player: organizing a space means organizing a metaphor of knowledge, an image of how we know and learn. In fact, if knowledge does not progress by formalization and abstraction but, as it seems, by the capacity to contextualize, to create relationships, to act and to reflect, then the spaces and the furnishings, the lights, the sounds must allow relationships, actions, reflections, sharing and collaboration. So here we have the concept of designing the environment that also means designing life, which means constructing a context in which it is possible to continue to live.

In my view, it is a concept that finds one of its highest expressions
in the meta-project. The antecedents are found in the years I was talking about before, the early 1970s; maturation occurred during our happy
encounters with architects like Tullio Zini. But the meta-project was the
moment where this positive fusion really took its highest form.

The keywords contained in the first part of the book were used to
formulate general criteria and contexts in an attempt to identify the
desirable characteristics for an environment for young children, based on
a critical analysis of the experience of the *nidi* and *scuole dell'infanzia*. But
they also represent the most effective synthesis of the trans-disciplinary
experience that led our thinking 'to think about itself'. If I had to illustrate the keywords I would use the helical form of DNA.

MICHELE: The meta-project is actually a sort of genetic project, a system of
conditions, qualities and values able to contribute to the identity of the
individual projects that derive from it. The hope is that ten different
designers who take inspiration from the meta-project produce ten different projects, but all with the same 'flavour'.

CARLA: The keywords of the meta-project are also the script of a pedagogical
curriculum vitae, or in any case I'd like to begin to rethink them in this
way, because they are much more 'secular' than all the technical terminology. They are keywords for inhabiting, and, therefore, for living... I just
got the desire to view them as *structuring elements* of a curriculum vitae,
or as *aims* for a curriculum vitae, and at the same time *outlines* for a curriculum vitae.

MICHELE: Another characteristic of that work was the involvement of many
people from different cultures and languages around the theme of designing environments for children: to create a network of thinking, a group
competency, a sort of collective intelligence that is mutually nourished.
In the meta-project, like in the more recent case of PLAY+ Soft, creating a network of people who offer their perspectives on the environment
becomes an objective in itself: *the means is the message*.

CARLA: In the book you are not able to identify who wrote what, whether the
author of a piece of text is the architect or the educator. We 'spread the
word' back and forth to each other, someone would throw out a word and
someone else would fertilize it.

VEA: In your daily professional activity as educator and architect, what role
has been and continues to be played by the research you carried out?

MICHELE: *Children, Spaces, Relations* is still used as a guide for our design
projects for *nidi* and *scuole dell'infanzia*, but also for the two lines of furniture we created in conjunction with Reggio Children and the other
spaces for children we've designed in public places (airports, shopping
centres, parks). Each project takes shape and identity also from the cultural context, the site, the historical period, just as the projects in other
countries – for example, the Takadanobaba nursery in Tokyo – are born

of a relationship between different cultures, from a dialogue that makes it possible to identify design elements that are not present in either of the two cultures but that arise from the relationship between them.

CARLA: The word 'relationship' is an important key for understanding. Why was this dialogue so fertile? Could it only have been so with a 'certain' architecture? Not by chance, the architecture represented in the meta-project is an architecture defined as 'relational', and ours is a relational pedagogy.

It is not by chance that we were constructing, talking and writing about relational pedagogy — Malaguzzi first and foremost — and they were writing about relational architecture, which highlights the 'soft qualities' and leaves to the architecture only the task of marking *fuzzy* boundaries. It is wonderful when you discover that you are a fish in an aquarium with other fish like you.

VEA: Michele, is there a particular characteristic always present in your projects that derives from what we have been discussing?

MICHELE: The search to give a multisensory dimension to the environment, which means working on identifying the materials, the lights, the colours (the so-called *soft qualities*), with the aim of providing not just comfort, functionality and easy maintenance, but also a sensory richness that is empathic with the children's cognitive processes. If children are a sensory laboratory and they know and interpret the world by engaging all five senses, then they deserve an environment that is rich from a sensory point of view with a design that enhances these aspects. A design for an environment for children that is poor from a sensory point of view is probably going to be an ugly design for children.

CARLA: It was evident to us that the younger the child, the more a relational pedagogy seeks a relational architecture, especially the 'soft qualities' because they are the ones to which the child is sensitive.

VEA: Michele, you've been collaborating with Reggio Emilia for fifteen years. What has changed in your way of working?

MICHELE: It has contributed to developing a way of looking, of thinking, and an enormous faith in children — a faith that is also nurtured by my daughters Alice and Mattia. Also, I've learned a 'reckless' and at times insane tendency to never be satisfied, a tendency, however, that generates quality and one that children deserve. And I've learned that it is truly naïve to think that a school, once the building is finished, is ready for use and the architect's job is finished. A good design project leaves some spaces (in both the real and conceptual sense) undetermined, so that the teachers and the children can determine their potentials. In reality, the designer should continue to work for a year or two in a group with teachers and pedagogistas to refine the design of the school, in a sort of relationship of 'design maintenance' that completes the realization of the project.

VEA: You have taken the research of the meta-project and the case studies of your architecture and furniture to many parts of the world. Which concept has turned out to be the most difficult to communicate and share with other cultures?

MICHELE: The concept of 'rich normality', a concept that I really love, but it is especially difficult to share in other countries. I am able to communicate the difference between simple and simplified, between complex and complicated, between multisensory and cacophonic, but I have a hard time translating from the Italian the concept of rich normality...

CARLA: The definition of 'rich normality' emerged from a discussion between Andrea Branzi and myself, where you were also present, Vea. I was discussing the idea of transgression as an 'escape from normality', and especially of always living outside the normal. But Andrea Branzi brought in this concept of 'rich normality', as the normality that also contains the anomaly, that is fluid, very difficult to inhabit, where there is beauty and ugliness, and we are called upon continuously to redefine beauty and ugliness, and so on.

Vea Vecchi in conversation about architecture and pedagogy with...

Paola Cavazzoni and Maddalena Tedeschi, pedagogistas who have worked with various architects, coordinating the development of new municipal schools; and Tullio Zini, an architect who has worked with Reggio since the 1970s, including designing the scuola dell'infanzia *in the Loris Malaguzzi Centre along with ZPZ Partners and Gabriele Lottici. The three have worked together on many projects (February 2009).*

VEA: You have all recently been involved in the opening of a number of municipal schools. For an architect and a pedagogista, what's most important in this collaboration? What are the roles and the meeting points, what difficulties might be encountered, and what do you learn from each other?

TULLIO: I think that designing involves envisaging many things – functional needs, quantities, possible future developments. But it also means a synthesis among different competencies; designing means coordinating and 'gelling' these different worlds to seek the most effective way to harmonize them and make them applicable to the everyday reality. As suggested by Vitruvius, the architectural theoretician of Imperial Rome, an architect has to know about mathematics without being a mathematician, about music without being a musician, about poetry without being a poet, and so on, because you have to be aware of all the different competencies that can be involved, in order to recognize their importance and fuse them together in a project. In my opinion, this statement by Vitruvius is close to your pedagogical theory of the *hundred languages* that children possess, and your rejection of hyper-specialization, and the ability to dialogue with other cultures and competencies that you consider to be such a rich resource. This concept can also be seen in the Renaissance, with the idea of the universal man whose culture encompasses all fields of knowledge.

So if you're designing a school you have to try to understand the pedagogical values. Designing a new school with this awareness is such a complex issue that, without the contribution of those who will inhabit it, those who are able to clarify the deep nature of what a school means, you risk creating projects that are worthless. There really must be an exchange, because there are many things you don't know: the daily life of the child, the child's relationships with his or her surroundings and with others, and so on. And if you don't ask these questions to those who inhabit the school on a daily basis, well, there's no way you'll ever know them.

We are talking about an exchange of competencies that is complex, and this is why I've always thought that creating a school is like creating a little city, because a school encompasses and reflects many of the themes of everyday life: the relationships with parents, food, sleeping, friendships, attachments, and many other things. So designing a school means confronting and resolving problems in a way that requires many and different competencies.

MADDALENA: I absolutely agree with Tullio about how designing requires that everyone involved comes to the table with their own competencies and curiosities, and that we have to be open to listening to competencies that we don't have and someone else does. Working with Tullio has been important as a professional experience but also a personal one, and I'll explain why. In terms of the relationships that we can glimpse and that we hypothesize in the school, what we are actually talking about is the relational life of the children, of their families, but also the life of the teachers, the cooks and auxiliary personnel; it's the life of many people for many hours a day.

So designing a school goes beyond the functional aspects of the environment, which naturally are important, and beyond the good organization necessary so that everyone can work in the best way. I believe that the most important goal is to ensure the best life to the people who live in that place.

I recall the emotion I felt when I first entered the *nido* Gianni Rodari, designed by Tullio, the fascinating plays of light, the *embraces* of the architectural forms and of the materials, the sensation of real pleasure. These feelings derive from qualities that are intrinsic to the environment and that emerge from an idea that values the people who inhabit the space. This attempt to imagine spaces and new possibilities in the children's living together helps create a new way of working and of teaching.

VEA: The relationship between Tullio and the schools is longstanding: to what extent have the pedagogy and the architecture evolved together?

TULLIO: I've always thought that to create a good architectural design, you have to take into consideration not only the structures of the buildings, but also the environmental qualities of inhabiting the space, such as the light, the sounds, the colours, the materials. All these elements must be part of the architecture. Talking about the 'soft qualities' in inhabiting spaces is easier now, because these concepts have gradually become more widespread, but back in 1989, when we began working on this type of project, they were not so common. Reggio Emilia has never just been content with the quantity of schools created, but as soon as one was finished, we would begin to examine the quality of living that it could offer.

When you design a building, you always try to get an idea of how someone might feel in the space you are proposing. You think about how people can move around in the space, with what rhythms and what ways of being they will be able to inhabit these new unexplored spaces. Then there's another aspect, a very complex one and also difficult to describe, which considers how to represent this new and growing culture of childhood without falling into 'infantilism', into a language that is simplified and banal.

PAOLA: I think that this idea of a complex design process has had an almost daily impact on the quality of inhabiting the environments; it also contributes to a greater awareness of how the children perceive, move around and inhabit the space, and this has given value to the culture of the children and their rights. Even the teaching practices were modified because looking at the furnishings and the objects as *words about the space*, looking at them as subjects in relationship, I think makes for a greater sensitivity, learned and expanded through the dialogue. All this helped the teachers to see the children's research and explorations in the space with new eyes, and to understand this as research and not just simply the manipulation of objects.

So I think that what you asked at the beginning is important: how did all this evolve, and what new elements did it bring to the latest architectural projects carried out? I think that what contributed to the evolution of the dialogue was primarily the idea of relationships: a pedagogy that believes in a child in relationship right from the start is the same as a relational architecture, so I think this indicates that you need to create places with strong relationships to each other, places in which there is not a hierarchical separation between different kinds of knowledge, between play and learning, between kitchen, hall and classroom, between inside and outside space, and the architectural culture has given concrete shape to this concept in the two most recent *nidi*.

Another evolution is represented by the use of different sized spaces. This had been experimented with in the *scuole dell'infanzia* built up to the 1990s but was not yet geared toward the younger children. It meant crediting very young children with the ability to use these spaces, and it also meant breaking down a number of stereotypes. A small child is not necessarily happier in small spaces; creating tall spaces with different levels, I believe, offers the child different possibilities. The space that Tullio created in the *nido* Iotti, its large size, is a strong provocation, but it also makes the centre a community space, where adults and children can be together. It can hold lots of people, it's a spacious meeting place, and for the teachers and myself this shifted our way of looking at the children.

Keeping the children in limited spaces certainly makes control easier, but perhaps it also reduces children's perceptions and questions. Being able to look at things from many points of view is a provocation, but also a metaphor. In *nido* Iotti, we saw very young children experiencing the *high space* in an extraordinary way, curious to encounter it, some also with caution, and I believe that this also led the children to a different way of relating with the teacher.

Designing is a creative act that becomes more interesting when carried out by pedagogy and architecture together, allowing our research and observations to evolve.

TULLIO: Over time, I have learned to value and to incorporate into my design projects the care that is typical of the feminine world, the importance that women's culture gives to gracefulness, to attention to details, and to low key furnishings, which are represented here by the flowers in that vase, the plant that is climbing up the building, and I think that these things are like enzymes that inadvertently change the architecture, without the need for introducing major structural transformations.

MADDALENA: I remember the discussion we had with you about what image to give of the *nido* as a public place for the community. How to give value to the idea of participation that is so important for us, the relationship with others, the possibility to involve everyone – children and adults, the neighbourhood, the town – in the choices made. And I remember how designing the entrance caused us to reflect on this idea. How to design an entrance that immediately expresses this idea of a public place, that cannot be confused with the entrance of a house or just any place; it had to make clear that this is a place of culture, open and public. The result was this entrance that is *important* but not oppressive, that is light and welcoming, with lots of windows, that also seeks harmonies with the surrounding environment, with a sage green column standing near a tall tree, a ginkgo that we recognized as the 'prompter' of that huge space.

I think this way of seeking connections is really precious, like the idea of designing these classroom spaces by highlighting their volume, their width, the different levels, and above all the thresholds, those intermediate places of contact. You enter the room and there's a lower ceiling that welcomes you and makes everything more familiar and private, and then suddenly you move and the perspective changes, because the ceiling rises, there's a much deeper volume; but that's not all, because wherever you position yourself your view is different. So they are places that in their way of being and presenting themselves, elicit and support research in those who inhabit them, children and adults alike.

PAOLA: I wanted to go back to the reflections on the language and codes of the physical space, of which children are very sensitive interpreters. An example, to clarify what I mean: the strong acoustics of a very large space can be a problem, but I noticed that at *nido* Iotti the use of the large shell-shaped dressing-up area assumes a special identity because dressing up is not just about putting on clothes: *Zorro* becomes even more *Zorro* if he runs, if there's a sound, if there's a big echo. Dressing up is also based on Mom's high heels, and the particular sound produced by a large space makes this a special dressing-up experience.

Children listen to the spaces and the places, they know how to listen to the languages of the space and I think that we adults can, too, if we consider this to be an important element that allows us to live better.

VEA: Has the actual use made of environments always followed the original design intention?

TULLIO: My idea is that in designing spaces you have to propose simple, basic landscapes, in which life can then evolve in a complex way, just as everyday life does. So you need the least possible number of constraints, to provide just some conditions of inhabitability and use, then allow the space to be used and changed in terms of function. You need to make suggestions but avoid overly specializing the spaces, because life evolves at a higher rate of speed than you foresee.

PAOLA: We have always tried to create a multipurpose space along with an idea of the relational aspect. So the stairway-play structure of *nidi* Rodari and Iotti was conceived by Tullio not only as an element of connection between the higher and lower levels, but as giving the possibility to have spaces for looking outside, terraces for being together. But it was also a space that the children themselves further reinvented; for some of the children, it's the niche where they can read or take precious objects, or a place where they can work on special construction projects.

MADDALENA: Tullio, I remember what you said about simple landscapes. And I think that the new school at the Malaguzzi Centre is also a challenge from that point of view, because this school is very large and rich, but then when you look at it you see the structures are minimalist and they seem to be waiting for the dialogue with the people who will inhabit the space. This is not the virtuosity of a structure that imposes on you a certain type of communication; instead, it's like a very light invitation, like whispering to the teachers and children to continue being interested and engaged, to verify things, to move things around, to invent new functions, to play with everything.

At the *nido* Iotti, we documented how in the room that faces onto the parking lot, the 6–8-month-old children who were starting to crawl would return to the windows, re-enacting goodbyes to their parents: after saying goodbye at 9 a.m., at 10.30 they would go back and confirm the farewell, 'Ciao!' As if they needed this sense of security, they would go back there and relive the emotion of that moment. During the initial period of attendance at the *nido* this was wonderful: the projecting windows became a sort of *security niche* to which the children could return, and this gives you a certain idea of the space.

TULLIO: The window sill is low and wide enough for the child to be able to sit inside it and look out...

MADDALENA: ...they were sitting there on the window sill like on a bench, and they would do the goodbyes, also collectively, all there close to each other saying 'Ciao!'...

TULLIO: ...these are the opportunities that you try to provide, then they are transformed, enriched. When we were assembling the last stairway at the *nido* Iotti, while the workers were still on the job, the intermediate landing had already become the place for dolls, it had already taken on a different use, already reinvented. You might not think of these things while you're working on the design, but when they happen, you learn to see the places anew, with different eyes, and you are happy about that. When we designed these stairway-play structures, we had also invented other interesting situations, like small windows through which the children who are crawling can look outside, lowered spaces and hideouts, but all this costs money and so you have to set limits, but there could be lots of opportunities...

MADDALENA: We are wondering how the children will live in the new school at the Malaguzzi Centre, because the school will be inhabited by children who have recently arrived from various parts of the world, who have lifestyles, maps, colours and mental images that may be different. It will be very interesting to experiment with these different points of view. We are imagining this kind of 'inter-language' that is not only verbal but in relationship with the environment and the materials. The documentation will be interesting because it will help the children to see themselves anew, to talk about themselves, and it will also help us as adults to open different spaces of thinking.

TULLIO: I believe that in this approach that I've taken, not overly defining spaces, there's the idea of a real dialogue, as if to say, 'Now it's your turn'. I think that the dialogue has to take place in this very free way, also working together to correct any design errors.

PAOLA: Oddly, all this research is often seen by others as a privilege, that in Reggio there aren't all the restrictions that other places have. How many times has someone said to me, 'We can't do this'? Our attention to the regulations and to safety is never separate from evaluations on well-being, quality and the rights of the child, never forgetting that the child is the protagonist.

MADDALENA: If we want to construct new spaces and interesting relationships for the children, we have to consider the furniture, the colours and the environment as a whole; there is a thread based on beauty that connects the parts, that creates harmonies and relationships. The multidisciplinary group set up to consider the furnishings at the new school in the Malaguzzi Centre consisted of pedagogistas, architects, interior designers, people with a special eye, but also the artisans who produce things, along with teachers and atelieristas of different generations. One choice we made was not to totally complete the new school but allow it to evolve, especially in the ateliers. There will still be the possibility to invent.

PAOLA: We continue to talk to Tullio about this, as one of the authors of this dialogue between pedagogy and architecture that has characterized our experience since the 1970s. This has involved not only architecture but also designing furniture and objects that derive from observations of the children, developing prototypes that were then tested. This design collaboration started with the inhabitable mirror triangle created by Tullio, which has been reproduced in many countries.

MADDALENA: Original objects were invented starting precisely from listening to the children. I remember that Malaguzzi himself had observed in the *nidi* that the children would learn to walk by pushing a small chair, so a group of teachers devised a sort of trolley with wheels with a mirror applied on one side.

TULLIO: We all contributed ideas and potentials, and now we have to continue to work together.

Chapter 8

Professional marvellers

Together with children and atelieristas, 'professional marvellers' as Malaguzzi once defined and prophesized teachers to be, are central characters in this book. In this chapter, in particular, I will attempt a deeper analysis of relations between ateliers and classes, between atelieristas and teachers.

As Sergio Manghi says, today's society and culture,

> have given us inescapable co-responsibility for everything that takes place, to ourselves and others, in contexts we are part of. The difficulty lies in giving ourselves to the historically new task of learning through others, reciprocally and uninterruptedly, starting each time from the beginning, however pleasant or unpleasant it may be.
>
> (Manghi, 2005: 18).

In Reggio Emilia, I believe we have managed the difficult process of learning through others in concrete ways; in the constant relationship between atelier and class; between teacher, atelierista and pedagogista. Perhaps the process has not always been fully and optimally achieved, however many our desires, the organization of our work, how we imagine things, have all been, and remain, centred on this objective.

For years, the teachers and myself learned to undo learning. We learned to modify a part of the mental framework we had learned previously in our respective cultural and educational backgrounds and listen to reflections and experience different from our own ways of thinking. However, the largest changes in mental framework and point of view were caused by observing and documenting children's strategies.

A person who completes their studies in an art secondary school, art academy or similar institution in Italy has hardly any knowledge of children, and the situation improves very little after sitting exams to qualify as a teacher in 'art education and history of art'. For this reason, I appreciate Malaguzzi's strategy towards me even more.

As soon as I started work in Reggio, he created the conditions for me to observe and reflect: I was to invite four children into the atelier at a time, ask them to paint at the easel and observe children of different ages working with paint in a non-figurative way which Malaguzzi called *stain games*. I believe it was highly unusual in 1970 to consider young children's non-figurative painting interesting and even more so to request that it become the object of observation and research by a secondary school teacher like myself. This form of observation lasted a considerable length of time because there were ninety children in the school: thirty aged three, thirty aged four, and thirty aged five. We need to consider Malaguzzi's courage and determination in making this choice in a situation, then, where there were thirty children per class and only one teacher.

Malaguzzi was aware that the role of atelierista needed to become *precious and necessary* to motivate the administration and defend schools from attempts at cutting funds. I have already said the profile of atelierista continues to risk extinction because often the schools that have such a worker are considered to have an unnecessary privilege, while Malaguzzi considered them to be an important presence, capable of collecting material and documenting original processes, and above all capable of producing different processes from those of traditional pedagogy. In his hypothesis, atelieristas would become much loved by children and families, and teachers would see them as allies, capable of giving value and visibility to work with the children.

At the same time, Malaguzzi gave me some books to read (Read, Lowenfeld, Stern, Piaget, etc.) which I used to get to know new theories and learn some practical methodology like offering children the seven colours advised by Lowenfeld. My educational offers quickly changed and progressively moved beyond these early suggestions, sometimes markedly so. However, when we start out it is necessary to start from those who know more than we do.

I still remember the many pages of notes I made as I observed the children (I did not yet use photographs and neither did anyone else in the schools) and how Malaguzzi read all these notes very carefully and then looked at the children's paintings again with the same attention. Then Malaguzzi discussed them with me, gave me his interpretations and asked me to write a report on the work, something I did at the end of the school year and presented to teachers in Modena and Reggio. All the talks given by teachers in Modena and Reggio schools on that occasion – both towns were supervised by Malaguzzi as pedagogical consultant at the time – were later published in a book entitled *Esperienze per una nuova scuola dell'infanzia (Experiences of a new school for early childhood)* in 1971.

I have related the episode because today it still seems indicative of the correct strategy for forming a new professional role such as atelieristas, or any other. Supply them with interesting and formative reading, immediately put them in observation and documentation situations to encourage their capacity for formulating hypotheses and developing interpretative antennae, then together reread and discuss collected material and make it shareable with others in presentations and publications. I have to say this journey is very similar to the one I still use today when coordinating new projects with atelieristas and teachers.

Different points of view

The different point of view of a teacher and atelierista interpreting the same subject was already obvious on that first public occasion. The teacher was one of the most able and expert in Modena schools and she delivered her entire talk without a single picture, using only verbal language to recount children's paintings. This might be possible if you are very good, but for this occasion I had immediately thought how indispensable it was to present an enquiry into visual languages with the support of pictures. I had, therefore, found an inexpensive way of visually supporting talks by creating large card albums containing the children's original paintings and I turned the pages of these as I gave my talks.

I have no idea why no one thought of taking photographs or projecting slides at that time, it is a mystery of those days which are now history. It is not possible for an atelierista to discuss images without using images. The differences in presentation that exist between two backgrounds like that of teacher and atelierista are not limited to communication, they also include how we observe and interpret.

Perhaps a person who has had occasion to paint has a greater practical sense, a sensibility for what it means, what a difficult, seductive thing, even for a child, it is to deal with being confronted with a large, white sheet of paper, making the first brushstroke, the first sign, entering a relationship with this empty, unknown space of the white paper. At the same time being aware how many ways a person can explore, caress and attack the paper, the large paintbrush steeped in paint, the *greediness* that takes a child in layering the colours that transform into the *impasto* as they merge. The material/colour that with 3 year olds often gets transferred from paper onto hands, can be a disturbing and unwanted presence for some children and they need to be certain it can be washed away and that their hands can go back to their original state.

I remember I *retouched* what a teacher was saying as she fastened the apron of a child who had doubts about beginning to paint, for painting is not a neutral action and though many children are enthusiastic, others are equally cautious. The teacher said, 'Put on your apron so you are sure you won't get dirty, this way you won't get your clothes dirty' and insisted on the benefits of the apron as protection against *paint which dirtied*.

I put it in this way, 'Look, the colour doesn't dirty, it colours. Colour is lovely, not dirty and if your hands get coloured you can wash them with water and the colour will dissolve and go away'. Perhaps it was not easy, even for very good teachers who had never painted, to fully understand the involvement a material like colour can produce, but as time has gone by and children, atelieristas and teachers have worked more and more together, the competency and sensibility of many teachers has increased markedly.

This sensibility still seems missing on some occasions, for example in situations in which teachers get carried away by an excessive enthusiasm for the value of colour and place children in situations that are, to say the least, embarrassing for them. I remember an episode in a school where as a *homage to the creative people* visiting from Reggio, we were shown to a small room with glass walls inside which a small group of children aged 15–24 months, completely naked, were using their hands and bodies to play with coloured paint. The children were covered in paint, their expressions not the least happy; they observed each other and us with an air of perplexity, one or two were crying. Fortunately, a good shower was already ready and the children's skin rapidly returned to its original colour.

Situations of this kind are extremely delicate. They are generally part of a performance by culturally aware adult artists highly conscious of the emotional implications of such a powerful chromatic impact. People probably believe children like to mess about and that is why they sometimes offer them certain types of material, like paint and clay, without a proper understanding of the emotional impact and sometimes disturbing imagery they can induce.

Another situation I often find when visiting schools, even in the area around Reggio Emilia, is a lack of attention towards quality, in particular the poor quality of materials made available to children for drawing and painting. Drawing activity is carried out on a regular daily basis in most schools, but generally it is used in superficial ways without careful evaluation of its enormous potential and the complex processes this visual language makes possible and which to my mind are extraordinary. The contexts children work in and materials available to them are often both underestimated due to insufficient understanding of how choices in these two areas can affect work progress from the very start. The size, shape, colour, grain and surface quality of paper are not neutral, nor are the nature and quality of tools used to produce drawings; we should not be indifferent to any of these.

At the Diana school, various sizes of paper were, and are, available to children: A4, A5, and off-cuts of various size and consistency given to the school by different printers. Larger sizes like A3 are used less because they are more expensive. Pencils are available in at least two hardnesses, rubbers, black felt pens with fine or large tips, grey felt pens and naturally, entire tins of felt tip pens in one colour, just one tin of many different colours used only on certain occasions, coloured pencils, pastel pencils which can be used in water, oil-based pastels and other types of equipment, when available. Savings are made by being careful with materials and this way children learn to respect the things they are given and consider materials precious. Small gestures of care and attention, like illustrating the potential of a tool with children, or letting children choose the size of paper or where they would like to sit are all elements predisposing children to work willingly, concentrate and feel pleasure. It is not always possible to obtain the results we hope for, but rites of care and attention are good starting strategies in any case.

If this all seems excessive to some people, that may be because not every-one is used to thinking of drawing as a language, and a highly complex one. So they are content with superficial drawing, done rapidly, to which they delegate the role of *baby sitter* to keep children occupied and quiet, because generally it is believed that children do not need much. Like all languages, visual language is learned through using it, especially in a cultured way.

Economic agreements

Sometimes Reggio schools ask families for a small supplementary financial con-tribution or sometimes Christmas presents become equipment that can be used with children and these end-of-year presents are almost always left to the school.

Families knew, or at least families attending the *scuola comunale dell'infanzia* Diana knew, that the school appreciated a tin of crayons or small tape recorder as a present much more than a traditional personal present for teachers. Donating presents to the school that make it possible for the intelligence and sensibility of children and teachers to grow and develop is a truly lovely present.

However, first and foremost it is the school that must be aware of the richness and educational possibilities offered by the various languages, and this awareness must involve the budgets decided by administration offices, to the point of detailed checks on the quality of materials purchased from vari-ous suppliers. The municipal schools stipulated an agreement with buyers in municipal purchasing offices so that while a part of the materials was bought centrally and distributed to schools specifically requesting them, a small sum of money was used by ateliaristas in schools to buy more specialized materials from shops accepting municipal vouchers. I get very indignant when I travel and see wealthy cities where school environments and equipment available to children are few and ill-cared for; on the other hand, I know how many very good teachers fight to obtain more and how inadequately they are heard.

Atelierista training

Reggio Children holds courses for atelieristas, lasting some months, in which we attempt to alternate theoretical teaching and practical experience, although it is impossible to simulate the experience of daily life in school communities in a completely effective way. The latest experience in these courses sug-gests to me that during the short months available for educating atelieristas, more time should be given to field experience, taking great care to constantly interweave theory with practical experience. It would be good for future atel-ieristas to be directly introduced into working situations with children, either alone or by the side of a teacher, to work on observing, understanding and annotating children's strategies. Theses phases of learning are already part of the current course but we need to invert the quantities of time dedicated to different activities to increase the part working with children.

An atelierista's work is similar to that of an artisan–artist, in which a deep and conscious experience of daily manual work can contain high levels of theoretical awareness. This is probably true of all professions but in the case of education, listening to children's strategies and the ability to relate these to the theory of pedagogy, the theory of art, and practical situations and processes that materials induce, determines the professional growth of educators to such an extent that work with children must become central. As De Chrico said, art is the fusion of hand and mind.

Although already mentioned in the chapter on school organization, I would like to remind readers that at the beginning of the 1970s, there were just four atelieristas. They were employed in the role of assistant with similar working hours to teachers and a slightly lower wage. Entrance was not by public exam as happened some years later and still happens today; Loris Malaguzzi chose people when he thought he had met someone who could do the work. A few years later, the number had already doubled, employment was based on public competition, working hours and salary were the same as those of teachers. A male presence was just beginning to be seen and the name 'atelierista' was coined. Writing towards the end of his life, Malaguzzi stated his position on the presence of the ateliers in schools, 'The atelier has always repaid us. It has, as desired, proved to be subversive – generating complexity and new tools for thought. It has allowed rich combinations and creative possibilities among the different languages of children' (Edwards, Gandini and Forman, 1998: 74).

In schools, together with other atelieristas I tried to find ways of mediating between what I had learned from art college and the world of art, which I felt to be important for their philosophical attitude and particular approach to reality, and ways of relating to the children I had before me. The 1970s were an exciting decade, there was so much to be done and invented both in the atelier and in educational work in general. Determinedly I pursued a certain type of journey of growth in my new profession; the environment of historical and contemporary art, its reflections and research, were reference points I turned to naturally and from which I took many suggestions in my work with the children because it was a world I belonged to culturally in terms of both educational and personal background.

One of the first things I proposed with 5-year-old children was a classical theme in art, self-portraits; recounting oneself in verbal language and then going back to recount oneself again looking into a mirror and representing one's face in a drawing or clay.

To do this, I bought at a flea market one of those small cases used by theatre actresses, it contained three small mirrors hinged together to simultaneously allow front and side views and I asked a parent to make some copies. Without realizing it, I was adopting a method used by Lorenzo Bernini who, when asked to sculpt people living far away from him, commissioned expert painters to make portraits from different angles to have documentation in drawing as a support.

Malaguzzi, who was highly sensitive, was doubtful about this proposal to begin with because he perceived that making self-portraits and reciprocally making portraits was a delicate process that could offend children in certain ways, given their young 'competencies'. His concern made me particularly cautious with the proposal and the way I worked by children's sides as they drew and worked with clay. Their work was a success and received praise from Gianni Rodari, an Italian writer and journalist, most famous for his books for children and whom many consider Italy's most important twentieth-century children's author. I do not know how Rodari found out about this work, but he wrote a very lovely article about it in a magazine interpreting children's words and drawings in more advanced ways than I had been capable of doing (Rodari, 1973b: 12).

What I often find difficult to get across when discussing suggestions from the world of art, is how these do not come from putting the products of children directly together with those of artists and suggesting they work on the same subject or imitate the same technique or forms as the artist, but by placing the child within similar processes to those of the artist.

To clarify this, I will go back to a point I made in the chapter on Aesthetics/Poetics. When I speak of processes which are analogous to those of artists, I mean for example the highly metaphorical processes in conceptual art; the creative and communicative use of the body in body art; how pop art uses images in series and transforms everyday objects into representations of markets and society; abstract art and all its hermetic language; and surrealist artists and their magical vision of the world. And again searching into the change light can make to landscapes in impressionist painting; the joyful use of brilliant colour in Matisse; the rhythm and simultaneous presence of more than one language in visual poetry. This is why I prefer to bring children and art together through processes, theories and the attitudes of culture and mind that have inspired work – and not through the products which in my view oversimplify the issue.

In actual fact, what we define as art is in certain respects closely attuned to children's ways of being: the way they look at the world with great intensity, their greediness to understand it and *inhabit it*. Synthesis, metaphor, the importance of physical qualities, attention towards repetition and variation, an attraction for colour, non-figurative exploration in drawing, inventing signs and forms to try and represent the world – these are all part of the children's world, but are also close to the artist's world. Children and artists, though for different reasons, have the same *completely new way of seeing* when they observe the world.

Physical simulations

To clarify this better in a simple way, I remember a heavy snowfall, the children's shocking physicality in the middle of the snow on this occasion, and the importance of their movements and bodies, which made the children enter the virtual space of a large canvas onto which images of snow were projected from slides. This happened at the beginning of the 1970s at a time when body art and the discovery of the body's expressive power and performances on this theme still had the energy typical of research.

I remember projections of fields of poppies onto a school wall and how a group of children became particularly excited by their relation to the projected flowers and the brilliant red of the petals and began a richly expressive dance accompanied by a song invented for the occasion. Since that time, in our schools children's bodies moving inside large images projected onto background surfaces have become the norm, and now video projectors in many schools have replaced the old slide projectors and supply new possibilities for expression, because with new technologies we can project moving landscapes and figures.

Naturally all experiences evolve: in my last years as an atelierista, we left out slides and CDs with different subjects and music, partly chosen together with the children, and available to them in a small room. The children used the projections and music as they pleased, and with the assistance of recycled transparent and coloured material, created superbly evocative and fantastical worlds. Recently I saw an interesting experience in Diana; the current young atelierista has had personal artistic experiences of working with video art and she projected a video of two tigers onto the whole wall of a small room sensorily saturating the entire space. One of the tigers stayed still while the other slowly padded backwards and forwards (in this case again, those with knowledge of the world of art, can catch glimpses of an intelligent suggestion taken from Bill Viola's video work). Children intervened as in previous experiences; it is clear, however, that the video's movement establishes a different perception and relationship.

Digital technology, with which I will later deal in more depth, has created extremely interesting possibilities for the imagination; however, these need to be managed very carefully. In the experiences recounted to this point, it was already necessary, is always necessary, to be careful not to invade children's imaginations with an excess of image and sound. Although children usually intervene to relate images, sounds and simulations of worlds in creative ways, I believe it is also opportune to sometimes silence technique and leave room for children's interior imagination, through whose power or lack they construct other realities. It is a question of alternating contexts and tools that put children in more stimulating contexts, with more neutral almost silent ones; extending references, travelling down different roads, always being very attentive towards children and also to contemporary social and cultural realities.

More then once, Malaguzzi, perhaps fearing I might overdo expressiveness and imagination, reminded me that with children we need to 'know how to lower the sails' at the opportune moment, because children also love very concrete situations.

It is an admonishment I have always tried to remember though I also consider myself very earthy and the relation I have to the earth and the things that inhabit it are very intense. This is *concreteness*, which has relations as its basis, an instinct that over time has become awareness, environmental and ecological.

For children empathy with surroundings is a kind of natural bridge to a relationship with the environment, and thus an indispensable basis for relations with others. But too often this is reduced and, therefore, diminished to a form of ingenuous anthropomorphism, an immature attitude, to be overcome.

Small gestures of solidarity

On a sunny February day, Alice (4 years old) discovered some prematurely flowering violets like unexpected treasure close to a low wall. The following day in place of the sunny weather, a cold wind was blowing insistently and Alice, remembering the violets, went outside to build a makeshift shelter for them from dry leaves. Again, a little boy (2 years old) in a *nido* found and gathered a rose from the ground as he was walking. He placed it on top of a low wall saying that it was 'going to sleep' and continued on his walk. A group of girls aged 5 years had 'adopted' a small apple tree which they cared for on a daily basis in the school's interior courtyard. They have an idea; to make some little clay birds to hang among its branches and keep the tree company, 'like dolls for her'.

All of us have had opportunities for observing similar attitudes in children: are we sure we should only smile and hurriedly write them off as infantile phases to be superseded? Or should we not instead support this tenderness and care for other lives flowing by our sides? Many of children's intelligent intuitions, including those on scientific topics, are generated by the particular sensibility they have for the beat of life which, if respected and opportunely supported, I am certain would help to construct knowledge that is not only more ethical and more based on solidarity but capable of a broader world vision.

The grammar of creativity

In the days Gianni Rodari spent in Reggio Emilia (in 1972) discussing the structure of his famous book *A Grammar of Fantasy* (Rodari, 1973a) with us, he made me better understand how suggestions from art can give us further occasions for inquiry and new journeys to make together with children, when we investigate them further and especially their processes. I do not remember who said 'creativity does not fall from the sky' but I made it the title of one of my talks. Being close to children and working with them makes it more natural to consider creativity in its *workday clothes,* so that one becomes less inhibited about analyzing it more deeply and working on the analysis to the point of creating a basic grammar which can stimulate creativity. Paraphrasing Gianni Rodari, I like to say, 'Art for everyone, not for everyone to become an artist but so that none should be its slave', and if creating and conceiving, as many of us believe, are innate activities in the thinking of humanity, these capacities need to have occasions for practice and being tried out.

An approach apparently of little account but important, was the one leading us to document, for example, the 'grammar of materials' from children's points of view; by which I mean the recurring basic forms they produce when using these materials; the grammar of clay, of paper, of drawing. In this way, the recurring movements and forms born from children's hands and imagination acquired new force and triggered 'educational relaunches'; by this I mean it becomes easier for teachers and atelieristas to use these basic forms to make interesting proposals for work. When using clay, for example, the snake-like shapes, small spheres, twisted shapes and spirals could be hung as pendants, or used to decorate various objects, or come to life and transform into the characters of a story. It was easier to see the importance of these 'basic alphabets' (see Figure 8.1) with various materials and support the children using them in interesting ways rather than destroying them and waiting for the arrival of more mature shapes.

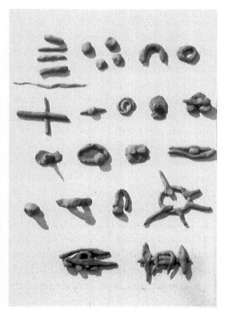

Figure 8.1 Alphabets in clay. Basic shapes constructed by children with clay

Gianni Rodari was one of the fiercest supporters of how fantasy and rationality, cognition and imagination take strength from each other and how above all in education, we must make them interweave, make them dance together.

Durer's rhinoceros

In those years, atelieristas worked a lot both with children and also with teachers. The latter came from a training for their profession in which visual languages were little considered; worse, what it was suggested they teach children in this area was damaging. I have stories from teachers about the nature of the exam for qualifying as an early childhood teacher more than thirty years ago and the method suggested by lecturers to get children to draw. These tales are full of humour but worrying and I am sure the kind of preparation offered to new teachers on the subject of drawing today is completely different. This is why I am always so surprised that I continue to see obvious distortions in ways of understanding visual languages during visits to early childhood services.

I think all of us have seen large trees on the walls of early childhood services, obviously drawn by teachers where children's contribution, when there is one, is to attach fruit and leaves. This contribution from children is in itself debatable, but more than that, the drawings made by teachers are hardly ever acceptable representations of *a tree* because in reality these have very different shapes and personalities, whereas very often teachers draw the *usual* stereotype of a tree. In this way, through a simple representation, not only is it explicitly declared that teachers have the correct scheme for trees; we give the children a banal stereotype even before they get to grips with constructing a personal image or personal scheme of what a tree is.

And all the terrible pages of exercise books in circulation! Pages that diligently bring together the worst images to be found, the worst stereotypes, that even an artist like Lichtenstein would find difficult to make acceptable. Is it possible teachers are not aware, that through the images they propose and use with such abandon they contribute to constructing mental imagery and figurative schemes? That figurative schemes are conceptual schemes, and if figurative schemes are of appalling quality then the quality of conceptual schemes will be affected.

Gombrich supplies us with an extremely clear example of this in an essay on the famous image of a rhinoceros engraved by Albrecht Durer (Gombrich, 1957), a leading artist of the Northern European Renaissance. Durer represented the rhinoceros without actually ever having seen one, using descriptions by other people. Some years later when the first specimens began to arrive in zoos, many artists continued to refer more to Durer's celebrated image for portraits than to the real life animal. In this example, Gombrich maintains that the power of an image to create reality is sometimes more powerful than the reality before our eyes. Even if the story were slightly exaggerated, I think there is universal agreement about how stereotypical images can become defective lenses we use to look at and distort reality.

This is all the more true when dealing with children. I have often seen children arguing over ownership of pictures reproduced in books, 'This is mine, I saw it first, you take the other one!' This seems strange only to those who are not familiar with children's great capacity for projecting themselves into *images*. I have clear memories of my childhood connected to this particular form of perception. Like many children, I loved illustrated books and there were many art and architecture books in my home that I adored to look through. I especially loved sculpture and adored the face of the Madonna in Michelangelo's *La Pietà* in St. Peter's Basilica in the Vatican City and villas I believe were by Palladio. I can remember exploratory journeys I took in my imagination around the rooms and gardens of these villas. I had enormous fun and whiled away many long hours, but I also remember the regret, almost fear, when I realized I was no longer capable of *physically getting inside the images*.

On various occasions afterwards, I tried to take those *strolls* again but I really was not capable. This is to say we should not underestimate children's ability for projection with visual imagery; and if we consider this strong ability in the light of Gombrich's story, we can easily deduce that greater care is needed with the quality of images we put in children's hands.

Once a year, parents and teachers from various Reggio schools visit bookshops to choose books for children, carefully evaluating both the text and images. These books are added to others bought in previous years and make up a small circulating library for all the children in a class to take home, a small library parents leave to the school as a gift after attending for three years. It should be remembered that books on art of different eras are also available to children in the school library.

Learning together

Going back to the lack of education in art and aesthetic dimensions for teachers and my extremely limited experience of pedagogy with children, together with teachers I had found certain strategies that seemed to be effective. Let us take the example of one of the many topics we chose in those years, the city and rain. The subject was chosen because it was situated in a cycle of change, transformation of dry city to *wet* city and we considered that an unstable and transitional situation, such as the arrival of rain might highlight certain aspects in the environment, in this case the city. Before beginning work with children, our attention was given to verifying adult knowledge on the subject.

One rainy day I set out with a teacher to visit the city and separately we photographed what seemed to us the most significant things to illustrate changes caused by the presence of rain. Then we discussed the pictures with the whole group of teachers. We made hypotheses together about children's interests, choices they might make, though we knew the children would probably surprise us and choose different things.

The road map we hypothetically charted became a kind of practice run for us in evaluating children's possible points of view, trying to understand which materials and techniques could be used most opportunely to have a better, deeper understanding of the expressive potential of each one.

This kind of journey led to us improving teachers' sensibilities and my own and also improved the educational work we did with the children. I realize now more than in the past how important is the time we dedicate to an exchange of ideas between adults before beginning work with children. And I understand it nowadays when I am coordinating phases of projects and make errors due to giving inadequate time for discussion and understanding.

From programmes to projects

In the 1980s and early 1990s, we used to organize subjects that we proposed to the children in chapters. For example, in the situation of the city changed by rain, chapters were: people's behaviour in the rain, the city's systems of defence against rain and rain-water collection, in particular lights and sounds, measuring rainfall, theories to do with the phenomenon of rain, etc. Then children moved around autonomously working on these topics, which had been chosen beforehand by teachers for the interest attributed to them. In this way, we interwove programmed data and project work that was open to emerging phenomena.

By 'programme' (*programmazione* in Italian) I mean establishing beforehand much of what will happen during work: topics to cover, contexts to prepare, work to assign to children, tools and materials for use and the time allowed for the work. By project work (*progettazione*), I mean work in which adults (teachers, atelierista, pedaogista) make initial hypotheses and seek to have a deeper understanding of an area or topic but where key elements for moving forward come from work with children and careful analysis by adults of what is happening along the way. Greater importance is given to some parts of a project than others, to images and thoughts slowly emerging in the children and which require agreements based on reflection and mediation, between the wishes and thoughts of the children and those of the teachers to decide which pathway it is most opportune to follow. Choices must not betray the thinking of the children or the nature of the theme they are working on.

As the 1980s proceeded, observation and documentation also proceeded, and children made us ever more curious and our trust in their culture and their interpretation of reality increased, so that little by little, even in the initial phases, the chapters of a project no longer strictly belonged to the teachers but were constructed together with children according to their point of view and the priorities they attributed to things.

So that, for example, puddles, extremely interesting micro-worlds which children love to play with, would perhaps assume greater importance than other elements connected with the rain. Initial phases of *progettazione* defined the topic for analysis, and tried to understand the potential it held for work with children; a sort of cultural and conceptual declaration of intents.

A fragment of a reflected world

I have always thought puddles were one of those subjects, or fields of investigation, one could propose with children without fear of being mistaken, because in them aspects of the unexpected, the imaginary and the cognitive come together in a fresh and happy way. An upside down fragment of the world, with perfectly reflected people, houses and trees is in itself already quite surprising; then with a small movement of the water these images fragment to the point of disappearing and then recompose. A micro-world we can enter and if we are alone or adults allow it, splash in with hands and feet. We can throw stones into them, float twigs and leaves. When we are on the edge of the puddle and a friend arrives, at first only a head appears in the water's reflection, then the image grows larger and larger until a whole person can be seen, and in reverse order the same phenomenon gets repeated when the person moves away. The landscape in the reflection changes when I walk around the puddle. If it is sunny a double image appears in the water; reflection and shadow. This double image, the result of different phenomena, is always quite difficult to understand and not only for the children. It is interesting to take time to investigate it.

When engaging with complex and interesting problems like these generated by a puddle, the problem always arises of how to deal with them in a class of twenty-six children, each with his or her biological clock. At the same time teachers, too, are not always fully familiar with problems and there arises a desire for a deeper understanding.

I will try to recount one possible way of working. Generally, we started with two groups, one of girls and one of boys, because among various individual differences gender was, and continues to be, an interesting one. We would often choose to have three children per group because it seemed to us the number made the dynamic of group relationships interesting. When we had documented and evaluated the ensuing processes, the difficulties and the solutions provided by the children, we proceeded with all the others, in groups again and often mixing boys and girls in groups of about six, bearing in mind all the material and the thoughts which had emerged from the work in very small groups. This way of working often improves the quality in the initial phases of work and our ability for listening to (observing) the strategies of children.

With all the children together, it was not always possible to document each group. Not because they were not interesting, but because in our everyday life with twenty-six children it is not possible to document everything with the same degree of rigour and this can be managed only during certain projects. Usually we tend to annotate and conserve the constants in children's ways of working and differences that seem particularly interesting. To my mind, this kind of documentation in which teachers note recurrences in the ways children deal with a problem and then makes them visible in a synthesis is extremely interesting. The following is an example.

Synthesis documentation

I will give a simple example about constructing trees in clay. We had made a clay forest where each child in the class had made some trees; a forest subsequently inhabited by people and animals, again in clay. Our observations concentrated mostly on the construction of the trees and anticipated difficulties in execution. At the end of the constructions we had observed, we made a synthesis of documentation about which problems of construction children have to deal with in a theme like this and how they resolve them.

There is a problem all children share when facing their first three-dimensional constructions in clay because they are not yet sufficiently aware of the consistency of the material and its behaviour. In this case, the problem involves the tree trunk, which has to support the weight of the branches and is generally too fragile and tends to bend (see Figure 8.2).

At this point, many teachers would intervene by explaining how to avoid the problem and the same explanation would be given to and adopted by all the children. A different thing happens if the children know that there is a feeling of trust in their capacities, and are used to trying to solve problems of construction in autonomous ways.

Here is the documentation about some of the strategies they used (see Figure 8.3). The fragile trunk was duplicated (a), or a series of pieces of clay are placed one on top of the other to form a sturdy trunk (b). In other cases, a clay snake is entwined around the tree thus making it more robust (c), or else bent completely over to double its resistance (d). Intelligent engineering solutions.

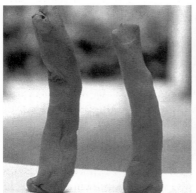

Figures 8.2–8.3 Synthesis documentation on constructing clay tree trunks with increased strength and stability. Children aged 5–6, *scuola comunale dell'infanzia* Diana

This documentation comes, as I said before, from teachers' notes. Images in the synthesis are made at a later date by the teacher (in this case using clay) to reproduce the strategies children used during their work.

Eyes and mind

Having a general picture of strategies used by children at the age when they face certain *stumblings on their construction pathway* gives teachers eyes that are better prepared for seeing other children's work too. Obviously if I were to propose again the same subjects mentioned here – the project of city and rain, or the forest project – even if I had documentation made on previous occasions available to me I would again observe and document the differences I am sure I would find, because the authors would not be the same ones, and compared with fifteen or twenty years ago (when this documentation was made) children have acquired other points of view through their viewing many media images: in short, the experiences and contexts of children have changed to some degree.

I have become aware that it is more common today than in the past to encounter in children's drawings different points of view representing the same subject. I was taken aback to see drawings produced by Alice, a little girl of three years, done in a hurry, but clearly demonstrating an attempt at representing a person in profile lying on a bed. I have usually found attempts at representing the human figure with a side view or profile, which is a different point of view compared to the more habitual front view, at a later age than this.

In my thirty years working at Diana school, I was able to observe drawings in which different points of view simultaneously represented the same subject. I remember a horse by Ivan (3 years 6 months), but at this age drawings of this kind are extremely rare. The question I have and would like to answer, is how much images seen on television, in films and in videogames, etc. have not only increased the quantity of images children see but also increased variables? For example, by supplying images of the same subject from different points of view, as often happens in film when the camera moves. Or given that Alice has a very good sense of spatial orientation, how much this influences visual perceptions and representations in drawings?

We all know that children tend to draw a subject by choosing a point of view that immediately makes it recognizable, but here I am describing a process of perception and representation that presupposes an imaginary view, and which moves through space to fix an image of the same subject from different viewpoints. The questions we could pose are many and there are many pathways to be taken where an attitude of research, or hypothesis, can produce interesting elements for reflection. Organization of the kind found in Reggio, with two teachers per class, an atelierista, a pedagogical team, makes it concretely possible to develop documentation capable of moving forward with new subjects and going more deeply into others – following some of the many pathways that are opened up by new questions.

Frequentations

Returning to the 1980s, together with the daily task of making teachers and atelieristas grow and develop together, Malaguzzi also organized many ongoing education initiatives. Some of these, for example firing clay, were specifically for atelieristas and we were always requested to take part in other initiatives, for example in mathematics and science. We listened to lectures on the latest discoveries in the field of neurobiology, which then we discussed among ourselves trying to understand the possible effects on our work. In the world of Italian education, I think we were among the first to discuss Edgar Morin's theories of complexity, the theories of Ilia Prigogine on entropy and time flow, Francisco Varela's theories on learning, Gregory Bateson's on mind and ecology, Mandelbroot's on fractals and other experiences. The working environment was a place of strong cultural growth.

I am convinced each one of us is extremely receptive towards places we frequent, their culture, atmospheres, conversations, friendships and loves. And during those years in the Reggio schools, 'the pleasure of thinking, the passion of ideas' was a strong presence, at least as I remember it. I believe it is underestimated and not fully understood how much a climate of cultural excitement, through stimulating interest, can be important in supporting the difficult and fatiguing work of staying with twenty-six or thirty children a whole eight hours a day every day for several years. Perhaps administrators, directors and unionists should reflect on this aspect and dedicate more attention to it.

I remember some of our trade union meetings in the 1980s in which union representatives tried to persuade us of the presumed enormous personal and social benefits to be gained from reducing our working week, going from the thirty-six hours a week we did in the municipal schools to the twenty-five hour working week in the state schools (provided by the national government, not *Comunes* like Reggio). In fact they believed it would be better to nationalize all municipal schools; making them all the same, as an important form of equality and democracy. And we tried to make them understand that certainly we would enjoy working nine hours less per week, but that this would mean working alone with twenty-six children and no longer in pairs with colleagues, except for a tiny amount of time of little significance, as still happens in state schools. This would have meant no longer being able to: work with small groups of children; make observations and documentation; prepare our own work programmes and weekly self-professional development; or to organize meetings with families, etc. And in effect the result of reducing our working week by nine hours would have taken the meaning out of the work and cancelled the dream of a difficult but intensely interesting profession. We managed to stop the union pushing for reduced hours, but I do not believe we convinced them of the implicit damage contained in their proposal.

Naturally on other important occasions we had the support of union organizations. As often happens, the identities and qualities of representatives matters in a large organization such as a union.

An urgent need for some reflection

For years now proposals have periodically been made for discussing the atelierista's role in schools. Above all it is atelieristas themselves who wish to discuss this, requesting better definitions of their tasks, and clearer shared rules in the relationship with the classes and with the entire teaching system. My impression is that this approach is mistaken; before we discuss the role of atelieristas we need to better evaluate what the presence of an atelier can bring into learning, to recognize poetic languages as important, indeed as fundamental; and then starting from these reflections to define the atelierista's contribution, her relationship to pedagogy and her tasks.

I have the impression we do not discuss these sufficiently, nor do we sufficiently discuss changes in learning caused by new digital environments offered to children, the quality of the educational system we find ourselves involved in today, what might be generated by the new Loris Malaguzzi International Centre, the importance of the large international network we frequent, the repercussions of very recent neurobiological discoveries and ecological philosophies. Taken up with doing so many things we run the risk of rushing our time for reflection and underestimating the extent to which we are involved in cultural and social evolution happening in the world.

The Reggio project, which includes continuity in public education between *nido* and *scuola dell'infanzia* (from birth to 6 years) with possible collaboration with the first classes in primary school, constitutes an extraordinary context for carrying out research for a better understanding of children today, what traits distinguish them from those of the past, and seeking to understand what educational hypotheses it would be best to use by their sides. How can we enter into dialogue with them if we do not continue to be informed about their possible mental imagery? Their strategies for learning? Their symbologies and their metaphors? 'The soul speaks above all in images. Images are its mother-tongue' (Hillman, 2001). Perhaps it does not only speak in images, but what do we know of children's images today?

Perhaps I particularly feel this lack of information, because I am no longer with children on a daily basis. However, I believe we need to know more, through gathering and discussing the many illustrations and impressions of teachers and atelieristas who for many years, with a high level of sensibility, have been living with children, respecting them, listening to them and, albeit in different ways, working by their sides and progressing together with them.

Growing together

In the relationship with classes, each atelierista acts in a different way, according to her personality and the traits of the group she finds herself working in. As far as I am concerned, I believe my role within the *scuola comunale dell'infanzia* Diana was that of *cultural exciter*, a role that found immediate and intelligent response in the sensibilities and activities of teachers: Magda Bondavalli, Marina Castagnetti, Sonia Cipolla, Laila Marani, Marina Mori, Giulia Notari, Laura Rubizzi, Evelina Reverberi and Paola Strozzi. These are the teachers with whom I reflected and worked most.

I do not know how much this was provoked or informed by the daily drive from Modena, where I live, to Reggio Emilia. Thirty kilometres of extremely familiar road, a trip during which I had occasion to reflect and advance new hypotheses for work. Once I arrived in school, I quickly went into the various classes, involving the teachers in my new ideas, they in turn gave me their opinions or new hypotheses and we grew together.

It was a question of together understanding the best way of continuing to develop our work in tune with the children, the projects we were carrying out, or if we were at the start of a new project our understanding of an article we had read, myself or the others, and that had provoked interesting thoughts. If school pedagogista Tiziana Filippini was present she would sometimes also get involved; she readily did so.

Naturally there were also more official, planned meetings, where projects were discussed with a different rhythm and in other ways. But this extremely rapid, slightly agitated start to the morning was a kind of light-hearted welcome to the day, a moment making room for new hypotheses and the possibility of doing interesting work with the children in a sharing way, work carried out in different ways depending on teachers' different cultures and personalities.

Atelieristas are less involved in the everyday responsibility of managing so many children and relations with their families, are less constrained than teachers who must organize the project of offering children interesting and varied activities and at the same time respect individual differences – a highly responsible and creative job. Given their different circumstances, I believe that atelieristas can take the role of conceiving and promoting new hypotheses for teaching in some areas. Because the atelier is in contact with the world of art, architecture and design and because the atelierista often has sensitive antennae for contemporary issues, it is her task to receive and bring these interesting cultural flows into school and, where possible, rework them in appropriate ways so that they light up areas which can be used for experimentation with children. It should not be thought that ideas derived from the world of art and design are distant from children's because children live immersed in contemporary life as no one else. Moreover, I have always had many of my intuitions from the poetic languages, and these have then enriched work on original school projects.

It is interesting to be aware of and know the verbal language used by the world of art to communicate its ideas. Interesting because pedagogy, like every other discipline, risks becoming closed in excessively self-referential language. This is what makes me suspicious and annoyed when I perceive the language in papers on the subject of professional development for teachers to be so distant from the world of children and the flow of life. What do education and pedagogy represent if they do not pulsate attuned to life?

Through simultaneously knowing what is happening in all the various classes in the school, it is easier for an atelierista to gain a general view of what is happening in the school at a given moment, and thus she has the possibility of relating apparently distant situations, redefining concepts, making interpretations and hypotheses about what is happening in classes at a particular time, and putting forward her perceptions to the whole group of teachers so that each one of them can become a resource for the others. I believe one of the roles of the atelieristas is exactly this: to act as go-between for the classes and contribute to keeping the group of teachers together and acting in solidarity – and I believe many atelieristas, although in different ways, do this on a daily basis.

Atelier organization

I am often asked about organization between the atelier and classes; do children go to the atelier in turns, for how long, how many children go at once? As far as Diana is concerned, the atelier never organized children to take turns coming in; we always did things in such a way that the atelier expanded out into the classes and school through enriched proposals in the classroom, above all as an approach. We always worked on projects and it was the progress of these that determined children's presence in the atelier. It would be difficult to say exactly how because the organization was not defined beforehand.

Naturally ways of working were different when there was one teacher and thirty children, compared with two teachers and twenty-six children. But taking turns, which apparently seems like a democratic solution, strongly risks being, in practice, a bureaucratic solution. If seventy-eight children from three classes of twenty-six want to paint at the easel and they can only do this in the atelier, then during a school year they will manage to do this activity on very few occasions; but if easels are present in classrooms and teachers are familiar with their use, then children's opportunities for experience in painting are multiplied and the same applies to other materials or activities. It might happen, therefore, that an atelierista works together with teachers in the classroom or that teachers work with children in the atelier.

A privileged situation and one much sought after is that of an atelierista and a teacher working together with a group of children, together observing and documenting what they do. This happens most often at the start of a project when we need to understand what direction to go in and 'live' exchange between atelierista and teacher is very useful, or during phases of a project deemed to be significant. Another important task for atelieristas in work carried out in school, is maintaining a certain way of seeing among both children and adults – how to define this? aesthetic, poetic? – highlighting the role of poetics in learning processes, or better still, appreciating the dance constructed together by cognition and emotion in all fields of knowledge.

Her contribution is particularly useful in all the work of theoretically and concretely framing projects, and again in phases of critical reading and interpretation of parts that have been documented. When possible, the school pedagogista also participates in these phases of work and self-development when it can be managed, and the entire collective contributes to the work of framing. Then it truly becomes 'a party for ideas'.

Figures 8.4–8.9 Borders of light. Children aged 35–36 months. Mini-story in *nido cooperativo* Girasole

Borders of light[1]

Among many kinds of experience accumulated in their work, teachers are familiar with some relatively simple but intelligent interventions that can light up children's curiosity and questions. One of these is creating the conditions for games of light and shadow to arise (see Figures 8.4–8.9).

Samuele and Camilla (2 years and 11 months) have stopped to observe cards with cut out patterns placed in the windows of their *nido*. The children become aware that these patterns are creating shadows on the floor:

SAMUELE: The sun is making them. They are all coloured white.
CAMILLA: The shadow here is a little bit darker.
SAMUELE: Look, it is a drawing in light. See, the light is all inside and stays still.

Samuele knows the sun is making the fascinating shapes on the floor; light and shadow together make a pattern he rightly defines as coloured. The shadow is all 'coloured' white. Only people who do not know how to see think shadows are black and white, do not realize the various shades of light and shadow. It seems he is attracted to the luminous area, and in fact he later defines it as a 'drawing in light'. What better, more poetic definition of a shadow?

The teacher becomes aware of the dialogue between the two children and intervenes:

'That "light drawing" is really beautiful! Can we manage to keep it here with us in the school? Can we manage to make it stay where it is on the floor?' Obviously the teacher's proposal of making the light stay still comes from her awareness that the shadow will move and to make the children notice this movement and perhaps to create an interesting question, she wants to mark the position of the shadow at that particular moment. The teacher is probably thinking of the book entitled *Everything Has a Shadow Except Ants* [*Scuole comunali dell'infanzia* Diana and Gulliver, 1999], produced in Reggio Emilia and published by Reggio Children, in which children of 3 years propose the game of stopping a shadow.

Documentation is useful because apart from making it possible to know children's strategies better, it makes adult eyes more sensitive and acute to what is happening.

The children go to the place containers of materials are kept and choose transparent glass pebbles of different colours.

SAMUELE: I'm taking these because they have light in them.

CAMILLA: I'm taking these because they have little holes and light goes through them. I think they will light up with the light.

Samuele and Camilla go round the edge of the shape on the floor placing their little objects around it.

SAMUELE: I'm closing it all up properly. To hold the shadow tight.

It is always surprising how empathy intervenes in children's choices; in this case the correspondence between material and light.

It is lunch-time. On returning the children go to check the shadow. 'It's a naughty shadow. It's run away from the pebbles. Look the shadow has moved, because the sun has moved.'

Samuele's initial awareness that the sun produces the phenomenon of the shadow, has led him to immediately relate the different position of the shadow to the movement of the sun in relation to the Earth. However, the phenomenon is not so certain as not to merit another test, or perhaps it is a nice game to play together and continue. So from containers children choose small transparent objects and this time they position them in the bright parts of the pattern.

CAMILLA: We'll put these larger marbles on the light.

Perhaps the little girl thinks the larger marbles will be more effective and that the areas of light are different to the areas of shadow, and more willing to stay where they are. Or perhaps she is also continuing with a lovely game. With great care the children place their marbles on the bright areas. Shapes of shadow, shapes of light, transparent objects enhanced by light, the combination constructs a fascinating composition, so much so that the children seem to forget their problem of stopping the shadow and more than anything else admire the aesthetic result.

SAMUELE: 'Look it is a light drawing'.

The teacher does not consider it opportune to intervene and insist on the initial problem, she will probably do this in another context using different elements. The seed has been sown and the children will very probably find ways of using it in other situations. Or it will be the teacher, using opportune 'provocations', who solicits further reflection in new situations.

Ordinary extraordinariness

It is also interesting with families to interpret small events in everyday life and look at them anew in all their ordinary extraordinariness. This episode was recounted to us by a father. Mattia has just turned 11 months and for some time has known how to get down from the sofa and bed; he turns round on his bottom and slides down backwards onto the floor. This particular day, after getting down he wants to get back up on the bed again but the side is too high and despite his repeated efforts, he cannot manage. He moves away and his parents think he has abandoned the idea but soon he comes back pushing a small plastic stool across the floor, which he places next to the bed and uses as a step to finally get up on to the bed.

Mattia is now 13 months old and uses a children's chair, kitchen steps and large boxes to reach switches and turn on household lights, which he loves like all children. It is easy to think the many elements in his first successful experiment contributed to the learning he has done; feeling his body reversing back through a journey and the effort of raising himself up, the sound of the stool being dragged (the same round stool he learned to walk with, pushing it in front of him on the floor at home, using it like a steering wheel to change direction), his stability, the emotion of climbing up high, succeeding in his venture independently. Motivation, emotion, physicality, the sound of dragging, stability. Which element was important for the learning Mattia now applies in a different form with so many variations? It would be difficult to establish this, but it is important to understand through what strange and sometimes indecipherable combinations learning takes place. This story also demonstrates the importance for parents, just as much as for teachers, of increasing their curiosity, observations and interpretations of children's learning – to know them better, to hold them in esteem and to grow together.

I spoke previously of atelieristas as *guarantors* that the dance between cognitive, expressive, rational and imaginative would always happen, or at least that it would be present as often as possible in processes of learning. I liked this idea of the atelierista guarantor of more complete educational processes and thought I was the first person to use the word. Then I discovered that Malaguzzi had already used it many years before.

The task is certainly not an easy one but Malaguzzi declared that it had been achieved more than he had initially hoped for. If this is true, it can only make atelieristas who worked with him very proud, but first and foremost we must give our thanks to him, and to all the teachers and pedagogistas with whom we have worked, culturally generous people willing to experiment and exchange their points of view. Not last the children, for whom the dance of ideas and sentiment is an absolutely natural process, and less fatiguing than the effort of keeping them separate.

Chapter 9

Visible listening

I believe the atelier's evolution, together with that of Reggio Emilia pedagogy, stems above all from the birth and diffusion of observation and documentation of learning processes. I will attempt to give an account of this journey from the inside, that is to say from the viewpoint of the atelieristas and teachers who transformed what was initially individual attention and personal documentation into strategies for observing and documenting that could be communicated and diffused to others in order to broaden the range and variety of interpretative points of view.

The 1970s and 1980s were years of research and invention in new ways of teaching, a different kind of school and a different role for the atelier than that of tradition; at that time a subject called 'art education' existed but only in middle schools for children aged 10–13 years. We put together an exhibition called *The Hundred Languages of Children*, first shown in Reggio Emilia, then first taken abroad to the Museum of Modern Art in Stockholm in 1981 and on a second occasion after further work in 1986. This illustrates our idea of the role of ateliers in education. As I have said before, the projects presented in the exhibition were divided into chapters decided by adults. We and the children moved freely through these without predefined programmes; we made notes of children's words but not recordings so they were undoubtedly rather approximate but interesting nevertheless; photographs already constituted an important part of communicating contexts and atmospheres.

Large groups of children were undisputed protagonists but due to the large number of children present at any one time, it was not possible to completely track processes, partly because attention could become distracted in this wider context. Our main interest was to illustrate the extraordinary, beautiful and intelligent things children knew how to do and sweep away (or so we hoped) the widespread work circulating in early childhood services at the time, where mostly teachers' minds and hands were central and children had a marginal role, which led to the same stereotyped products for all. Even though this way of documenting gave a rather general view of children, it led to a much greater sense of respect for them and a desire to know them better, and our attention and interest was confirmed in neurological research and its discussions of neurons and synapses in movement and brains being shaped in different ways.

The 1990s saw much detailed investigative work and close attention to working with small groups of children, which could only be done because we had two teachers working simultaneously, and for this we had to modify our organization of the school day and environments. As I have already discussed in Chapter 7 on Environments, we created small spaces called *mini-ateliers* adjacent to the classrooms after research we had done on environments, and these allowed us to divide children into smaller groups and offer proposals, materials and equipment in new and different ways. In those years, we worked hard on organizing our environments, especially in a school like Diana, which had very small spaces made more numerous over time through small and inexpensive miracles of invention.

Space multiplied

An important basis for observation and documentation is the design of inter-esting contexts. One of the many features we planned, for example, was a multiple space for construction. The space we equipped for constructions was an example of possibilities and variations in perception and discovery; walls were normally covered with white sheets but these could be raised to reveal large mirrors that reflected constructions in an interesting and surprising play of replication and inversion. We made a small trolley and positioned a spotlight on it; when this was switched on, it created together with the con-structions atmospheric and fascinating landscapes of light and shadow. The trolley could be moved back and forth and left and right to enlarge, reduce and vary the play of shadows.

We have always done a lot of experimental work with light and shadow in the schools in Reggio. In a small environment like the *scuola comunale dell'infanzia* Diana, we were aware of the risk of saturating it with too many possibilities. It was a real risk, but at the same time we needed to imagine how seventy-eight children with different needs, characters and strategies could go on exploring new and interesting things, every day for three years either alone or in groups. In such restricted spaces with so many objects dis-played and available, it becomes important to have some rules – not so much written but made effective by everyday practice – for example, caring about the environment and orderliness. Everyday staff and children were together responsible for putting games and materials in their place and creating order in spaces in careful, aesthetically pleasing ways. There are many ways of tidy-ing and just as many ways of making an environment pleasant to live in, and we tried, and continue trying, to do this in our everyday life.

Crossing the border

The first *officially recognized* project documenting and observing a small group was a long jump competition organized by 5-year-old children. Laura Rubizzi was the teacher who coordinated the work with Loris Malaguzzi providing consultation, and I think for her this work represented the border between her previous way of working and a new way. In this project, my work was above all the photographic documentation of group strategies. I do not entirely recall my thoughts because many years have gone by since 1984 when the project took place. However, almost simultaneously, we also began a project on drawing, which naturally involved the atelier to a greater extent and in this I had a better taste of the differences between the approach to topics and documentation used up to that point and the new approach in which listening to the strategies of children was more central.

A new *type of observation* and documentation in photographs was created that we called mini-stories because they were based on brief episodes. Many of these mini-stories appeared in the last edition of the *Hundred Languages of Children* catalogue (Malaguzzi, 1996) and in *Making Learning Visible: Children as Individual and Group Learners* (Rinaldi, Giudici and Krechevsky, 2001), written with researchers from Harvard University's Project Zero.

What are mini-stories? They are ways of catching, in photographs and recordings of children's words, a synthesis that gives the essence of the context and strategies children use and, more importantly, a deeper sense of what is taking place. Through visual images we try to pause on children's expressions and actions with one another and in the work they are doing, seeking to convey as much as we can of the learning and atmosphere, the sense of life flowing within a group. It is not a simple thing at all, and one learns by doing it. The person documenting must be highly alert, *antennae vibrating*; she needs to understand rapidly and make live interpretations about which image best represents the significance of what is taking place.

Film director Wim Wenders has said that the shooting of a camera is a 'time' that flows between photographer and the subject photographed. It flows out and returns. This time establishes a contact for seeing and interpreting. Many photographs tend to give simple, didactic explanations of a situation without looking into the deeper meanings.

At that time we made great use of slides because they facilitated communication with the public and this for us was an important basis for exchange and discussion. Computers and computer programmes that handle photographs did not exist then and so the cropping and exposure of a photograph were not easy for us to change. Slides were also expensive and images, therefore, were particularly sober and careful. For me, and many others, these were twenty years of intense practice in listening *to situations*.

We were all enthusiastic and understood we had found a study tool for understanding children better and a form of communication that was easy to disseminate and pleasant to use. At that time, Howard Gardner came to Reggio Emilia for the first time to present his recently published book on the eight intelligences; it was an interesting thesis and one that involved us in discussion long after his departure. As soon as Gardner arrived, Malaguzzi wanted to present some of the research we had done on drawing and communicated through mini-stories, because they represented something new for us and we were proud of them. Gardner was interested but he was also very tired and jet lagged from his journey; narrating stories through an interpreter did nothing to facilitate communication. I remember how embarrassed I was, because while I was speaking, probably not in an entirely synthetic way, I could see how tired our visitor was, but Malaguzzi was so excited at being able to discuss new and exciting aspects of drawing with a scholar like Gardner, that he continued undaunted. From this episode, it can be understood how much we perceived each new documentation strategy to be an achievement for understanding and an opportunity for reciprocal exchange.

At the same time another atelierista, Mirealla Ruozzi, was working on documentation of the first mini-stories in a *nido*, for children under 3 years. As Malaguzzi said, over time the atelier becomes ever more a place for research, a territory where research and documentation produced in classes was gathered together and selected to create new connections. Over time, teachers at Diana (and naturally also all other teachers in all municipal schools) became more sensitive to visual languages, more skilled in observing and documenting and I, like other atelieristas, learned to know children a little more.

The archive

A group of teachers growing together in an attitude of research becomes a very compact, stable group and, during the time that the Diana teachers and myself worked together, we produced an enormous quantity of material and documents, for the most part interesting. Perhaps one of the most positive aspects that contributes to keeping a group united is the sense of discovering new things, moving forward together in understanding shared work. Marina Castagnetti, a teacher at *scuola comunale dell'infanzia* Diana, had found a system for archiving material so that it could more easily be consulted. The very little space available to us in school and the multitude of material were elements that soon made the archive room into a sort of depository. Some of us took turns in attempting to re-establish order because we believed it to be extremely important. However, this work of tidying required a lot of time and we always had so little.

When I left Diana school, the archive had become an unimaginable layering of projects and material that was impossible to consult. This year, Marina Castagnetti, who left the school years ago and is now pursuing a vocation caring for environments and other things, returned to the Diana school to try and create a system for this archive, which we believe bears traces not only of Diana history but, at least in part, represents the history of educational work done in Reggio's early childhood centres. The Documentation and Educational Research Centre of *Istituzione Scuole e Nidi d'Infanzia*, where Marina has been working for years, is thanks above all to those who inhabit it, one of the loveliest places in the Malaguzzi Centre.

A learning group

It is truly difficult to understand the ingredients that made the group of teachers in the Diana school such an effective learning group. Individual identities were very different and we rarely mixed with each other outside school because our friendships, interests and reference points were different. And yet at school solidarity between us was enormous, and I have great esteem and affection for all of them. We had learned to understand our best characteristics, which we used with awareness, and our weak points, which as a group we tried to remedy. The names of teachers who worked at the Diana school are many but the ones I worked with longest are Magda Bondavalli, Paola Cagliari, Marina Castagnetti, Sonia Cipolla, Tiziana Filippini, Laila Marani, Marina Mori, Giulia Notari, Evelina Riverberi, Laura Rubizzi and Paola Strozzi (I hope those not quoted will excuse me). All ready to *turn on* in order to try out new things, willing to recognize lovely ideas, optimistic about children's intelligence and attentive in different ways to politics, perhaps more on a national level than in the city. No one watched *the clock*, all were ready to put in extra hours at work, curious to better understand things happening in our work with children. A truly beautiful group adding ethical intelligence, to use Gardner's definition, to individual traits and making the profession of teaching an interesting individual and social adventure.

In 1991, the American magazine *Newsweek* dedicated its cover to Diana – as the representative of an entire network of municipal schools – and defined it as the school with the most advanced pedagogy, 'the most lovely school in the world'. I was in Germany for a cycle of conferences with pedagogista Tiziana Filippini. What I remember most are the telephone calls I received from Diana teachers who were confronted by a crowd of news reporters and photographers the morning after the magazine was published and this media exposure continued for some weeks. Teachers' professional backgrounds do not include abilities in communicating on television or in interviews; schools and children do not anticipate invasion by television crews, but I have to say the staff were very capable, especially at maintaining a situation of normality with families and children inside school.

I believe the recognition met with widespread agreement and support in Italy, but there were also various types of opposition. The schools in Reggio Emilia and Loris Malaguzzi were not well-loved or recognized for innovation by the university world or official academic pedagogy. They were too different, standing too far outside schemes people use to reflect themselves.

Observation as evaluation

In one of her essays on observation and documentation, Carla Rinaldi speaks of documentation as a kind of evaluation in process, in the sense that we gather and pause on things to which we give value (Rinaldi in Rinaldi, Giudici and Krechevsky, 2001: 84). This is absolutely true, and even more so for documentation in photographs because a situation in a photograph is not repeatable. This unrepeatable quality of a situation, its uniqueness, engenders a strong sense of responsibility that increases with experience rather than decreasing, because when we reread transcriptions of recordings or discuss and interpret what took place with other people, we realize we should have added other pictures to the ones taken, and how different interesting opportunities have been missed in our documentation.

Precisely because documentation makes it possible for us to reflect more deeply, there is a phase of documentary post-production where we sometimes feel the need to add to our live accounts. These are generally details of documented processes being reconstructed at a later date to give greater completeness to an analyzed topic. For example, it might happen that we rephotograph an object to frame it in such a way that it communicates the concept we want to express with greater force. We must remember that visual documentation is expressed in more than one language and we need to know some of the rules for communication in these.

I attach a lot of importance to the communicative power of mini-stories, alone or as part of a more complex project, because they give educational work *a face* that too often only gets reported verbally or through photographs with captions, giving us certain facts at the most but never feelings. The cognitive and expressive feedback experienced by the person documenting should also be considered, because documentation is too often underestimated from the point of view of professional growth; it is often seen or done simply as information about what has taken place, and not particularly important for teachers' professional development.

Some months ago at a public conference, I heard a university teacher from a Faculty of Education Sciences, after listening to a talk given by a primary school teacher who, I imagine, had made great efforts to visually document her account, make ironic comments about the 'mania' of giving reports a *beautiful visual form*. Taking this comment to the limits of its logic, we would come to maintain the uselessness of visual communication as expressed in the Trajan Column or Giotto's Cappella degli Scrovegni, and many others. Clearly visual languages are not generally considered important in school culture; in primary schools a subject called *Arte e imagine* (Art and Images) exists, which usually consists in teaching some art techniques and a knowledge of some artists. I am sure that as with all school subjects it is taught excellently by some teachers and terribly by others, but it is relegated to a certain number of hours in the school timetable, little related either to the culture of teachers or the culture of other disciplines.

All this seriously contradicts the Italian art tradition and contemporary culture where images have an important role in information and communication. For this reason, at least, visual languages should receive greater attention in school education, in order not to be dominated by them or receive them passively, without the ability to analyze or reread them. I fear that as in the past, the real problem is that artificially and superficially separating disciplines is part of school and that in the education of both pupils and teachers, an aesthetic dimension is not considered in the least important; most certainly it is not considered to be an epistemological structure. We need to truly reflect on how much this has diminished the thinking and formation of younger generations.

A photographic way of seeing

In one of the latest projects we have coordinated (the photograph exhibition *A Mysterious Glance of Children on the City*, 2008, see also Chapter 10), children from the municipal schools photographed the historic centre in Reggio Emilia and chose elements that in their opinion represented the city's urban identity. We were all struck by the visual culture and sensibility children demonstrated in capturing original and non-conformist images of the world. Children of different ages showed a capacity for reading environments and recounting them in truly surprising pictures (see Figure 9.1–9.3).

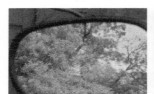

Figures 9.1–9.3 Photographs taken by children aged 5 and 6, *scuola comunale dell'infanzia* Munari (atelierista Barbara Quinti)

What we should be asking is why should children aged 10 or 11, capable of capturing the essence of reality with such originality and awareness, write about and explain the same reality in such conformist and uninteresting ways? We cannot get away from a question of this nature. It is important to society that schools and we as teachers are clearly aware how much space we leave children for original thinking, without rushing to restrict it with predetermined schemes that define what is *correct* according to a school culture. How much do we support children to have ideas different from those of other people and how do we accustom them to arguing and discussing their ideas with their classmates? I am quite convinced that greater attention to processes, rather than only the final product, would help us to feel greater respect for the independent thinking and strategies of children and teenagers, and would substantially improve the reciprocal respect between pupils and teachers.

Making notes

In the *scuola comunale dell'infanzia* Diana, we tried as teachers to reflect and document our own strategies for observation and documentation. But this is not at
all simple and immediately we realized the difficulty of really achieving it; the
interventions and evaluations we make as we go along are numerous, and not
always easy to capture and define. However, it is an interesting test, if only to
become aware that what we call *documenting of children's processes* are only conscious fragments (it could not be otherwise) of the process we are interpreting.
This does not detract from the importance these efforts had and still have for us,
in bringing us closer to the strategies of children and, therefore, to an understanding of how to frame proposals we make with them; in short, how to make
the relation between learning and teaching more culturally productive.

The most frequent form of documentation is one using only organized notes;
after various trials and research, the Diana group of teachers invented a system of
documentation which simultaneously allowed us to follow individual and group
processes (naturally I include the teacher documenting in the 'group') and later
reconstruct a larger number of happenings, so that we could communicate processes being investigated as completely as possible (see Figure 9.4). As time went
by, we came to realize that notes became more effective when they resembled
stage directions, introducing small, rapid icons agreed on beforehand: eyes looking, mouth smiling, etc. Naturally the completeness of various forms of notes
depends on context, the number of children, the number of adults present, etc.

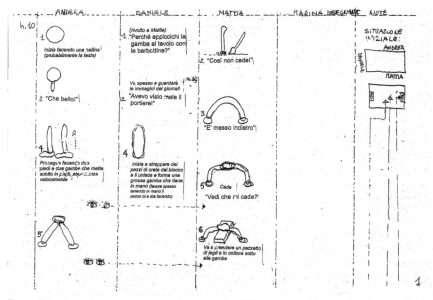

Figure 9.4 Notes by a teacher, *scuola comunale dell'infanzia* Diana

Often observations are not thorough and organized because there never seems to be enough time. But even when notes are hurried, which frequently happens, like the ones shown here (see Figure 9.5), they let us look back and discover things which happened on the way, and which we would never know about if we only ever see the finished drawing.

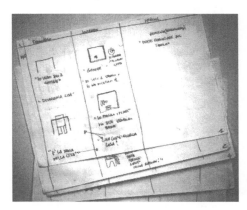

Figure 9.5 Notes by a teacher, *scuola comunale dell'infanzia* Diana

The teacher proposes to the children to represent a group of people eating together at a table, aware of some of the difficulties the children will encounter but confident she is placing them in a situation where they can exercise their good powers of invention to come out on top (see Figure 9.6).

Figure 9.6 Drawing of a table. Lorenzo and Francesco, aged 5–6 years, *scuola communale dell'infanzia* Diana

Each drawing contains secrets; here are just some of the many we discover on reading the notes. Children are attentive to the work of companions and always open to borrowing knowledge: Lorenzo has drawn a table leg upside down, Francesco intervenes, running his hand down the leg of a real table he says, 'Look it goes down, not up, try and draw it... good, down, down, now stop and go back up, good, now it's fine'.

We realize how the nose of a person drawn in profile has first been placed in a frontal position and then later in the right position (see Figure 9.7).

Figure 9.7 Details of notes, *scuola comunale dell'infanzia* Diana

Above all we discover the strange and unexpected procedure of a little girl who, after drawing the first person at her table, finds it difficult to position the person sitting opposite. What does she do? She begins rotating her drawing of the chair thinking that this way she will get to the position she wants. At a certain point either she realizes the final result will take her back to her starting point, or... well, we are not completely sure what happens, her rotation is modified and the girl succeeds in her intention, so that in the end the two people are sitting opposite and facing each other (see Figure 9.8).

Figure 9.8 Details of notes, *scuola comunale dell'infanzia* Diana

We discover so much busy thinking! So much intelligence and invention! All these elements put together over time give us new eyes for seeing children, and more ideas for proposals with them.

Over time we felt the need to construct other tools for observation that we called *piste osservative* (observation pathways), which are a sort of written guideline for orienting and supporting specific observations like constructions in clay or drawings. Taking clay as an example, certain sections of the *pista* will focus the teacher's attention on individual attitudes in children; how they handle the clay, the shapes they make, to what extent they perceive its three-dimensional potential and issues of stability and balance intrinsic to the nature of the material. Others will focus on the things children say as they work, the similarities and differences between girls and boys, what part of their hands and what actions they use most frequently when shaping the clay. The list is a long one and the type of observation can go from very simple to very deep.

Can these *piste osservative* support the work of inexpert observers? Only partly. I am not against disseminating work tools but the quality of their use is strongly connected to the cultural and conceptual understanding that generates them.

After rather a long phase of deep documentation with small groups, in which we identified some similarities and differences between groups of girls and boys, we went back to documentation examining the whole class and attempted to synthesize some of children's recurring strategies on the same topic. We alternated this general view with closer views of certain processes. We became aware that, following our experience of documenting small groups, our general view was no longer the same – as if we had the gift of multiplying eyes and ears. The book entitled *Everything Has a Shadow Except Ants* (Municipality of Reggio Emilia, 1999) and the *Crowd* project (see also Chapter 3) recall and represent that period very well.

It was interesting in both projects to go back and work again on topics we had worked with years before and observe how much our approach to the theme had changed, become richer. Children suggested so many new and original projects through observing and documenting them! To break with certain schemes in drawing which became repetitive or a little lazy, we noticed it was sometimes enough to suggest variations on a proposal, such as including movement in the subject of the drawing or a variation in the artist's vantage point. For example, a little girl running, chased by something she is afraid of; or two children playing with a ball; or people seen from above; or rotating the point of view for drawing an object (see Figures 9.9–9.12).

Figures 9.9–9.11 Drawings from life of a person observed from front and side. Alice 5 years 6 months. December

Figures 9.12–9.13 Person observed from front and side, taken from an illustrated sequence. Alice aged 5 years 8 months. February

Different points of view

Representing the same thing from different viewpoints is a theme we often explore through proposals of different kinds that we make to the children. It is very effective to my mind, because it moves imagination through space, and some areas of neurological research have shown that when our mind imagines an object rotating through space, what we 'see' conserves analogies with what actually happens. I think analyzing the same object from different points of view is a lovely, intelligent game and also represents an ethical attitude towards awareness of the plurality of ways of seeing the same problem.

In proposals and games apparently distant from moral attitudes and concepts, we can often transmit and educate much more than only using words. If imagining and seeing an object from different points of view is considered to be an important approach, then it should be included in the everyday planning of proposals. In Reggio, we often speak of project-based thinking in our everyday life. It means a way of seeing that projects us into the future, hypothesing, anticipating. Project-based thinking is a permanent aspect in our way of thinking, thinking which develops through the connections between things. It includes environments, tools, procedures (meaning that it thinks of these as important elements). It does not isolate the phases of a journey but projects them into connective networks. I will attempt to give some illustrations of all these points through some work done by a teacher.

Drawing from life[1]

This is an interesting situation with children aged 5–6 years old, who have been invited to sit round a classmate acting as a model. If they wish, they can move to another viewpoint on the same day or the following day. I have already illustrated a situation of this kind in the previous chapter to underline how certain proposals are interesting even when a situation is rather difficult. However, in this example, observation has been carried out adequately.

In this type of research, two very different materials can be used side by side; drawing and clay, with two different, parallel underlying processes. I will only recount some particularly interesting parts in my opinion from this very long documentation.

At a certain point, Federica experiences difficulty in drawing her profile and repeatedly asks Giovanni to help. Giovanni initially concentrates on his sculpture and limits himself to encouraging Federica to 'look properly'.

But then he gives her his attention and some verbal advice, 'You know by now that there's only one eye in a profile and the nose sticks out from the head'.

These few words are sufficient and Federica draws the profile of the little girl modelling.

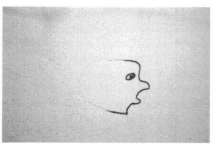

At this point Giovanni intervenes and completes the mouth.

The finished drawing.

Federica is highly satisfied with her drawing.

Friends around her participate in her satisfaction and congratulate her. Effort and pleasure often coincide and are individual triumphs in which groups generally participate and learn.

Drawings from four points of view.

Some comments on the clay models. It cannot be taken for granted that a three-dimensional material makes it possible to get a three-dimensional vision of the object being reproduced. The observer's point of view sometimes conditions reality and the possibilities offered by a material.

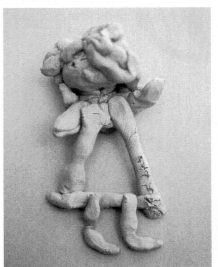

Both children positioned in places where they see the model from the side, make sculptures that only have the arm they can see. Camilla resolves her side view in this way.

The group of children has a final feedback session in which they make comments, evaluations, self-evaluations; they express the difficulties they have encountered and reasons for the choices they have made; individual and group awareness are both developed.

The children comment on the reality of the situation they have worked in, 'With clay you have to do everything – not just what you can see. You can do that in a drawing, but not with clay'.

Many faces for the same subject

In our city, bicycles are a frequently-used means of transport and an interesting subject for live investigation. Generally speaking in two days children represent the side, the front and the back of a bicycle they draw from life; drawings are then photocopied and given back to the various authors together with the proposal of positioning a person on the bicycle seat. Another proposal, which is great fun for the children and which can be proposed with 4- and 5-year-old children, is to take off their shoes, put them on the table and draw the shoe from the side, the front, from behind, above and below (see Figure 9.28).

LE·MiE·SCARPE

ALICE

Figure 9.28 Drawings of shoes: side, front and back views. Alice aged 5 years 10 months

Our attitude in this and other proposals is to understand a little more of children's strategies and to get to know them better, but what we are most interested in is that the child should come out successfully, or at least feel that way. Our work at the side of children, which is different from child to child, always has this in mind. It should always be remembered that children have a strong sense of evaluation and self-evaluation we need to be careful of, and though we should not deceive children with gratifying flattery, at the same time we must not humiliate them or make them feel inadequate.

Esteem, surprise and gaiety

I have already said how aware we are, because we understand its complexity, that the documentation we collect represents only small fragments of processes, and how these are in any case modified by the documentor's presence and intervention (Heisenberg's theory of indetermination). However, we are also aware of the richness this documentation gives teachers, the implicit esteem it encourages for children and their intelligence, including their many unexpected creative inventions, and the climate of affection and complicity that is created. Observation and documentation make us feel we are opening small chinks offering glimpses into the world of childhood; a world we have had access to in the past but whose memories are difficult to hold onto; its times, rhythms, ways of organizing work and forms of democracy often unanticipated and not always easy to understand or accept when they happen; different strategies in approaching problems and stumblings, solutions that almost always manage to surprise us. Is it this sense of surprise, continuing over time, that makes us so persevering in pursuing this journey of observation and documentation that is not always easy to realize? Or is it the need to give meaning to what we do?

It is true that from our documentation we have learned to listen a little more to the world of children, and have become more familiar with the individual and group strategies employed by children we work with daily for some years. Above all, perhaps, we have learned to betray them a little less and make proposals that are more attuned to their interests.

Do I never doubt the real need and value of all this work we do observing and documenting all our busy work? Certainly these doubts come, partly because this activity is not immune to tiredness, tension, often requiring complex organization. But then it is enough for me to observe and document, or for a teacher to show me her notes from observations with the children, and I feel a sense of gaiety and interest overcoming all my doubts.

I would say gaiety and surprise are the feelings that have perhaps most accompanied my work with children. For thirty years, when I set foot inside the *scuola comunale dell'infanzia* Diana, I experienced the strong sensation of stepping into a parallel world, with special rules, atmospheres and ways of thinking. On my way through the school to the atelier, there were always unanticipated and amusing encounters: some child dressed up with flippers on their feet (the children loved dressing up in these, and hats and gloves) would be taking a walk around the school, or a child would approach, stop in front of me and I had to guess what was new, but it was not always clear what it was, and so attempts at guessing began, and maybe it was a pair of shoes, or a new haircut or a tooth missing. In the atelier, I would always find a group of children who were there more or less officially and the impact of their tales would often make me forget the problems of the outside world.

This does not mean that schools are detached from reality; rather it means seventy-eight children is another reality, very often a highly amusing one, where you talk in deep ways about difficult topics, or I should say topics the adult world considers difficult.

Naturally this came together with hard work, irritability and misunderstandings, because children are also tiring, awkward, perseverant and, as Malaguzzi used to define them, betrayers, because so often they betray our expectations. But then this is one of the most amusing and interesting aspects of the work.

Practising attunement

Something that scares me somewhat is that since 2000 when I left Diana, I have not had opportunities for directly following observations with a group of children in a normal everyday school context, and I am certain it would take some time and practice before I became attuned to observation in the way I was before. I know that in the beginning I would probably be irritated by children's times and rhythms – so often different from our own – not so much the way they slow down and accelerate, but such different rhythms; concentration and interests rapidly alternating with distraction that is sometimes not real but only apparent. I would have to try and refind the verbal language, facial expressions and tones allowing me to communicate with them, to be accepted, to be respected.

A well-known and admired woman writer from abroad had proposed doing a little inquiry with children in the school and insisted on being left alone with them. After the meeting she left the room rather vexed and angry saying the children did not understand the questions she asked them and that they had also been very rude. Since we had prudently put her in contact with a group of very calm, well-behaved children we tried to understand what happened from the children's perspective. Probably the writer acted in too self-confident and hurried a way with the children, expecting and wanting the children to confirm her ideas on the subject she was interested in, without taking into consideration children's attitude of independence and *betrayal*. At the first, predictable provocation from a little boy she reacted by saying she would not give him the promised award at the end of the discussion and he angrily answered that she was old and when she was even older he would go and steal his award from her. In short, neither friendship, liking or trust had been created – all difficult things to achieve.

I do not know why working with small children is deemed to be simple. Very often only physical fatigue associated with the work is taken into consideration; not all the mental juggling that must be done to have their attention, interest, concentration, trust and friendship. But when you manage to have their friendship then children are courageous, you can propose difficult projects and they will stand by you in trying them out, get enthusiastic, get their parents involved, be willing to stay on longer at school. When children are motivated, they like doing difficult things.

I often recall an incident that took place during work on the theatre curtain for the Ariosto Theatre, one of the city's historical theatres (see also Vecchi, 2002). The large painting we were working on for the creation of the curtain was inside the Sala dei Pittori in the Valli Municipal Theatre because it was 3 × 4.5 metres and too big to fit inside the school. Each morning a small group of us would go from Diana school to the theatre. We were at a point with the curtain where, in order to continue the work, we needed to make decisions about certain important things.

As we walked one day on our journey from school to theatre, Giulia, a little girl in the 5-year-old class, came and took my hand saying, 'Vea you do remember don't you, I'm the youngest in the class?' Her message was clear and I gave her a reassuring smile, told her of course I remembered and as we continued walking along calmly we began to think about some of the decisions we needed to make in order to continue our work on the painting. Another child in the group, Leonardo, often became emotional when he had to work on something important and, in this case, before he began painting he would always ask to go for a 'pee pee' after which he was calmer. The children were aware we were working on an important and very difficult project, but if I had suggested to either of these children that they should stay behind at school that day instead of coming to paint, they would have been very disappointed. They knew perfectly well they could ask to stay behind, but they never did so.

Children have an excellent sense of evaluation and self-evaluation, they are aware of the things requiring a greater, out-of-the-ordinary commitment. But they accept the extra work because they know the results will be immensely gratifying for them. Leonardo himself, at the end of each day's work, was always very satisfied and would often exclaim, 'There! We've done a really good job today'. Effort and joy can be compatible in learning too; they must be carefully measured out and above all motivated.

Doubts

Doubts that create clouds over issues of observation and documentation essentially have to do with their effects on children. How much does seeing themselves represented and recounted in our observations and documentation constitute an element of disturbance? As always, I believe we need to reflect more deeply on children's possible points of view.

Perhaps doubts are greater than in the past because of the times we live in, and the new technologies available expose all of us to being continuously documented. Observation and documentation have great potential benefits. Certainly, like all of us, children need to be seen and recognized for their individuality and they need to be regarded with respect; I am convinced children should clearly feel the interest and esteem in which they are held. And when observation and documentation are capable of high levels of solidarity with children, they help and support more intense and affectionate relationships between children and teacher, and this keeps at bay the risk of indifference – one of the worst risks in any relationship.

But if on the one hand documentation can lift us from anonymity, on the other hand it can bring an excessive visibility, which is not always judged positively by the person being observed. I am convinced, however, that doubts arise above all in people outside the situation, because when adults and children are in a group working together, the cognitive and emotional involvement are so strong that all doubts are forgotten and fade into the background. At the same time, it is well to be careful not to let observation and documentation become simply an educational technique and lose their ability for pushing forward our way of thinking or switching it on. It is also important to maintain an attitude of solidarity with the children and not to transform them into the subject of laboratory experiments. It is obvious, too, that observation and documentation, like all strong flavours, should be used in careful doses.

Subjectivity

Films made with video cameras were used as study material but because they required longer times for viewing, they were used less frequently than notes and photographs. However, it was probably exactly this need for watching and rewatching videos that prompted us to use them in observing and documenting different individual processes more deeply in the 1990s. A video exists from that time which focuses on the hands of two little girls aged 5 years 6 months as they are making little clay horses; we were interested in looking at how the ability of the hands assists and helps the ability of thoughts. To my mind, this video demonstrates some interesting aspects, one of which is an adult prejudice in film that makes us linger over active hands and be less interested in hands that are still, suspended in reflection, or in doubt, or 'listening' to materials. Documentation of this kind causes a shift in the teacher's thinking and ways of seeing and lets her know certain children better whose traits are less evident.

The making of some little clay horses by two girls aged 4 years 6 months at that time became something of a symbol for this interest we had in broadening our research into different 'subjectivities', the specific characteristics and points of view each person or thing has (see Figures 9.29–9.39).

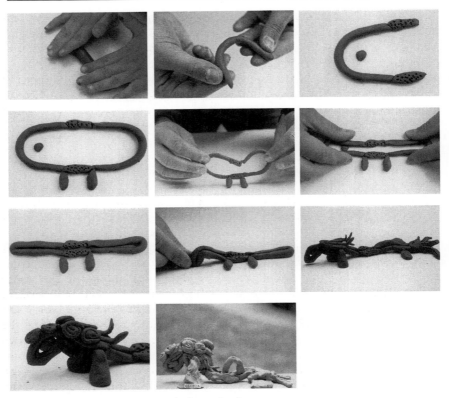

Figures 9.29–9.39 Construction of a horse in clay

I remember that when he saw this documentary material for the first time, Malaguzzi scolded me for having printed the images small and, therefore, in his opinion, giving little importance to the entire documentation. He had immediately intuited that documenting individual processes in such a detailed way would bring new information and new, precious points of view to interpretations of the children's world. Each new phase we tackled, to be communicated clearly, brought new ways of documenting. To illustrate the individual processes in the case of the clay horses and some others, the technique we felt most suitable at the time for capturing the different and complex passages was for adults to make a reconstruction of the process at a later date.

In order not to have a video camera continuously pointing at the same subject, considering the invasive nature its presence could assume, and at the same time not to miss any phases during the making of the product, we needed more discreet, intelligent and highly detailed notes, or else a film camera positioned at a distance when the type of work or context made it possible. With a careful eye on the process filmed by video camera or annotated in sketches done by hand, the child's *product* was subsequently reconstructed by the teacher, carefully observing the original piece of work. During the remake, photographs were taken of phases in construction considered significant for understanding the process.

This investigative work where teachers' hands, following the tracks of children's hands, attempt to reconstruct, give shape and image to children's thoughts is an extremely interesting journey that can be used to arrive at deeper intuition about individual children's choices and pathways.

New documentary structures

At about this time, we became aware of the impossibility of communicating with others about the projects using our usual tool of traditional exhibitions because of the limited space available and the summarized reading required of the observer. In documenting processes we could not skip too many phases of the journey otherwise the aim of the operation was betrayed and made incomprehensible, meaning that for correct documentation we needed more space for showing and opportunities for slower kinds of reading. So we conceived of a form of in-house publishing we called *quaderni di studio e ricerca* (study and research notebooks) (see Figure 9.40) and these have proved to be one of the best tools for teachers' and atelieristas' evolution; apart from involving two languages, visual and written, this type of publication allows us to communicate a greater number of interpretations than wall documentation. Copies can easily be made – at that time with photocopiers, now using computers – and distributed to several people for greater returns in interpretation and contributions from multiple points of view.

Figure 9.40 Study and research notebooks

It is not easy to get those who have never tried to understand the difficulties, to appreciate how much care and synthesis of interpretation is required for this type of documentation, in order to gain a better understanding of work done together with children and the legacy of learning acquired in this way for both teachers and children. A project is the flowing together of many things, the concurrent appearance of interesting events; there are many crossroads where we are forced to choose which direction to go in, at the same time as seeking not to prevaricate, for example not to betray the children's strategies and thinking, but to constantly choose which elements are most important to highlight and develop. There are probably different strategies that can help us with this process of evolution but in my experience we become better at it when we are able to continuously interpret and conceptualize events taking place during (and not at the end of) the journey.

In our most recent exhibitions, much work has been done on this aspect, which I will discuss in greater depth in the final chapters on two new exhibitions: *Dialogues with Places* and *The Wonder of Learning*. When the work of documenting and revisiting is finished, further interpretation and synthesis are needed in order to keep only what we consider to be the main elements, namely those capable of communicating the meaning of the completed work, because otherwise documentation can turn into a thorough and sequential chronicle of phases in a journey, something less interesting and far removed from what we should be able to understand and communicate through documentation. I believe this is another case in which exchanges of points of view as we work is one of the things that helps most, allowing us to increase the quality of our processes of interpretation.

Children making documentation

In recent years, children have themselves tried out the role of document maker, being offered opportunities for documenting the work of their classmates, something that was facilitated by the simplicity of using digital cameras. As always when we work with children, the results have been extremely interesting but, as ever, each time we go down a new road we need to find the time for a better discussion and understanding of what has taken place. I have not, we have not, yet sufficiently reflected on what it means to the children to deal with a process of documentation as document makers, and evaluation is still being done. Proposals exist, like this one, in which it is as well to define boundaries from the start to keep risk at a distance; for although it is right to wonder what changes might take place in learning pathways if children become used at an early age to paying more attention to their own individual strategies, it is just as right to be cautious.

I confess I have my doubts. I always fear the attitude of imitating typical adult roles is far removed from children's identity. Children are so perspicacious, so capable of interpreting the requests we believe we have not expressed, so skilled that misunderstandings on the subject would be easy. Perhaps with children of compulsory school age it might be a good way of working, but before any kind of evaluation we first need to try, retry and reflect on effective benefits.

New ways of seeing

After these experiences, in 1997 we felt sufficiently well prepared to start work on an enquiry to be carried out with the University of Harvard's Project Zero, *Making Learning Visible: Children as Individual and Group Learners* (Rinaldi *et al.*, 2001). This research was looking for more information and understanding not only on the subject of children working in groups but on how much individual children were enriched or conditioned by the group itself. What conditions made a group into a learning group?

A small work group was formed from Harvard University and the Reggio municipal schools and there were various meetings and discussions to create a framework for the research. Following this, the Diana and La Villetta schools became the environments in which atelieristas and teachers conducted their field research, which was then interpreted in a series of meetings by the entire research group. I remember we immediately applied the reflections generated during the course of the first meetings in a project we were beginning with 5-year-old children, in which they were designing decorations for the school's interior courtyard – in fact this became *The Beautiful Wall* – from the title children gave to the work in ceramic still decorating Diana's courtyard. It is incredible how our ways of seeing can change when they are oriented by new thinking!

The camera helped me to discover and communicate a series of aspects that I did not appear to have captured in previous documentations – and another piece in the mosaic of understanding children's strategies was added to previous ones. I discovered and documented how, within a learning group, sub-groups were often formed and I was able to catch glimpses of their different rhythms and strategies.

Perhaps the aspect that personally struck me most was a sort of etiquette, perhaps more, perhaps a social pact with governance lying somewhere between the formal and the ethical, that supported the group's work and was constructed through using verbal language, body language, tone, facial expression and proxemics. All this was on a democratic basis, again with rules not always easy for the adult world to understand and accept, and which can sometimes appear cruel. Such as the meeting in which the children established a rule whereby each person present had to verbally give their opinion on a certain issue. In this case, everyone was *forced* to give an opinion, even if they did not wish to. I must add, however, that even the most timid of children, after accepting a rule established by the group, managed to express something and were afterwards very happy about doing so, usually feeling more confident.

In order to make each person's participation in a work group visible in the final product, children are prepared to propose quite extraordinary strategies, like some of those that I documented in the book *Making Learning Visible: Children as Individual and Group Learners* (Rinaldi, Giudici and Krechevsky, 2001). These things are, perhaps, already known but I saw them unravelling and being made clearer in front of my eyes as I took the photographs. Once again new thinking and an attitude of curiosity and research demonstrated their ability for *guiding eyes* and advancing and evolving knowledge.

An important work for the city

An important project we worked on soon after was further opportunity for testing and documenting group work — we were to design and create a theatre curtain for a historical city theatre. Although I have already mentioned this project, I would like to add a little more. It was 1998 and the project was a courageous one, both for Antonio Canova who was director of the Reggio Theatres and suggested the project with Mayor Antonella Spiaggiari's enthusiastic approval, and for us who accepted because it was by no means a simple thing to create a work beautiful enough to be housed in an important nineteenth-century theatre like the Ariosto.

For those who would like to know more about the project work and the creation of the curtain, there is a book that recounts the story (Vecchi, 2002). But here I wish to underline just two things. The first, and I think this is obvious, is that in order to receive a request of this nature, which I believe to be the only one of its kind in the world, Reggio schools and, in this particular case the atelier, had gained the trust of part of the city; secondly, this project was the result of many years of observation and documentation.

Aside from being a quite exceptional project, it is the story of a group of children and adults closely followed from the beginning of the project to its end. We tried to make visible, as much as is possible, how ideas are generated and how they unravel, the roles of different individuals in the group and the adults by their side, their periods of crisis when the project came to a standstill and the struggle to find a path and continue. Reading it again, with all the criticism that can be made (some parts are better than others, some of the writing could have been more careful or gone deeper), I still believe it is a useful tale for those wishing to work in groups and work together with children on a collective piece of work. Those wishing to make the journey should be aware of how difficult it is to let children be the *authors* of each phase of the design and creation of a piece of work and not simply the executors of beautiful individual forms.

To end

We have recently revisited pedagogical observation and documentation during work to realize a new exhibition entitled *The Wonder of Learning*. In this phase of our long journey, some issues have emerged with special force:

- the importance of a narrative structure in which communication is developed as a significant source of feedback for understanding work carried out.
- the importance of working documents, made as work is ongoing, which can be consulted for a deeper and fuller understanding of children's processes and the choices made by teachers.
- documentation and communication which takes into account the various aspects of the environment it will be shown in so that it develops on different levels – writing, pictures, objects.

Chapter 10

We take up the walk again

In 1994, Malaguzzi died leaving us orphans, having lost an important reference point. However, after a brief period of disorientation it appeared that the entire system of municipal schools had remained steady in the face of losing our maestro and we courageously faced new problems such as funding Reggio Children, which had been envisaged by Malaguzzi but still remained to be invented and constructed. At that time, as I have said before, Carla Rinaldi and Sergio Spaggiari, in their joint role of directors of early childhood services and Sandra Piccinini, as the new *Assessore* for schools and culture, found themselves making decisions which were not easy, as new things never are, but perhaps the very attitude of research stimulated by the unknown, and the uncertainty and doubt which it gives rise to, not only held together a very complex system of organization but led it to evolve and become interested in cultural and organizational aspects not usually contemplated by traditional pedagogy.

I believe an important role at the time in the way things evolved positively was played by the existence of a political administration that was especially friendly towards the schools, in particular in the person of Mayor Antonella Spaggiari, an intelligent and capable woman, with an enviable capacity for communication and optimistic faith in our cultural possibilities.

I did not participate in all the issues that might have been part of the political and administrative discussions and choices. But I do know that feeling sure of an administration's esteem and friendship makes one assume a trusting attitude towards the choices being made. This trust we placed first in Loris Malaguzzi and then in the pedagogical team and administration that took over after his death. This does not mean we did not have a vigilant attitude towards choices being made, or were unwilling to intervene in the case of disagreement. However, we did not expect to be betrayed on basic values and this allowed us to continue our work with interest and pleasure. In these first difficult phases of transition, the atelier was particularly important for continuing to make visible work done in the municipal schools, through exhibitions and publishing, illustrating how the loss of a maestro, as Malaguzzi undoubtedly was, was not the end of an educational philosophy.

Visual writing

Rolando Baldini and Vania Vecchi, graphic designers, have for many years been by our side testifying to the fact that the graphics contained in books, posters and exhibitions are never simply illustrations but the processing of a language; visual writing. The presence of this couple has been important for the atelier and our entire visual communication system. Over the years, their graphics have contributed to giving our work continuity and a recognizable quality and to communicating in new, cultured and poetic ways a different image of the child than ones traditionally communicated. Their long-standing collaboration continued to remind us that in order to be of quality, visual language must be a blend of metaphorical synthesis and knowledge of the elements of perception and technical competency, and it is difficult to imagine their culture has not also influenced the work of atelieristas, teachers and pedagogistas with children.

Without doubt the work done by these two graphic artists over many years and continuing to this day has contributed to evolving our culture and giving an original identity to our pedagogy in our communications. Above all, they have ensured the identity of visual communication has been finely tuned to pedagogical identity. They have given their constant attention to never betraying the culture of children, nor simplifying it into schemes unacceptable to those who work together with children and hold them in esteem.

Changes

Since Malaguzzi's death, important developments have taken place in the management of Reggio schools and Reggio's relations with the wider world (discussed in Chapters 5 and 11). Interest in Reggio Emilia's pedagogical philosophy has grown further and expanded over time internationally, building new pathways that have partially modified the work of atelieristas and teachers, increasingly called upon to communicate work they carry out with colleagues from other parts of Italy and abroad. This growing national and international role for Reggio's pedagogical philosophy has been supported by Reggio Children in different ways; through showing the exhibition entitled *The Hundred Languages of Children*, which now exists in four different digital editions simultaneously shown on four continents; through the organizing of a publishing house with sometimes unanticipated success; through working on professional development for groups coming from around the world; through national and international conferences and seminars; through various consulting work; and more recently through courses for those who wish to become pedagogistas and atelieristas. All these activities have seen a large contribution from ateliers in giving visibility to work with children, and as always happens, sometimes risks have been run.

Accelerated journeys

The third generation of atelieristas has been added to the first of which I was a part, and to the second, and have found themselves in environments where documentation is an integral part of pedagogy and educational work. However, professional development routes inside schools risk becoming accelerated courses, with insufficient time available for truly *understanding and listening*. At the same time, and this also happened to us, new atelieristas know little or nothing about children or pedagogy in the beginning, with the partial exception of people attending Reggio Children courses for atelieristas. Such courses of three months or thereabouts constitute only a start, however important.

To date, three courses have been held for atelieristas with funding by provincial administration and, therefore, free for participants. A background in art is an entrance requirement, particularly in the visual arts or music, and participants must be aged under thirty. There are always many applications and we make a selection on the basis of curricula and portfolios. An interview tries to establish the group of participants (about sixteen) most suited to the job.

To date, the three-month course has been divided into weekly modules on subjects such as pedagogy and educational philosophy in Reggio Emilia, environments, observation and documentation, *progettazione*, children's multiple languages, visual languages and musical languages. Naturally disciplines are not separate but seen as subjects for deeper discussion, always trying to weave together theoretical and more concrete parts. At the end of each week, testing takes the shape of a workshop for an evaluation of individuals and the group in the area of the week's topic. There follows a period of some weeks working in schools in direct contact with children. At the end of the course, a final evaluation is made of a written project given as a presentation and an interview. Participants must acquire various competencies during the course, in observation and documentation, photography, music, graphics, environments and digital technology. The course is intensive and rather difficult for the young people who participate but it is also culturally exciting.

When their course finishes, almost all students are asked to work as atelieristas in Reggio Emilia and in other municipalities in its surrounding province. This is the start of a difficult time because teachers and pedagogistas expect them to have experience, which cannot be acquired in three months of course work. Atelieristas sometimes find themselves in environments little suited to continued professional development. It takes time and quality to make good atelieristas and to make ateliers the place in schools traversed by a multiplicity of languages.

Perhaps this professional development is simpler in Reggio Emilia than elsewhere but it still cannot be taken for granted. New atelieristas find themselves in pedagogical contexts possessing an accumulated experience of educational work, ready and willing to help on journeys of professional development and pass the baton. However, it is not easy for atelieristas to participate in new journeys in creative ways, to work by the side of expert teachers who are not always willing to listen to proposals they have gone beyond or already decided against, or perhaps to find themselves working with less expert teachers, freshly employed and often oriented in the direction of educational work that is distant from that done in Reggio's municipal schools. It may happen to begin with that atelieristas are involved in the final documentation of a project without having had the opportunity to follow children's work sufficiently, or perhaps their contact with children is too brief and hurried.

Without ignoring work done in the past, young atelieristas, by virtue of their age, have the task of bringing new techniques, materials, sensibilities and concepts into schools and, in order to do this in original ways, two issues are particularly important. First, attentive participation in the culture of their time; second, learning to listen to children's strategies so that necessary inventive connections can be made between the stimulus of poetics in new, contemporary art and the imagination and culture of children.

The right professional development for the atelierista's complex profile (the same is true for teachers and pedagogistas) is very urgent at the present time because of the turnover in generations working in Reggio's schools. The need for them to mature in a shorter space of time makes adequate responses more difficult.

Atelier, exhibitions, the city

I left the *scuola comunale dell'infanzia* Diana in 2000 after working there for thirty very beautiful, very interesting years and I urgently felt a need to contribute some of my experience to new generations of atelieristas, teachers and pedagogistas; or perhaps I still desire the experience of cultural excitement that the profession continues to give me. Projects I have coordinated most recently, working together with other atelieristas and pedagogistas, have attempted to make the role of poetic languages in schools more explicit, dealing with and attempting to clarify difficult subjects such as relations between pedagogy, art and artists, the relationship to the environment, the strategies of children as photographers and other subjects apparently more distant from my profession such as learning to write. At the same time, we have reaffirmed how attention for things taking place in the city can stimulate and orient interesting educational projects, inviting the schools and city into a relationship important for the whole community.

Children, art, artists: The Burri exhibition

In the project entitled *Children, Art, Artists*[1] (2002) opportunities afforded by a large retrospective exhibition of work by Alberto Burri, an important late twentieth-century painter, were used in a course of professional development with a group of municipal early childhood centres, primary schools and middle schools (that is with children aged 20 months to 14 years) and staff in Reggio Emilia's Civic Museum, which reflected on what things are common to children and artists or what might be different. We argue in this project that juxtaposing children and artists is advantageous when we work on their processes and put them side by side, while on the contrary a comparison of finished products makes for equivocation and distorted evaluations. The result was an exhibition and a catalogue (2004) that recount and visualize, through projects with children, the attention and reprocessing we feel is necessary for a dialogue with art and artists leaving important traces in each child's personal strategies.

Figure. 10.1 The Children, Art, Artists exhibition

In this way of working, adults reapproach the work of artists or art contexts and attempt to capture their emerging sense and significance, then rework these to propose situations with children in which they can try out and explore processes close to the artist's but which let children piece together their own mental imagery. At a later date, children have opportunities to see the artist's work in the hope of increasing curiosity and understanding. Whatever happens though, children will have experimented with interesting processes in sensitive, intelligent actions.

An analogous situation was the project entitled *Invitation to...* conceived by artist Claudio Parmiggiani and promoted by Reggio Emilia administration in 2002. The project with children concluded with an exhibition entitled *Dialogues with Places* which I will not discuss at length because it is covered in Chapter 7 on Environments.

The magic of writing

Another project arose from the seductive power of an exhibition in the city entitled *Alphabeto in Sogno* (2002), again conceived and curated by Claudio Parmiggiani and examining the subject of figurative poetry in all its unpredictable aspects; writing in which words and imagery come together to make new, different and more complex meanings. We worked on an educational project, which became part of a journey in learning to write and read in *scuole dell'infanzia* and the first and second years in elementary school, years when children are building up competency in written text whilst needing to keep alive the magic of writing.

We are aware that learning to read and write is a fascinating and extraordinary adventure in itself; however, in Reggio Emilia we also believe that playing with words, using them to invent visual metaphor or make short *visual poems* can be a stimulus for the mind and forms of expression. It is no coincidence that highly *seductive* writing has been produced in this way in different eras and cultures.

In figurative writing, multiple meanings can be attributed to one word (or letter, or sentence) through using the communicative, metaphorical and symbolic potential in the language of drawing. Text and image interweave and accentuate the identity and meaning of an object or concept. There is an obvious relationship between writing and visual language because drawn signs are the basic element of writing. Writing is always image and removing it from this natural, aesthetic context probably means we impoverish one of its communicative possibilities for expression.

 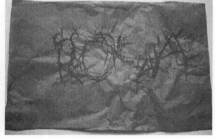

Figure 10.2 'Devil'. Writing on sandpaper with red background

Figure 10.3 'Pink'. Writing on fuchsia silk paper

This was an opportunity for reflecting and thinking again about children, written and spoken words, communicative expression in written text, the relationship between traditional and digital writing, and about the separate or combined participation of many languages in processes of learning and constructing knowledge.

The language of photography

A Mysterious Glance of Children on the City[2] (2008) is a small but interesting exhibition of photography in which the language of photography by children artists, to date only sporadically worked on, started to become an educational experiment, probably on an international level. On other occasions, we noticed how children's ways of seeing are capable of capturing and giving identity to place through collecting details going from signs of an environmental nature to textures in walls, highlighting one shade of colour, shadows and light. In this exhibition, we received confirmations and some surprises, such as the heightening effect of different points of view on the same subject (perhaps something of the work done in our schools passes into their approach), a marked use of the zoom lens (used more by 3–6-year-old girls and 10–11-year-olds boys), and many other elements which will be reported and commented in the exhibition catalogue. However, the aspect my colleagues and I find most interesting is getting inside and participating in children's ways of seeing through elements they photograph, to understand their interests and perceptions a little better. We are interested in bringing together children in different age groups, different countries and different cultures and believe the research will be interesting.

Another element of a socially important nature, which is important to report, is how a children's exhibition of this kind was made part of a European photography festival held in Reggio Emilia each year for some years now. The significance is obvious: it appears the city of Reggio and its administrators truly hold the children in esteem and trust the intelligence and creativity of both children and teachers, continuing with new Mayor Graziano Delrio, the traditional relationship of respect that has always existed in administrations since the end of the last war (with all the normal ups and downs). A good relationship with the municipal administration and the Mayor are too important for our school culture, the culture of Reggio Children and the International Centre for us to leave to chance.

As always these projects all have in common a wish to do lovely, interesting and educational things with children, together with the added aim of clarifying and illustrating more clearly relations between the worlds of art and pedagogy or education, a subject which we have been working on for many years. Or, at least, I have been working on for I do not wish to make others guilty for things they are not responsible for.

Finding analogies between work produced by children and primitive art work and work produced by artists is something Malaguzzi always avoided doing in an explicit way, probably out of a fear that it prompts many misunderstandings. However, I am certain (almost certain) that he would have done it, because so often we are asked questions about this area. I am very sorry I have attempted to theorize on and clarify some aspects of this issue without being able to discuss them with him and if I had been able to without doubt my reflections would have been deeper and more complete. I say this to take responsibility for the ideas I have expressed, not all necessarily shared by everyone in Reggio schools.

The first time I presented the thesis of my theory for bringing together children, art and artists was in a talk for a very large study group visiting Reggio, I forget what nationality. My hypothesis, then as now, is that the relationship between children and artists is highly productive on an educational level – the juxtaposition comes about through certain processes which must be present and unfold in the creative act; curiosity, courage, synthesis, metaphor and symbolic invention.

Professional development courses

Because the projects I have discussed were part of professional development with teachers and atelieristas, strategies were adopted during these journeys that I believe are still valid:

1. Initial workshops for adults to enable preliminary discussion and possible experimentation with the subject to be treated. This first phase preceding work with children should not be underestimated as it prepares us to 'listen' more carefully to the contexts we will be working in and situations we will encounter; it makes our capacity for interpreting more acute. It is important to provide a basic bibliography for deepening the knowledge of project participants.

2. Intermediate points in journeys with children where, either in small groups or all together, participants come together to communicate how work is progressing, including presentation of visual documentation. Teachers and atelieristas are obliged to make documentation during journeys and not wait until the end of the project. Ways of documenting must necessarily be comprehensive, clear and capable of synthesis. In *Dialogues with Places* (Filippini *et al.*, 2008) we worked extensively on documentation in process. Critical revision along the way is a tool for exchange and fundamental evolution in professional development; it is as indispensable for new generations of teachers and atelieristas as it was for ours.

3. A final exhibition for communicating with the public, a reminder for school and city communities to participate and be involved because education cannot be just for teachers to reflect on. The process of *writing a synthesis* of a project, which must also be *visual* in order to include it in an exhibition, gives us important, deeper insights into the project itself.

4. Visual documentary material such as videos and PowerPoint presentations are of use with the public. Each visual tool creates a communication context with its own rhythms that we need to understand if we are to use their full potential. All these different forms of documentation and communication are exercises in *writing* – both theoretical and concrete – that give us practice in catching the essence of experience and teach us the use of different narrative structures. They are exercises in interpreting and arguing what we do with children, which have a public resonance and are extremely effective in the complex processes they induce.

All these projects, presented briefly above, were occasions for professional development with study groups from Italy and overseas.

Exhibitions as litmus paper

Each exhibition, though in different ways, was a sort of litmus paper for the current phase of education in Reggio's schools. Each highlights what we have managed to achieve and diffuse in a large number of schools; and each makes evident which things are missing, what we need to do more work on. For example, we have managed to make more visible the child–teacher relationship and the development of projects; but this is much less true of individual and group learning, and we need a deeper focus on these subjects.

The digital environment, by which I mean the synergy and relationship between different tools such as computers, scanners, digital cameras, recorders and projectors has increasingly entered schools as an everyday working environment and we have made considerable advance in its use at theoretical levels together with some interesting and innovative experimental applications with children. Some analysis and documentation of learning processes in this area is just beginning to be seen but I think much remains to be done.

Chapter 11

The Loris Malaguzzi International Centre

In 1998, the *Comune* of Reggio Emilia decided to purchase a complex of industrial buildings dating back to 1936 and covering an area of roughly 10,000 square metres. These included a small villa, offices and industrial warehouses used for maturing Parmiggiano-Reggiano cheeses, all situated in the city's first industrial area north of the centre. The decision, a courageous one not least for the financial commitment required, has opened up new and ambitious projects.

A national architecture competition was held to choose a design for the new centre and in 2003 work began on the first phase of building. The first part of the International Centre, dedicated to Loris Malaguzzi, was opened in 2006; spaces created from renovating the industrial complex included a small building with offices for administration and courses, a lecture theatre for 400 people, exhibition halls and laboratory/atelier areas initially housing the *Raggio di Luce* (Ray of Light) atelier. A second phase of work began in 2007 and, at the time of writing (in 2009), construction work is underway on a large entrance and reception area to welcome visitors and study groups, a *scuola dell'infanzia* with three classrooms, additional areas for an experimental first two years of primary school, areas for older children and a large garden. The entrance will be accompanied by a large, sinuous sculpture by Richard Serra (at least this is the initial idea).

Once completed, the centre will be a place for hosting and promoting 'research and innovation, on city, national and international levels', with people of all ages. This is what has been declared. These objectives and dreams are ambitious and will not be easy to realize. For now the centre, although not yet complete, is opening new possibilities and commitments that are very interesting but rather difficult, and has highlighted the urgent need for renewal and a more comprehensive philosophy of relations, in order to manage unforeseen new projects and dreams.

The new president of Reggio Children is Carla Rinaldi, whose important role in the story of Reggio Emilia's municipal schools has already been mentioned. Working by her side are a group of seven people including myself – 'directors of operations' – responsible for different areas. I have been entrusted with the area of publishing, exhibitions and ateliers, without forgetting projects closely interwoven with other areas, especially ones to do with research, professional development and consulting. All my professional activity over forty years of work was practice for building new connections between the culture of pedagogy, contemporary arts events and projects with children, and we will see how much this work will be useful for new themes confronting the International Centre.

One of the most difficult and delicate aspects is finding the right way of interweaving cultural products with economic return for the centre would have a short life without funds to support it; and at the same time, it will lose its declared identity without innovative and high quality cultural products. Only those who think theoretical and practical elements can be separated could imagine this to be an easy task to realize. However, ideas exist and I believe they are quite good ones; the process leading to quality products, working within budgetary discipline, requires a network of competencies we are slowly building up.

Over the years, there has been good international dissemination of Reggio pedagogy and the International Centre can continue to represent and support this. But through its work with increasingly international relationships, it must also find sources and voices to support the development and changes taking place in Reggio Children and contribute towards them. I always fear an attitude of critical 'repose', which is satisfied with itself, thinks of itself as good enough, refines certain words and certain aspects but generally stays still, with no evolution, no *cultural excitement*.

One of our greatest sources of credibility is our desire and ability for building up an international network of interesting multicultural and multidisciplinary voices.

Beyond school culture

A cultural credit, which has grown over time, is leading us to cross the boundaries of school and extend into the spaces of childhood in general. Many of the most recent requests for collaboration have come from outside school environments and take us into the world of sensitive, culturally advanced industry. We have pedagogically supervised and supported ranges of furnishings for childhood, Atelier3 and Play+ (discussed in Chapter 7) and, where used, these have truly altered school landscapes and public spaces for children. Professional development initiatives with IKEA have been held and continue. There has been consultation for a table setting with Alessi. Currently there are professional development courses for trainers in companies such as Unicredit, a large financial institution that is trying to create connections between children and adults in innovative ways. In an initial meeting recently, apart from the more usual talks in meeting rooms, a workshop was held in the *Raggio di Luce* atelier with a group of employees and their children. One hypothesis behind all this work is that creative situations improve people's capacities in the workplace and outside it; another hypothesis is that knowing children's strategies, how they tackle and resolve problems, how they work in groups, the rules they establish for themselves, the forms of democracy they act out, all extends an awareness of what civil society should offer to people. A society that does not welcome children with respect and the right forms of attention is a society that has distorted many values and does not respect itself.

Many of the topics discussed in the book up to now – ateliers, pedagogy, environments, observation and documentation, family and city participation – must be reconsidered and developed in the light of the new experience of the International Centre. We have to be capable of holding on to the best parts and renewing them – and to conceive new ones. No small challenge!

The three areas I have been entrusted with – exhibitions, publishing and ateliers – are part of Reggio Children's educational and cultural activities with the public. They are situated in contexts of research and reciprocal exchange in the city, and on national and international levels, and draw attention to the importance of education as a fundamental element for democratic growth. They are closely interwoven; each one generative of the others, each having a different level of priority according to the subject treated. Each exhibition, book, atelier, by consciously approaching it as part of a project, can simultaneously be a time for research, communication, professional development and dissemination.

Looking to the future: a new travelling exhibition

I would like to conclude with some notes on three cultural products I consider to be a hope for the future and in which the areas for which I am responsible at the International Centre have played an important role.

The first is the creation of the new travelling exhibition called *The Wonder of Learning* (see Figure 11.1). The authors of this collective work are children, atelieristas, teachers and pedagogistas in Reggio Emilia's schools and two schools in Sant'Ilario d'Enza, a small town in the Reggio Emilia province with whom we have worked with for some time.

Figure 11.1 The exhibition *The Wonder of Learning* preface: reference theories

The new exhibition both sits with and replaces the older one, *The Hundred Languages of Children*, which has been produced in six different versions since 1981: Italy/Europe, North America, Australia, France, Holland and Japan. The exhibition has been much loved by different cultures and countries and in an International Network meeting was declared one of the most effective places for professional development and pedagogical dissemination of the Reggio Approach. We asked ourselves if an exhibition was still the most effective tool for communication and narrative, if it was the best representation of us today; and we answered that a travelling exhibition was potentially a *piazza* for discussing education and allows more than one *language* to be simultaneously used for communication and narration. Considering these times of such accelerated social and cultural change, and the difficulties schools and education are experiencing everywhere, it seemed important to us to create something that made it possible to create cohesion and vitality among an international public interested in schools and education. Reggio pedagogy has always had a public and democratic vocation, maintaining the balance between popular success and aspects of a more intellectual and elitist nature.

It was the second time I had found myself in the situation of organizing an international travelling exhibition, first in 1981 and now again in 2008, and perhaps this second venture is the one I felt to be most difficult in all my years of work. In the previous exhibition *The Hundred Languages of Children*, there was the energy of inventing practices that did not exist then (or at least were unknown to us, our attitude was slightly that of teaching pioneers) and presenting them in a structure for communication that was both beautiful and unusual for a children's exhibition. All the projects were discussed with Malaguzzi and this made us feel calmer because we had enormous faith in him. We were in a small group of schools working on the exhibition and all my memories seem simple and full of fun. I know very well that memory is highly selective and highly interpretative, but in my mind the exhibition had the right rhythm in its phases of growth, which almost followed a natural evolution in our growth in the schools.

The decision to create a new exhibition, capable of continuing to tell the story of children, teachers and education today and positioning educational processes in a context of cultural and social contemporary life, is a responsibility that we took on but is not at all easy. We feel less pioneering than in the past in that, fortunately, many educational aspects and proposals have been disseminated and been experimented with in other places around the world. So it was less simple to find an immediate consensus and a sense of wonder as with the previous exhibition. Every exhibition is an act of courage, one realizes what is acceptable and also what is missing or still fragile; but this time we did not have Malaguzzi to reassure us and decisions about whether projects were interesting enough to be exhibited in an international show were entirely ours.

Some questions and choices

How have observation and documentation taken part and been expressed in the way the new exhibition communicates with the public? How could we make the importance given to poetic languages in Reggio Emilia *transparent* in the exhibition? Here are just some notes.

The exhibition is not only intended for the world rotating around schools (teachers, pedagogistas, psychologists, families) but for all sectors and all people interested in the world of childhood. We chose subjects that seemed among the most interesting, and our approach, as always, was to weave several languages together in one theme, interweaving cognitive and expressive aspects. One theme we wanted to emerge was how intense relationships with things can modify learning; relations with environments and materials. Perhaps we over used the word 'dialogue' – 'dialogues with places', 'dialogues with materials', etc.; we know very well to what extent true dialogue comes of listening, which is not easy to put into practice. But we were not able to find another word which would be clearer and more understandable when translated into many different languages, and which would represent a hope and an objective. The entire exhibition, like the previous one, is full of pedagogy–atelier *dialogue* and clearly represents new things this has produced in practice. This can be seen in themes like learning to write and approaches to science.

Some projects sketch out new languages and issues like celebrating the empathetic physical approach children have when connecting to an environmental space, to the point where children of 5 and 6 years designed and realized a choreography, with movements and gestures closely related to elements in the space where the dance took place (see Figure 11.2). This project, with some others, tentatively entered into fields not yet properly explored or reflected upon, with ambitions and interest in opening up new frontiers.

Figure 11.2 The Wonder of Learning exhibition: Notes for a Choreography project

Perhaps the most innovative aspect was work we did on the narrative structure of projects. Never before had we felt so clearly that working on narrative structure effectively means reflecting and working on interpretative processes and meanings. The work was done in an interdisciplinary group (see Figure 11.3): apart from ourselves (teachers, pedagogistas and atelieristas), the group included our long-time graphic artist Rolando Baldini, who also accompanied us in the previous exhibition, and two architects, Stefano Maffei and Michele Zini who are particularly attentive to contemporary communication. Meetings were extremely interesting and helped us to see the educational projects with less insider language and eyes and, therefore, to extract new meaning.

Figure 11.3 Interdisciplinary group

First, the group analyzed each project in an attempt to gain deeper understanding of its phases and emerging meanings and to discuss the theme of how to communicate these to the public. Work continued in an exhibition hall at the International Centre where we set up provisional environments that we called 'spaces for reflection' (see Figure 11.4) using simple paper 'sails' to separate them. Here we met in small groups, retracing the steps of the previous interdisciplinary discussion to sketch a new outline, paper proofs for a simulation of how communication would appear in the exhibition.

Figure 11.4 Rooms for reflection

This was a way of showing and making public the process of change that some projects in the new exhibition underwent. This process of change and transformation is difficult to communicate to the outside world and frankly I am not sure to what extent our intention of showing how projects are transformed by interpreting documentary material can be understood or appreciated. It is difficult to convey how the projects being examined ceased to be a simple chronicle of events and how the parts we considered most significant increasingly emerged. Although there were legitimate doubts about these 'spaces for reflection', they were certainly a good metaphor for the world of education and the opportunities afforded by good documentation for deep examination at a later date.

With the consultants mentioned above we held further meetings to decide on the materials to use, then to develop the professional communication of projects in the group of graphic artists and architects working on the exhibition structure.

Different levels for reading

During these meetings, the concept that the exhibition should suggest and allow different levels of reading and deeper study was better defined. Including space, reflections and the tools used by Reggio educators for their work (the different forms of finished and unfinished documentation made during the life of projects in the exhibition) makes the documentation 'production line' more explicit. Increasingly we find ourselves examining and analyzing the entire journey leading to a final project. Monitors are included in the exhibition and these provide an extra 'snapshot', moving photographic images, and convey general atmospheres that are otherwise very difficult to illustrate. We would have liked a greater presence of interwoven language – written text, photographs, video, music, the environment – but the short time available to us and the high operational costs only made this partially possible.

I am certain the exhibition will form the basis of professional development for teachers, pedagogistas and atelieristas, and that it will contribute to renew parts of our thinking especially on the processes of documentation. Including all the documentation from a journey of work makes the crossroads encountered along the way, the choices made, even the mistakes, more visible than in previous exhibitions or documentation currently created and shown in *nidi* and *scuole* in Reggio Emilia.

The first exhibition display map discussed by the project group was not simply a proposal for layout, but reflected a conceptual orientation: microenvironments situated side by side or connected in different ways allowing and communicating a non-univocal narrative structure (see Figure 11.5). Each micro-place has an image and identity related to the project housed and visited. It is a three-dimensional idea of communication, using all the possibilities offered by a space.

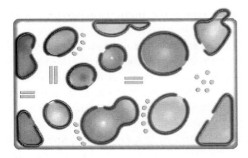

Figure 11.5 Exhibition display map

All these choices reflect and underline the educational philosophy: subjectivity, dialogue, connection and autonomy. An element for discussion and professional growth, which to my mind should be clear to those using the exhibition when it is properly understood and used, is how it shows ways in which educational philosophy must be reflected in the different phases and practices of pedagogy. How theoretical parts, project parts, documentation and ways of communicating, despite all having their own specific features, belong to the same cultural and ethical landscape and are, therefore, interreferential in a way which mutually strengthens them.

The exhibition was inaugurated in Boulder, Colorado, in June 2008 and for a whole week 700 people looked, listened and debated with a group from Reggio Emilia and between themselves on themes of education and learning among children and teachers. The exhibition will remain in the United States for five years moving from city to city and state to state, stopping in each one for at least six months so that communication and professional growth are as deep as possible. In the meantime talks are underway in other countries for producing multiple versions of the exhibition, or sections of it.

A collective autobiography

At the same time as this new exhibition, another important exhibition was inaugurated entitled *One City, Many Children*. This recounts the history of Reggio's municipal schools against the background scenarios in the city, in Italy and around the world. It is a collective autobiography dealing specifically with how our schools were born, and more generally with the growth of early childhood education in the city of Reggio Emilia. This is situated in a narrative structure maintaining an awareness of cultural and political contexts in Italy and abroad over the years, which were contemporary with choices made in Reggio Emilia. Although the timings and methods are different, and different choices were made, it is a history reflecting that of many Italian cities.

Constructing this tale was a long and delicate journey. It is a courageous story because it deals with living people who have experienced the same history in different roles and with different points of view — sometimes very different. I regret that Loris Malaguzzi – one of the main protagonists – was not able to give us his interpretation.

It has been said that the present shapes history and not always vice versa. Memory among other things is a rather complex process based largely on interpretation. However, although the exhibition takes us through the history it is not an exhibition on the past; it is strongly contemporary, and gives us a sense of the energy, perseverance, courage, ethics, hard work and risks which were part of the innovative choices made down the years.

It is on the whole a beautiful story; dense pages of a book unfolding in the International Centre galleries, a place at the beginning of its life. So that the presence of this history is also a warning, reminding us of something I believe to be important, that would have grave consequences if we were to forget it. To express this idea I will use the voice of Loris Malaguzi, pedagogista, in *The Hundred Languages of Children* exhibition, 'Utopia, dreaming and wishing need to be part of our everyday quality, allowing us to bring about a *rich normality* going beyond ideas of exceptional experiences to re-establish a new, positive value for normality'.

This is a beautiful augury for schools, education and life; for when we lose sight of these elements, normality is quick to dissolve into mediocrity and conformity.

Looking to the future: the first atelier in the International Centre

Workshops offering children and adults opportunities for working with their hands are often connected to the idea of people modelling inert materials as they please. Good artisans know this is not the case, 'they know they do not have the right to use violence on materials, but must patiently try to understand them, stimulate them cautiously, almost seduce them'. These words are not my own but reflect my thoughts exactly; they were written by the famous anthropologist Claude Lévi-Strauss in his eulogy to manual work (Lévi-Strauss, 2008: 46). 'This is also why manual work, less distant than would first appear from the work of thinkers and scientists, constitutes an aspect of the enormous effort made by humanity to understand the world' (Lévi-Strauss, 2008: 46). In the culture of the atelier, whatever subject matter or material it treats, there must be awareness of theory *made flesh in the material* that gives body to theories, anticipates them, suggests them, or in some way illuminates them.

The International Centre includes atelier areas and the initial project was entrusted to atelierista Giovanni Piazza and myself. We started out knowing most of all what we did not want it to become, i.e. a space for people to pass through, offering a stimulus to be responded to rapidly, organized around questions and answers, for one-off visits without returning. We had in mind many children's museums which, although they often house intelligent and interesting contents, are generally organized in a way we did not find convincing; we wanted something different.

We searched for a long time for the right name to give our new place of experimentation and in the end we confirmed the name 'atelier' because we felt it was the most suitable metaphor for a place of research where imagination, rigour, experiment, creativity and expression would interweave and complete each other. We decided to organize this first atelier around the theme of light because light is fascinating, allows different approaches, and is an element we have explored for many years in our municipal schools in the form of natural daylight and artificial light. Having spent so much time 'frequenting' light was precisely what persuaded us to choose an approach we were less familiar with – a scientific approach – and here we found ourselves to be less knowledgeable. Olmes Bisi, Professor of General Physics at the Faculty of Engineering of the University of Modena and Reggio Emilia, worked by our side. I believe quite a long time went by before we came to know each other and understand each other's language.

I was completely enraptured by written formulas, which I found beautiful but knew I did not understand them. Stepping outside the field of art I found myself in another area of learning for which the school I had attended offered very few analytical tools. Here I personally experienced and became clearly aware of what Howard Gardner theorizes in his writings as the difference between understanding and comprehension. I felt I could understand some scientific explanations of light given by Olmes Bisi; some, like the theory of colour, I knew superficially. But I realized I did not understand enough to be able to carry out operations of invention and interpretation that come to me so easily for visual and artistic languages. It was the first time since starting to work in Reggio schools that I was capable of producing some educational theory, but could not put it into practice in satisfactorily innovative ways. This disoriented me because the true nature of the atelier's identity lies in practical production, be it visual, sound-based, using body language – or scientific.

After much discussion and collaboration with architect Tullio Zini on the physical space, and with pedagogistas Paola Cagliari and Maddalena Tedeschi on the pedagogical work, the atelier finally emerged, despite the fact that some of my initial doubts remained. We gave it the name *Raggio di Luce*. Running the atelier was entrusted to a group of young people who had completed a Reggio Children course for atelieristas.

The *Raggio di Luce* atelier has participated in the Genoa Science Festival three times with great success. There is an experimental group of *nidi*, *scuole dell'infanzia* and primary schools working on continuity between the atelier at the centre and ateliers in their schools in three research areas: reflection, refraction and diffraction. The atelier is open to the public on Sundays so that children and families can explore and try and understand light phenomena. Experimentation with light has taken place in schools in other countries such as Japan, Sweden and the USA.

Figures 11.6–11.7 Raggio di Luce atelier

Experimenting

The *Raggio di Luce* atelier is an experiment, in culture and organization. It has been complex and has included professional development for the atelieristas who conduct the atelier and educational support for a new scientific approach involving 'continuity' projects both with schools and for family visits with children. Light and certain light phenomena are central protagonists and highlight the extent to which expressiveness and beauty can accompany an understanding of scientific thinking. Science is almost always missing from educational work with small children, or taught in ways that are mostly to do with facts teachers want children to learn. It is a challenge to be by children's sides with an approach to reality and its phenomena that gives *meaning and strength* to *scientific thinking*. This already belongs to our species in a natural, biological way, but needs practice, needs to be supported and informed through proposing stimulating contexts and situations so that it can develop along children's typically unanticipated pathways.

I was waiting to begin seeing the children at work, counting on my ability (or presumed ability) for working by children's sides and proceeding with them with explorations and points of view that are often interesting and not conformist. This was not possible because I was taken up with many other commitments. What I managed to do on a practical level, remarkably little by my usual standards, was identify and advise which parts of documentation coming from municipal schools were to my mind most suited to being shown in the light section of the exhibition and to being interwoven into its narrative structure. This narrative structure was then taken up and concluded by part of the atelier project group (Olmes Bisi, Paola Cagliari, Giovanni Piazza and Maddalena Tedeschi).

With time, the *Raggio di Luce* atelier has become an evocative environment, and conveys an identity that is attuned to the pedagogy in the schools, however, much remains to be dealt with in better ways. We are too used to new educational approaches to accept work to date in the *Raggio di Luce* atelier without critical reflection, and this is especially true of the work being done with older children. We need to get to know them better, have closer collaboration with their teachers and more opportunities for research together. We have also seen how much time is needed for adults to work by children's side, in exploratory work, fine tuning their listening and proposals. It is this element that is perhaps what most distinguishes the quality of certain educational environments from others. It is also one of the most difficult things to achieve.

I believe the most innovative part, something that should be continued in ateliers on other themes, has to do with the 'continuity' projects between the *Raggio di Luce* atelier and school ateliers, or other spaces in schools. How do these work? First we come to agreements with teachers about general procedures, then there is a first visit to the atelier during which we observe how children of different ages approach luminous contexts and equipment, the strategies they use, their interests, the first things they wonder about and their first discoveries. The second phase is based on all these aspects; we hypothesize how work can be continued back in the school environment. Further meetings inside the atelier follow (depending on the distance from school) where the project continues to evolve. We feel the 'continuity' aspect of these projects comes from having them continue and alternate across different places, such as the light atelier and school (although others could be added), a relationship that activates dynamics through which everyone becomes engaged and involved together with interesting cultural products.

After two years of experiment with light, we are considering developing further exploration on this theme through using other languages: the languages of photography, theatre and sound. Atelieristas in the *Raggio di Luce* atelier are doing experimental work I feel is very interesting, juxtaposing light effects with those produced by sound waves and creating unusual phenomena that stimulate curiosity and a desire to investigate for a better understanding.

Travelling atelier and exhibition

In the meantime, we have come to a metamorphosis of the *Raggio di Luce* atelier: from permanent atelier inside the International Centre to travelling atelier. Practically speaking this consists of equipped areas (we call them 'illuminatories') already used in the centre and an exhibition of educational projects representing work done with children over the past two years. It is a travelling atelier exhibition that can visit different places and simultaneously provide professional development for the people managing it. At the time of writing, it is in Udine, in the North-East of Italy, and appears to be highly successful with school groups and families.

The combination of atelier and exhibition came about because we do not agree with the idea of giving out only the equipment and tools we have invented and created. We fear the rapid spread of projects and ways of working, which at the centre and in our schools are given quality through an extremely careful approach. This is not an easy thing to improvise, as it requires time and accompanying theories. So it seemed to us the least dangerous and most effective way was an environment communicating some of the theses in our approach to scientific thinking and documentation, to illustrate work done in the past two years. Supporting these is other equipment for further exploration and experimentation. They open the way for work which can be done outside the atelier – in schools or independently.

The requests we receive from various different places for ateliers and workshops, going from ateliers on specific subjects (such as encounters with material or light) to workshops related to artistic events in museums, bookshops or other places, pose old problems and new. New problems consist in not knowing the children and teachers we meet and the short time made available for the projects; an old problem, which becomes amplified in this new situation, is the preparation of atelieristas and teachers. However correct the project and procedure we agree on may be, it cannot guarantee the quality of an offer or process alone. The specific character of individual adults working with children continues to be a condition that makes a difference, and so the choice of person and their professional development are things to be born in mind when considering the feasibility of projects requested of us and on which we are currently working.

In the whole process of a strong and international reorganization of the Reggio Approach in the context of cultural and social change in the outside world, which I have briefly and superficially outlined, ateliers and atelieristas must naturally also partly rethink their work, examining their effectiveness and the contemporary nature of their role. For the objective of renewal that the centre proposes, however, I believe it is important they should try and further develop their original role of forty years ago, which defined their presence in schools: bearers of projects for freedom, and persevering defenders of *non-obedient* processes, supporters of the importance of poetics in learning and in education.

Chapter 12

Blue flowers, bitter leaves

In summer in many parts of Italy, in fields and the least welcoming of places, along the sides of roads and in small pockets of arid land, there blooms a wild flower of the most startling azure blue, challenging our perceptions of the surrounding colours. This is wild radicchio, common chicory; a plant with slightly bitter leaves, which women collect in late spring in the fields and which is prepared together with other salad leaves and hard-boiled eggs. This blue summer flower is a mutation of the cultivated form and has very strong, tenacious stalks with small flowers of an intense blue colour, made even more striking by the fact that the plant spreads in a myriad of clusters to form drifts of a special blue, surrounded by an even more brilliant green; a most appropriate metaphor for summer.

If these flowers are gathered and put in water, they lose their intense colour and do not last very long. Like poppies they are not flowers for picking, they are better left where they are, and their presence transforms any place into somewhere special. Like poppies, chicory flowers seem fragile, but the seed is strong and the plant is really a weed, and has the strength to invade and grow.

The presence of ateliers in Reggio schools is of this nature; an intense and visible presence, but which becomes less strong and visible when the atelier is taken out of a pedagogical context to a place that cannot embrace it or use it in an instrumental way. It is not art, and does not look for infant art, but possesses a way of seeing that marvels and feels emotion on observing things. It knows how to be a robust herb but then ineluctably it becomes a blue flower, unexpected and poetic.

The philosophy and experience, which have been put together over these years, represent the resilience of the atelier. Transplanted into other contexts, the more it finds terrain and environments possessing some of the elements that made its birth possible in Reggio Emilia, the more it will break new ground and be capable of carrying out its role participating in innovative education. Elements such as pedagogy that are sensitive to listening and the poetic languages; organization that is creative on a daily basis; quality in education entrusted with a cultural, social and political role.

In Reggio Emilia's schools, there is still much to be discovered, learned and discussed. We need research groups that involve a greater number of external voices, belonging to other disciplines, contributing to the birth of new thinking and new practices; cross-pollination between new tools and old is needed to better confront old and new problems.

Ateliers must continue, in some cases must go back to being, places of research, suited to contributing to the changes being acted out in our society. They must use and develop the approaches and tools that belong to them: processes of freedom, distancing conformity, emotional participation. Ateliers and atelieristas will continue to be a fundamental presence if they are able to support empathetic processes; they must not be shy of rational approaches but must also be able to feel excitement and excite; to perseveringly pursue the poetic languages as necessary indispensable values; to be bearers of a more complete knowledge and creators of relations of solidarity with the surrounding world.

Notes

1 Introduction

1 The Italian 'confronto' is completely opposite to the English 'confrontational', though it can sometimes entail being confronted with something. It is seeking people out because we want their point of view or 'to look at' something we are or do 'in the light of' another way of being or doing. It is an important word in Reggio.

3 A general overview

1 Conversations taken from Malaguzzi, 1996: 143.
2 Project entitled 'Light riddle' by *scuola comunale dell'infanzia* Gulliver, children aged 4–5 years, teacher Lucia Levrini, atelierista Anna Orlandini, pedagogista Maddalena Tedeschi.
3 Project by *scuola comunale dell'infanzia* Diana, children aged 5–6 years, teachers Sonia Cipolla and Evelina Reverberi, atelierista Isabella Meninno, pedagogista Tiziana Filippini. This synthesis has been put together using documentation by atelierista Isabella Meninno. The complete documentation can be found in *The Black Rubber Column: From Conception of an Idea to Realisation of a Final Model*, Reggio Emilia, Reggio Children, 2009.

4 The bicycle metaphor

1 The Video Centre was created in the 1980s in the *scuola comunale dell'infanzia* La Villetta premises. It supports documentation of projects and activities taking shape in Reggio Emilia's schools with video and audio material.

5 The long view of organization

1 The *Assessore* for Schools and Culture has a political role and is nominated by the mayor to be responsible for educational and cultural policy in municipal administration.
2 The first cooperative *nido* opened in Reggio Emilia in 1987 with an agreement between the Comune and two cooperatives working in the area of community services. Over the years many more cooperative *nidi* have opened in Reggio Emilia.

6 An ethical community

1 The *Consiglio di Gestione*, currently named *Consiglio Infanzia Città* (Community Early Childhood Council), is an elected body in each *nido* and *scuola dell'infanzia*, which is composed of staff, parents and other community members. The Council is a democratic body whose task is to promote participation and social management as well as the co-responsibility of the families served and the citizens for educational issues. The Councils are elected every three years.
2 Enìa is a utility formed by merging various municipal service industries. It provides gas, electricity, water, centralized heating and waste collection services to the public.

7 Environments

1 Domus Academy was born in Milan in 1982 as an open project around the Italian design and fashion experience. During the years, Domus Academy also asserted its importance as a school, a place of post-graduate training and research laboratory in design and fashion design. Since the beginning, DA set up a Research Centre, DARC – Domus Academy Research and Consulting – to develop knowledge in the relationship with industries. *www.domusacademy.com*

8 Professional marvellers

1 Project by *nido cooperativo* Girasole, children aged 35–36 months, teachers Lorena Sala, Silvia Montruccoli and Consuelo Faietti; pedagogical consultant and project coordinator Elena Bega.

9 Visible Listening

1 Project by *scuola comunle dell'infanzia* Diana, children aged 5–6 years, teacher Evelina Reverberi, atelierista Vea Vecchi.

10 We take up the walk again

1 A project promoted by the Civic Museum of Reggio Emilia, Reggio Children, The Documentation and Educational Research Centre, REMIDA. The catalogue of the exhibition, curated by Vea Vecchi and Claudia Giudici, is published by Reggio Children (2003).
2 A project promoted by *Assessorato Cultura del Comune di Reggio Emilia*, Reggio Children, in collaboration with *Istituzione Scuole e Nidi d'Infanzia del Comune di Reggio Emilia, Reggio Scuola* – Education and Professional Development Service

Bibliography

Agostini, F. (2003) *Deleuze: evento e immanenza*. Milano: Mimesis.

Alfano Miglietti, F. (1997) *Identità Mutanti*. Genova: Costa & Nolan.

Aristotle (2007) *Poetica*. Roma-Bari: Laterza.

Arnheim, R. (1954) *Art and Visual Perception: A Psychology of the Creative Eye*. Berkeley, CA: University of California Press.

Arnheim, R. (1969) *Visual Thinking*. Berkeley, CA: University of California Press.

Atiyah, M.F. (2007) 'Senza bellezza non c'è verità'. *Corriere della Sera*, 14 March 2007, pp. 47–48.

Augé, M. (1992) *Non-lieux*. Paris: Seuil.

Barbaras, R. (1994) *La perception: Essai sur le sensibile*. Paris: Hatier.

Barbiana School (1967) *Lettera a una Professoressa*. Firenze: Libreria Editrice Fiorentina.

Bateson, G. (1972) *Steps to an Ecology of Mind*. San Francisco, CA: Chandler Publishing.

Bateson, G. (1979) *Mind and Nature: A Necessary Unit*. New York, NY: E.P. Dutton.

Bateson, G. and Bateson, M.C. (1987) *Angels Fear: Towards an Epistemology of the Sacred*, New York: McMillan.

Bauman, Z. (1993) *Postmodern Ethics*. Oxford: Blackwell.

Bauman, Z. (2001) *The Bauman Reader*. Oxford: Blackwell.

Bauman, Z. (2005) *Liquid Life*. Cambridge: Polity Press.

Bauman, Z. (2008) *Individualmente insieme*. Reggio Emilia: Diabasis.

Bauman, Z. and Tester, K. (2001) *Conversations with Zygmunt Bauman*. Cambridge: Polity Press.

Becchi, E. and Bondioli, A. (eds) (1997) *Valutare e valutarsi*. Bergamo: Edizioni Junior.

Berardi Bifo, F. and Sarti, A. (2008) *RUN: Forma, vita, ricombinazione*. Milano: Mimesis.

Bocchi, G. and Ceruti, M. (eds) (2002) *Le origini della scrittura: Genealogie di un'invenzione*. Milano: Bruno Mondadori.

Bocchi, G. and Ceruti, M. (eds) (2007) *La sfida della complessità*. Milano: Bruno Mondadori.

Bodei, R. (1995) *Le forme del bello*. Bologna: Il Mulino.

Bondioli, A. (1996) *Gioco e educazione*. Milano: Franco Angeli.

Brandi, F. (1994) *Mutazione e cyberpunk: Immaginario e tecnologia negli scenari di fine millennio*, Genova: Costa & Nolan.

Branzi, A. (1984) *La casa calda*. Milano: Idea Books.

Branzi, A. (1997) *La crisi della qualità*. Palermo: Edizioni della Battaglia.

Branzi, A. (2007) 'Un'idea di Reggio Emilia'. In Molinari, L. (ed.) *Reggio Emilia: Scenari di qualità urbana*. Reggio Emilia-Milano: Skira-Comune di Reggio Emilia.

Bronfenbrenner, U. (1979) *Ecology of Human Development: Experiments by Nature and Design*. Cambridge, MA: Harvard University Press.

Bronowski, J. (1978) *The Origins of Knowledge and Imagination*. London: Yale University Press.

Bruner, J.S. (1964) *On Knowing: Essays for the Left Hand*. Cambridge, MA: Harvard University Press.

Bruner, J.S. (1966) *The Relevance of Education*. New York, NY: Norton.

Bruner, J.S. (1983) *In Search of Mind: Essays in Autobiography*. New York, NY: Harper & Row.

Bruner, J.S. (1986) *Actual Minds, Possible Worlds*. Cambridge, MA: Harvard University Press.

Bruner, J.S. (1990) *Acts of Meaning*. Cambridge, MA: Harvard University Press.

Calvino, I. (1959) *Il Barone rampante*. Torino: Einaudi.

Calvino, I. (1972) *Le città invisibili*. Torino: Einaudi.

Calvino, I. (1988) *Lezioni americane*. Torino: Einaudi.

Carroll, L. (1998) *Alice's Adventures in Wonderland*. Oxford: Oxford University Press.

Casula, T. (1981) *Tra vedere e non vedere*. Torino: Einaudi.

Cavallini, I. and Tedeschi, M. (eds) (2007) *The Languages of Food*. Reggio Emilia: Reggio Children.

Ceccato, S. (1987) *La fabbrica del bello*. Milano: Rizzoli.

Celli, P.L. (1997) *L'illusione manageriale*. Roma-Bari: Laterza.

Ceppi, G. and Zini, M. (eds) (1998) *Children, Space, Relations*. Reggio Emilia: Reggio Children.

Ceruti, M. (1989) *La danza che crea*. Milano: Feltrinelli.

Ceruti, M. (2007) *Cultura scuola persona*. Talk given at the 'Infanzia: cultura, educazione, scuola' Conference, Reggio Emilia, 11–13 October 2007. Available: http://www.edizionijunior.com/inrete/page_scheda.asp?ID=373 (accessed 30 July 2009).

Changeux, J.P. (1983) *L'Homme Neuronal*. Paris: Fayard.

Chomsky, N. (1968) *Language and Mind*. New York, NY: Harcourt-Brace and World.

Clark, A. (1997) *Being There*. Cambridge, MA: MIT Press.

Colombo, I. (1998) *Comunicazione esperenziale: La scrittura dinamica*. Milano: Corso di Laurea in Disegno industriale, Facoltà di Architettura, Politecnico di Milano.

Dahlberg, G. and Moss, P. (2005) *Ethics and Politics in Early Childhood Education*. London: Routledge

Dahlberg, G., Moss, P. and Pence, A. (2007) *Beyond Quality in Early Childhood Education and Care: Languages of Evaluation*, 2nd edn. London: Routledge.

Dal Lago, A. and Rovatti, P.A. (1993) *Per gioco: Piccolo manuale dell'esperienza ludica*. Milano: Raffaello Cortina.

Davoli, M. and Ferri, G. (eds) (2000) *Reggio Tutta: A Guide to the City by the Children*. Reggio Emilia: Reggio Children.

Deleuze, G. (2000) *La passione dell'immaginazione*. Milano: Mimesis.

Deleuze, G. and Carnet, H. (1977) *Dialogues*. Paris: Flammarion.

Dolci, D. (1970) *Il limone lunare*. Bari: Laterza.

Dri, P. (1994) *Serendippo: Come nasce una scoperta*. Roma: Editori Riuniti.

Eco, U. (1962) *Opera aperta*. Milano: Bompiani.

Edelman, G.M. (1989) *The remembered present*. New York, NY: Basic Books.

Edelman, G.M. (1992) *Bright Air, Brilliant Fire: On the Matter of the Mind*. New York, NY: Basic Books.

Edwards, C., Gandini, L. and Forman, G. (eds) (1998) *The Hundred Languages of Children*, 2nd edn. Norwood, MA: Ablex.

Enzensberger, H.M. (1997) *Zickzack*. Frankfurt am Main: Suhrkamp.

Fabbri, D. and Munari, A. (1984) *Strategie del sapere: Verso una psicologia culturale*. Bari, Dedalo.

Filippini, T., Giudici, C. and Vecchi, V. (eds) (2008) *Dialogues with Places*. Reggio Emilia: Reggio Children.

Freire, P. (1967) *Edução como prática da liberdade*. Rio de Janeiro: Paz e Terra.

Galimberti, U. (1997) *Il corpo*. Milano: Feltrinelli.

Galimberti, U. (1999) *Psiche e techne: L'uomo nell'età della tecnica*. Milano: Feltrinelli.

Galimberti, U. (2007) 'Due punti di vista, per un obiettivo: trovare soluzioni ai conflitti', *La Repubblica delle Donne*, 7 July 2007, p. 59.

Galimberti, U. (2008a) 'Generazioni a confronto', *La Repubblica delle Donne*, 5 March 2008: p. 278.

Galimberti, U. (2008b) *Il segreto della domanda*. Milano: Apogeo.

Gallese, V. (2007) 'Dai neuroni specchio alla consonanza intenzionale. Meccanismi neurofisiologici dell'intersoggettività'. *Rivista di Psicanalisi*, LIII, 1, pp. 197–208.

Gardner, H. (1982) *Art, Mind and Brain*. New York, NY: Basic Books.

Gardner, H. (1983) *Frames of Mind: The Theory of Multiple Intelligences*. New York, NY: Basic Books.

Gardner, H. (1989) *To Open Minds*. New York, NY: Basic Books.

Gardner, H. (1991) *The Unschooled Mind: How Children Think and How Schools Should Teach*. New York, NY: Basic Books.

Gardner, H. (1999) *The Disciplined Mind: What all Students Should Understand*. New York, NY: Simon and Schuster.

Gardner, H. (2005) *Development and Education of the Mind*. London: Routledge.

Gardner, H. (2006) *Five Minds for the Future*. Cambridge, MA: Harvard Business School Press.

Gardner, H. (2007) 'The Ethical Mind'. *Harvard Business Review*, March, p. 2.

Giani Gallino, T. (1993) *Il bambino e i suoi doppi*. Torino: Bollati Bordigheri.

Givone, S. (2003) *Prima lezione di estetica*. Roma-Bari: Laterza.

Goethe, J.W. (1991) *Zur Farbenlehre*. Frankfurt am Main: Deutscher Klassiker.

Goleman, D. (1995) *Emotional Intelligence*. New York, NY: Bantam Books.

Gombrich, E.H. (1957) *Art and Illusion*. Washington DC: Bollingen Foundation.

Gombrich, E.H. (1963) *Meditations on a Hobby Horse and Other Essays on the Theory of Art*. London: Phaidon Press.

Goodman, N. (1978) *Ways of Worldmaking*. Indianapolis, IN: Hackett Publishing.

Gregory, R.L. (1966) *Eye and Brain: The psychology of seeing*. London: Weidenfeld and Nicolson.

Hall, E.T. (1966) *The Hidden Dimension*. Garden City, NY: Doubleday.

Hawkins, D. (1974) *The Informed Vision: Essays on Learning and Human Nature*. New York, NY: Agathon Press.

Hillman, J. (1999) *Politica della bellezza*. Bergamo: Moretti & Vitali.

Hillman, J (2001) *Il piacere di pensare*. Milano: Rizzoli.

Hillmann, J. (2004) *L'anima dei Luoghi: Conversazione con Carlo Truppi*. Milano: Rizzoli.

Hölderlin, F. (2004) 'Patmos'. In *Poems of Friedrich Hölderlin*. Selected and translated by James Mitchell. San Francisco, CA: Ithuriel's Spear.

Hoyuelos, A. (2004) 'A pedagogy of transgression', *Children in Europe*, 4, pp. 6–7.

Humphrey, N. (1986) *The Inner Eye*. London: Faber/Channel Four.

Itten, J. (1961) *Kunst der Farbe*. Ravensburg: Otto Maier Verlag.

Johnson, G. (1991) *In the Palaces of Memory*, New York, NY: Alfred A. Knopf.

Kellog, R. (1969) *Analyzing Children's Art*. Mountain View, CA: Mayfield Publishing.

Lenz Taguchi, H. (2009) *Going Beyond the Theory/Practice Divide in Early Childhood Education: Introducing an Intra-Active Pedagogy*. London: Routledge.

Levi, P. (1994) *Il sistema periodico*. Torino: Einaudi.

Lévi-Strauss, C. (2008) 'Elogio del lavoro manuale', original text read at the ceremony of conferring the Nonino International Prize, 1st February 1986, and published in *La Repubblica*, 4 May 2008, pp. 46–47.

Lévy, P. (1995) *Qu'est-ce que le virtuel?* Paris: La Découverte.

Lévy, P. (1996) *L'intelligenza collettiva: Per un'antropologia del cyberspazio.* Milano: Feltrinelli.

Lilli, L. (2007) 'A scuola senza amore', interview to Edgar Morin, *La Repubblica*, 4 April 2007, p. 49.

Lorenzetti, L.M. (1995) *La dimensione estetica dell'esperienza.* Milano: Franco Angeli.

Lurcat, L. (1996) *L'enfant et l'espace: Le role du corps.* Paris: Presses Universitaires de France.

Malaguzzi, L. (ed.) (1971) *Esperienze per una nuova scuola dell'infanzia.* In *Atti del seminario di studio* tenuto a Reggio Emilia il 18–20 marzo 1971. Roma: Editori Riuniti.

Malaguzzi, L. (1972) 'La nuova socialità del bambino e dell' insegnante attraverso l'esperienza della gestione sociale nelle scuole dell'infanzia'. In *La gestione sociale nella scuola dell'infanzia*: *Atti del I convegno regionale di Modena*, 15–16 maggio 1971. Roma: Editori Riuniti.

Malaguzzi, L. (1975) 'Il ruolo dell'ambiente nel processo educativo'. In *Arredo Scuola 75: Per la scuola che cambia.* Como: Luigi Massoni Editore.

Malaguzzi, L. (1981) 'Significati e finalità della gestione sociale'. In *La gestione sociale come progetto educativo: Partecipazione e corresponsabilità da subito.* Reggio Emilia: Comune di Reggio Emilia.

Malaguzzi, L. (1983) 'Che posto c'è per Rodari?'. In De Luca, C. (ed.) *Se la fantasia cavalca con la ragione: Prolungamenti degli itinerari suggeriti dall'opera di Gianni Rodari.* Bergamo: Juvenilia.

Malaguzzi, L. (1995) *Una carta per tre diritti.* Reggio Emilia: Comune di Reggio Emilia.

Malaguzzi, L. (1996) *The Hundred Languages of Children: Catalogue of the Exhibition.* Reggio Emilia: Reggio Children.

Malaguzzi, L. (1998) 'History, Ideas and Basic Philosophy', 2nd edn, In Edwards, C., Gandini, L. and Forman, G. (eds) *The Hundred Languages of Children.* Norwood, MA: Ablex.

Manghi, S. (2005) 'Apprendere attraverso l'altro', *Animazione Sociale*, 12, pp. 13–23.

Mantovani S. and Musatti T. (eds) (1983) *Adulti e bambini: Educare e comunicare*, Bergamo: Juvenilia.

Marcuse, H. (1955) *Eros and Civilization.* New York: Vintage Books.

Massumi, B. (2002) *Parables for the Virtual: Movement, Affect, Sensation.* Durham: Duke University Press.

Maturana, H.R. and Varela, F.J. (1990) *El Árbol del Conocimiento: Las Bases Biologicas para el Entendimiento Humano*, Santiago: Editorial Universitaria.

Morando, S. (ed) (1963) *L'Almanacco letterario: La civiltà dell'immagine.* Milano: Bompiani.

Morin E. (1999) *La tête bien faite: Repenser la réforme, réformer la pensée.* Paris: Editions du Seuil.

Morin, E. (1973) *Le paradigma Perdu.* Paris: Editions du Seuil.

Morin, E. (2002) *Educare gli educatori.* Roma: Edup.

Munari, B. (1977) *Fantasia.* Roma-Bari: Laterza.

Munari, B. (1981) *Da cosa nasce cosa.* Roma-Bari: Laterza.

Negroponte, N. (1995) *Being Digital.* London: Hodder & Stoughton.

Nonveiller, G. (1992) *Le arti visive e l'educazione.* Venezia: Accademie di Belle Arti.

Olsson, L. M. (2009) *Movement and Experimentation in Young Children's Learning: Deleuze and Guattari in Early Childhood Education.* London: Routledge.

Pagnin, A. (1977) *La personalità creativa.* Firenze: La Nuova Italia.

Parmiggiani, C. (2003) *Invito a... Claudio Parmiggiani: Catalogue of the Exhibition.* Cinisello Balsamo (Mi): Silvana.

Penose, R. (1997) *The Large, the Small and the Human Mind.* Cambridge: Cambridge University Press.

Piaget, J. (1945) *La formation du symbole chez l'enfant: Imitation, jeu et rêve, image et représentation.* Paris: Delachaux et Niestlè.

Piaget, J. (1964) *Six études de Psychologie.* Paris: Editions Gouthier.

Piaget, J. (1970) *Psychologie et epistemologie*. Paris: Denoël.

Pierantoni, R. (1998) *Verità a bassissima definizione: Critica e percezione del quotidiano*. Torino: Einaudi.

Plutarco (1995) *L'arte di ascoltare*. Milano: Mondadori.

Pontecorvo, C. Ajello, A.M. and Zucchermaglio, C. (1991) *Discutendo si impara*. Roma: Nuova Italia Scientifica.

Pontecorvo, C., Ajello, A.M. and Zucchermaglio, C. (eds)(1995) *I contesti sociali dell'apprendimento*. Milano: Ambrosiana-LED.

Popper, K.R. (1994) *Knowledge and the Body–Mind Problem: In Defence of Interaction*. London: Routledge.

Prigogine, I. (1988) *La nascita del tempo*. Roma-Napoli: Teoria.

Rabitti, G. (1984) *Alla scoperta della dimensione perduta: L'etnografia dell'educazione in una scuola dell'infanzia di Reggio Emilia*. Bologna: CLUEB.

Radice, L.L. (1962) *L'educazione della mente*. Roma: Editori Riuniti.

Read, H. (1943) *Education through Art*. London: Faber and Faber.

Ricco, D. (1999) *Sinestesie per il design*. Milano: Etas.

Rinaldi, C. (1999a) *I processi di conoscenza dei bambini tra soggettività e intersoggettività*. Reggio Emilia: Comune di Reggio Emilia.

Rinaldi, C. (1999b) *L'ascolto visibile*. Reggio Emilia: Comune di Reggio Emilia.

Rinaldi, C. (2006) *In Dialogue with Reggio Emilia: Listening, Researching and Learning*. London: Routledge.

Rinaldi, C. and Cagliari, P. (1994) *Educazione e creatività*. Reggio Emilia: Comune di Reggio Emilia.

Rinaldi, C., Giudici, C. and Krechevsky, M. (eds) (2001) *Making Learning Visible: Children as Individual and Group Learners*. Reggio Emilia: Reggio Children.

Rizzolatti, G. and Sinigaglia, C. (2006) *So quel che fai: Il cervello che agisce e i neuroni specchio*. Milano: Raffaello Cortina.

Rodari, G. (1973a) *Grammatica della fantasia*. Torino: Einaudi.

Rodari, G. (1973b) 'Io chi siamo?', *Il giornale dei genitori,* November/December, pp. 10–14.

Rose, S. (1993) *The Making of Memory*. New York, NY: Anchor Books/Doubleday.

Rousseau, J.J. (1762) *Émile, ou de l'éducation*. Paris: Rey.

Scalfari, E. (2008) 'L'opinione pubblica è rimasta senza voce'. *La Repubblica*, 17 August 2008, p. 1.

Scuola comunale dell'infanzia Diana (2009) *The Black Rubber Column: From Conception of an Idea to Realisation of a Final Model*. Reggio Emilia: Reggio Children.

Scuole comunali dell'infanzia Diana e Gulliver (1999) *Everything Has a Shadow Except Ants*. Reggio Emila: Reggio Children.

Stein, E. (1980) *Zum Problem der Einfühlung*. Halle: Buchdruckerie des Weisenhauses.

Steiner, G. (2006) *Lectio Doctoralis*, Bologna University, 31 May 2006. Text collected by Michele Smargiassi and published under the title 'La verità è sempre in esilio', *La Repubblica*, 1 June 2006, p. 43.

Stern, A. (1984) *Les enfants du Closlieu*. Paris: Hommes et Groupes Editeurs.

Tanizaki, J. (1933) *In'ei raisan*. Tokyo: Chuo Kouron Sha.

Thaut, M. H. (2009) 'The musical brain – an artful biological necessity', *Karger Gazette*, nr. 70.

Thomas, G.V. and Silk, A.M.J. (1990) *An introduction to the psychology of children's drawing*. New York, NY: Harvester Wheatsheaf.

Trevarthen, C. (1998) *Empatia e biologia*. Milano: Raffaello Cortina Editore.

Vattimo, G. and Rovatti, A. (eds) (1983) *Il pensiero debole*. Milano: Feltrinelli.

Vecchi, V. (1998) 'The Role of the Atelierista', 2nd edn. In Edwards C., Gandini L. and Forman G. (eds) *The Hundred Languages of Children*. Norwood, MA: Ablex.

Vecchi, V. (ed.) (2002) *Theatre Curtain: The Ring of Transformations*. Reggio Emilia: Reggio Children.

Vecchi, V. and Giudici, C. (eds) (2003) *Children, Art, Artists*. Reggio Emilia: Reggio Children.

Vygotskij, L.S. (1934) *Myšlenie i reč'. Psichologičeskie issledovanija*. Moskva-Leningrad.

Weick, K.E. (1995) *Sensemaking in Organizations*. Thousand Oaks: Sage.

Zoja, L. (2007) *Giustizia e bellezza*. Torino: Bollati Boringhieri.

Zolla, E. (1994) *Lo stupore infantile*. Milano: Adelphi

Index

Page numbers in *italics* denote an illustration